UNCOMMON SCHOOLS

UNCOMMON SCHOOLS

The Global Rise of Postsecondary Institutions for Indigenous Peoples

Wade M. Cole

Stanford University Press
Stanford, California

Stanford University Press

Stanford, California

Printed and bound by CPI Group (UK) Ltd, Croydon, CR0 4YY

Library of Congress Cataloging-in-Publication Data

Cole, Wade (Wade M.) author.
Uncommon schools : the global rise of postsecondary institutions for indigenous peoples / Wade M. Cole.
pages cm
Includes bibliographical references and index.
ISBN 978-0-8047-7210-5 (cloth : alk. paper)

1. Indigenous peoples—Education (Higher)—Cross-cultural studies.
2. Indigenous peoples—Legal status, laws, etc.—Cross-cultural studies.
3. Indigenous peoples—Government relations—Cross-cultural studies.
4. Higher education and state—Cross-cultural studies. I. Title.

LC3727.C54 2011
378.1'9829—dc22

2010049966

Typeset by Thompson Type in 10.5/15 Adobe Garamond Pro

To Karen,
for setting me on this path,
and Johanna,
for taking it with me

CONTENTS

LIST OF TABLES

LIST OF FIGURES

LIST OF ABBREVIATIONS

ADB	Asian Development Bank
AIHEC	American Indian Higher Education Consortium (United States)
BIA	Bureau of Indian Affairs (United States)
BIITE	Batchelor Institute of Indigenous Tertiary Education (Australia)
CEGEP	*Collège d'enseignement général et professionnel* (Canada)
DIAND	Department of Indian Affairs and Northern Development (Canada)
FNU	First Nations University of Canada
HBCUs	Historically Black Colleges and Universities (United States)
IIG	Institute of Indigenous Governance (Canada)
ILO	International Labor Organization
IRA	Indian Reorganization Act of 1934 (United States)
ISCED	International Standard Classification of Education
NVIT	Nicola Valley Institute of Technology (Canada)
PTE	Private Training Establishment (New Zealand)
SIIT	Saskatchewan Indian Institute of Technologies (Canada)
TAFE	Training and Further Education (Australia)
TCCUAA	Tribally Controlled College and University Assistance Act (United States)
TCUs	Tribal Colleges and Universities (United States)
TEI	Tertiary Education Institute (New Zealand)

TWoA	Te Wananga o Aotearoa (New Zealand)
TWoR	Te Wananga o Raukawa (New Zealand)
TWWoA	Te Whare Wananga o Awanuiarangi (New Zealand)
VET	Vocational Education and Training (Australia)
UNDRIP	United Nations Declaration on the Rights of Indigenous Peoples
UNESCO	United Nations Educational, Scientific, and Cultural Organization
WINHEC	World Indigenous Nations Higher Education Consortium

A NOTE ON TERMINOLOGY

IN DISCUSSING INDIGENOUS PEOPLES, I SEEK TO BALANCE THE politics of naming and the imperatives of precision with the interests of style. So, for instance, I use *indigenous* and *Aboriginal* interchangeably, ignoring precise technical differences that distinguish the terms. According to Guntram Werther (1992: 6-7), "the term *indigenous* is most commonly used to denote the original inhabitants [of a region]. . . . The word *aboriginal* adds to indigenous by denoting a specific claimed political, cultural, economic, and legal relationship between an indigenous people and a colonizing state." I dispense with this distinction. Moreover, for reasons discussed in the Introduction, "indigenous peoples" or "Aboriginal peoples," in the plural, refer to corporately organized political groups, whereas "indigenous people" or "Aboriginal people," in the singular, denote an apolitical collection of individuals claiming indigenous or Aboriginal racial, ethnic, and/or cultural descent.

Adding to the terminological confusion, indigenous peoples are called by different names cross-nationally, and these names have changed over time. In Canada, the Department of Indian and Northern Affairs (Canada 2002) has established exceedingly detailed guidelines regarding the appropriate lexicon to use when writing about the indigenous peoples of Canada. "Aboriginal peoples" and "First Nations" refer collectively to all indigenous peoples who currently reside in Canada, including Indians, Inuit, and Métis. Three categories of "Indian" exist. "Status Indians" comprise those individuals whose names are listed on the government's Indian Register, as defined by the Indian Act; "non-Status Indians" are individuals who consider themselves to be Indian, but who are not recognized as such under law; and "treaty Indians" belong to a First Nation that signed a treaty with the Crown. "Inuit," formerly known as "Eskimos" (a term that is now considered pejorative), are the original Arctic peoples of northern Canada. The Supreme Court of Canada decreed in 1939 that Eskimos/Inuit belong to the same legal category as Indians (*Re Eskimos* 1939). "Métis," French for "of mixed blood," describes individuals of mixed Aboriginal and European ancestry.

In the United States the terms "American Indians" and "Indians," although based on an infamous and grossly inaccurate historical misnomer, have recently enjoyed a revival among academics and indigenous peoples. "Native American," conversely, seems to be falling out of favor, although it is still sometimes used to describe American Indians, Alaska Natives, Aleuts, and Native Hawaiians *in toto*. I prefer "American Indians," but restrict that usage to indigenous peoples living in the contiguous forty-eight states.

In New Zealand, "Maori" replaced "Native" in official discourse after 1947 (Armitage 1995: 145). In quoting official sources or citing specific acts of government prior to 1947, I retain the usage "Native," but otherwise employ the term *Maori* to describe the original inhabitants—*tangata whenua*—of New Zealand. "Aotearoa," which translates as "land of the long white cloud," is the name given by Maori to New Zealand and is commonly used in academic and official discourses. I, however, continue to use "New Zealand" for the sake of clarity (except when Aotearoa forms part of a proper noun, as with "Te Wananga o Aotearoa"). Finally, *Pakeha* is the term adopted by Maori to describe New Zealanders of European descent. Because it enjoys widespread usage in New Zealand, by Pakeha and Maori alike, I adopt it, too.

Indigenous peoples in Australia are collectively denominated "Aboriginals" or "Aboriginal peoples," and individual indigenes are correspondingly referred to as "Aborigines." Torres Strait Islanders are also indigenous to Australia, particularly in a cluster of small islands north of Queensland. Blood quantum has been especially important in determining aboriginality in Australia, so that categories such as "half-caste," "quadroon," and "octoroon" are also common. Indeed, race has been the dominant trope in Australia's official discourses regarding Aboriginal peoples, and the issue of legal status was, until recently, much less important than it has been in other countries (Armitage 1995: 22–27; Chesterman and Galligan 1997: 92; Wolfe 2001).

PREFACE AND ACKNOWLEDGMENTS

THIS BOOK DOCUMENTS AND EXPLAINS THE EMERGENCE OF postsecondary institutions for indigenous peoples around the world, with particular emphasis on the Anglo-derived democracies of North America and Australasia (Australia, Canada, New Zealand, and the United States). But readers should be warned: I do not begin to unearth the *specific* factors that gave rise to these institutions "on the ground"—the very crux of my analysis—until Chapter Four. So just what is going on in the first half of the book?

Much. Beyond an examination of what, admittedly, are obscure and peripheral institutions, *Uncommon Schools* represents a study in comparative politics, world history, and organizational innovation. My central thesis is that indigenous peoples differ from most other racial, ethnic, cultural, and linguistic minorities by virtue of their exceptional claims to sovereignty under international and domestic law, and that this unique political status accounts for the existence of indigenous postsecondary institutions. Rooting out the source of these sovereignty claims took me on an intellectual journey I had not anticipated when I started the project, one that required, among other things, a survey of 500 years' worth of international legal developments and a comparative analysis of the colonial experiences, political structures, and court decisions of countries around the globe. I spend a great deal of time addressing these matters, as they constitute the core explanatory thrust of the analysis.

It is also important to be clear from the outset what this book is *not*—a detailed historical or ethnographic account of particular countries, indigenous groups, or postsecondary institutions. Rather, in broad and necessarily selective brushstrokes, I emphasize how mutually constitutive changes in global discourses and national policy environments fostered the creation of indigenous-controlled colleges, universities, and other postsecondary institutions as novel organizational forms. The establishment of these institutions offers a specific empirical context in which to examine much larger social, political, and legal processes, including the incorporation of indigenous peoples into nation-states, the rise of a global indigenous rights movement, and the worldwide expansion or "massification" of postsecondary education. I wrote the book as a political, historical, and comparative sociologist, motivated by a desire to understand the effect of globalization on political relationships between minority groups and their respective states. It is therefore my hope that readers who have no direct experience with or interest in indigenous postsecondary institutions per se—not to mention those who, like myself a dozen years ago, lack even a basic awareness of them—will nevertheless find much of interest in these pages. If this is the case, I will count my efforts a success.

In both substance and process, this book is a testament to path dependence, the idea that distant choices and events—no matter how serendipitous—can profoundly affect future outcomes. The project began more than a decade ago, when Karen Bradley hired me as a research assistant at Western Washington University. Karen's project analyzed the participation of women in higher education worldwide, and my first responsibility as her assistant was to compile information on the structure of higher education systems in countries belonging to the Organisation for Economic Co-operation and Development (OECD). While perusing New Zealand's entry in the *Encyclopedia of Higher Education*, I discovered, buried in a footnote, that three postsecondary education institutions for Maori students had recently been established. I was vaguely aware of tribal colleges and universities in the United States—one of them, Northwest Indian College, was located near the university I attended as an undergraduate—but did not know that similar institutions existed elsewhere in the world. With Karen's encouragement and mentorship, I embarked on a comparative-historical analysis of what I came to call "indigenous postsecondary institutions." I owe my decision to pursue graduate studies, my present career as an academic, and the existence of this book to her. I also extend my gratitude to John Richardson, who fostered my nascent comparative and historical sensibilities. His influence pervades this book and continues to shape my sociological outlook.

I wrote the bulk of this book at Stanford University, where I had the good fortune of studying under the guidance of John Meyer and Francisco Ramirez. They understood the promise of this project before I did and helped me bring it to fruition. John tirelessly provided (and continues to provide) feedback at every turn, while discussions with Chiqui profoundly shaped my thinking on the dynamics of inclusion and exclusion. I also thank David Baker, David John Frank, Susan Olzak, Woody Powell, and Matt Snipp for their suggestions and encouragement as the book took shape. Thanks as well to Kate Wahl, Emily Smith, and Joa Suorez at Stanford University Press, who made this book a reality, and to Margaret Pinette, who helped make it more readable.

Books, I have learned, depend on much more than intellectual stimulation and assistance to be written. They also require a great deal of time and money. Financial support for this project in its various stages was provided by the National Academy of Education/Spencer Foundation postdoctoral fellowship program; Montana State University; and the American Educational Research Association, which receives funds for its "AERA Grants Program" from the National Center for Education Statistics of the Institute of Education Sciences (U.S. Department of Education), and the National Science Foundation under NSF Grant #REC-0310268. I gratefully acknowledge the support of these institutions, while also recognizing that they are in no way responsible for the content reported herein.

Most importantly, writing a book also demands a great deal of emotional and moral support. For this I thank Joanne Cole, who has been a constant source of love and inspiration in my life; Karl and Evelyn Kraft, for their enthusiastic support of this project and my professional endeavors; Johanna Cole, for gracing me with her unwavering patience and unconditional companionship; and Adam and Nora, who cheerfully shared their dad with his computer.

UNCOMMON SCHOOLS

INTRODUCTION

Indigenous peoples throughout the world survive policies and practices ranging from extermination and genocide to protection and assimilation. Perhaps more than any other feat, survival is the greatest of all Indigenous peoples' achievements.

The Coolangatta Statement on Indigenous Peoples' Rights in Education, §3.1

FREE, PUBLIC, AND COMPULSORY SCHOOLING was designed to be not only a great equalizer but also an efficient homogenizer. A robust democracy and a functioning economy, it was thought, required that citizens speak a common language, share common values, and profess a common identity. The task of generating these commonalities fell largely to schools. In France, free and compulsory village schools sprang up in the nineteenth century to convert peasants into Frenchmen (Weber 1976). In the United States, "common" schools of the same era assimilated the working masses and immigrants into the national polity (Tyack 2003).

By whatever name—common, village, or something else—schools played an integral role in nation-building enterprises. They were predicated on the notion of replacement: Traditional cultures and mother tongues had to be discarded before one could gain entry into the imagined community of nationhood (Anderson 1991). It simply was not possible to speak patois and be French, or Wampanoag and be American. For indigenous peoples as for immigrants and peasants, common schools obliterated native languages and cultures with startling efficiency.

The belief that common schools could (and should) transform "ignorant" indigenes into "civilized" citizens had remarkable staying power and geographical reach. In 1880, the Board of Indian Commissioners in the United States reasoned that "if the common school is the glory and boast of our American civilization, why not extend its blessings to the 50,000 benighted children of the red men of our country, that they may share its benefits and speedily emerge from the ignorance of centuries" (Adams 2005: 18). Nearly a century later and an ocean away, government officials in Australia issued a policy report declaring that "a major instrument of assimilation is education of aboriginal children" (Hasluck 1961: 4). Assimilation would be achieved more effectively, the report continued, if Aboriginal children were educated in "normal" schools—the same schools as white children—rather than in "special" schools catering exclusively to Aboriginal communities. As in American and Australia, this was the policy also in Canada, New Zealand, and virtually everywhere else European colonizers displaced indigenous peoples.

Much has changed in recent decades. The use of schools to expunge minority cultures, once a core element of national assimilation policies, offends contemporary standards of propriety. Common schools have largely abandoned their assimilationist designs in favor of pluralism and multiculturalism (Feinberg 1998). But if states have relinquished the goal of cultural homogenization, they have also not ceded it to racial or ethnic groups. The appropriate antidote to Eurocentrism and nationalism is the celebration of diversity, not the valorization of difference.

In this book I argue that indigenous peoples have turned the tables on *both* assimilation *and* multiculturalism by establishing their own "uncommon schools" charged with preserving traditional languages and cultures, promoting local economic development, and fostering political autonomy. The past forty years have witnessed the emergence of postsecondary institutions established by and/or for indigenous peoples around the globe. The first such institution, Diné College in Arizona, was chartered as the Navajo Community College in 1968 by the Navajo Tribal Council. Similar institutions currently serve indigenous peoples in Australia, Canada, New Zealand, Scandinavia, Russia, Latin America, and throughout the western United States.

By most accounts, these "indigenous postsecondary institutions" should not exist. They serve exceedingly small, destitute, and poorly educated populations that until recently were targeted for wholesale assimilation. Moreover, their existence contradicts an otherwise general trend toward integration in higher education. In an era when the legitimacy (and, indeed, the legality) of race-based admissions policies is suspect, it is fairly commonplace for indigenous postsecondary institutions to restrict admission to indigenous students.

Against these odds, postsecondary institutions for indigenous peoples are now a standard, even mandatory, feature of existing or aspiring democracies with an indigenous population. In other words, indigenous postsecondary institutions have become *institutionalized*, such that a state's failure to establish one—or at least to support indigenous peoples' efforts to establish their own—is considered "negligent and irrational" (Meyer and Rowan 1977: 350). But it would be a mistake to attribute their existence to the magnanimity of national governments. In establishing their own postsecondary institutions, indigenous peoples have overcome seemingly insurmountable obstacles, due in large measure to their exceptional status as "quasi-sovereign" political groups under international and domestic law.

This book accounts for the emergence and institutionalization of post-secondary institutions for indigenous peoples. Briefly stated, I contend that the nature and purpose of indigenous peoples' education have changed in tandem with their legal standing and normative status, which in turn reflect broader structural, political, and cultural transformations in the global polity (Thomas, Meyer, Ramirez, and Boli 1987; Meyer, Boli, Thomas, Ramirez 1997). The right of indigenous peoples to self-determination as currently recognized under international law, rooted in their claims to precontact sovereignty and traceable to fifteenth-century legal discourses, empowers them to establish and control their own postsecondary institutions. A complete understanding of indigenous postsecondary institutions, which first emerged less than fifty years ago, therefore requires an analysis extending back 500 years. It also necessitates a comparative analysis of the conditions that facilitate the establishment and shape the development of indigenous postsecondary institutions in different countries. Finally, it compels an explanation as to what makes these institutions different from other colleges and universities. These are the central tasks of this book.

After World War II, two global processes—the destigmatization of "peripheral" groups such as women and minorities and the massification of higher education—combined to produce the expanded participation of underrepresented students in tertiary education (Trow 2006) and the increased representation of marginalized cultures and perspectives in formal curricula (Frank, Schofer, and Torres 1994; Frank, Wong, Meyer, and Ramirez 2000; Olzak and Kangas 2008; Rojas 2007; Wotipka, Ramirez, and Martinez 2007). These twin processes gave women and minorities access to educational institutions from which they were previously excluded. As a consequence, separate institutions that had been established to accommodate women and minorities during their segregation from "mainstream" institutions began to close.

Without question, indigenous peoples have also profited from improvements in the status of minorities and from the expansion of mainstream higher education institutions to include underrepresented groups. But unlike the situation of women and other minorities, the efforts of indigenous peoples to establish and control their *own* postsecondary institutions are increasingly permitted and in many cases actively supported by states. In fact, postsecondary institutions for indigenous peoples arrived on the scene just as separate colleges for other groups came under scrutiny for their role in perpetuating racial and gendered segregation. The rise of tribal colleges in the United States during the 1960s and 1970s, for instance, coincided with the closure of many women's and black colleges. What accounts for this anomaly?

In addition to destigmatization and massification, which promote the integration of disadvantaged groups into mainstream institutions, indigenous peoples also lay claim to a distinctive political and legal status—sovereignty—that supports the creation of separate institutions. Participation in the mainstream political process is a *human* right, whereas control of the political process itself is a *sovereign* right. Likewise with education: Equal access to and participation in mainstream educational institutions is a human right, whereas control of separate institutions is a sovereign right. Sovereignty, I argue, is the crucial variable accounting for the contemporary emergence and continued sustainability of postsecondary institutions for indigenous peoples. In liberal societies that privilege individualism, equality, and nondiscrimination, groups without claims to sovereignty find it difficult to establish or maintain separate institutions.

CONCEPTUAL FRAMEWORK

Indigenous Sovereignty

Unlike racial, ethnic, or cultural groups that immigrated (voluntarily or involuntarily) to existing states, indigenous peoples occupied their lands prior to the arrival of colonizers. They had historical precedence in a territory now dominated by culturally different "others," typically European colonizers and their settler descendents, and they remain culturally, socially, and legally distinct from the ambient settler and migrant populations.[1] Prior occupancy, in turn, implies claims to prior sovereignty that most racial or ethnic minorities lack (Werther 1992; Macklem 1993; Kingsbury 1998). American Indians, for example, are accordingly treated "not as a discrete racial group, but, rather, as members of quasi-sovereign tribal entities" (*Morton v. Mancari* 1974: 554), and international human rights discourses clearly delineate between indigenous peoples and other minorities (Daes 1996).

In addition to the putatively objective criteria of historical continuity, colonial subjugation, and cultural difference, contemporary international discourses also underscore the importance of subjective self-identification. The Declaration on the Rights of Indigenous Peoples, adopted by the U.N. General Assembly in 2007, asserts that "indigenous peoples have the right to determine their own identity or membership in accordance with their customs and traditions" (United Nations 2007: Article 33[1]). In the American context, the Supreme Court ruled in *Santa Clara Pueblo v. Martinez* (1978: 72, n. 32) that "a tribe's right to define its own membership for tribal purposes has long been recognized as central to its existence as an independent political community." The prerogative of self-identification therefore applies to indigenous peoples as autonomous political communities, not as members of racial groups.

Today, many indigenous peoples contend that the sovereignty of their ancestors remains intact because it was either never extinguished or else illegitimately usurped. Not surprisingly, some commentators deny that indigenous groups currently possess, or ever had, valid claims to sovereignty as currently understood (Boldt and Long 1984; Corntassel and Primeau 1995; Flanagan 2000). Part of the problem is that the very nature of sovereignty has evolved over time. Max Weber might have concluded that precontact indigenous peoples (and, for that matter, premodern Western polities) exercised traditional sovereignty, whereas sovereignty is now understood distinctly and exclusively in legal-rational terms. Rather than view sovereignty as having an all-or-nothing quality—either an entity is or is not sovereign—I propose to reconceptualize it as a continuous variable supporting a variety of possible claims.

Take, for instance, the Montevideo Convention on the Rights and Duties of States (1933), Article 1 of which identifies four criteria for sovereign statehood: (1) a permanent population, (2) a defined territory, (3) a government, and (4) the capacity to enter into diplomatic relations with other states. The standard approach treats each criterion as a necessary condition of statehood. Sovereignty, in this view, is a binary qualitative state: Entities satisfying all four conditions are sovereign, while entities lacking even one of them are not. A different approach, one that I advocate, treats the criteria as additive. Thus, sovereignty varies as a matter of degree rather than kind. Most indigenous peoples satisfy the Montevideo requirements in some fashion:

- They have distinct populations, delimited and regulated by their own principles of membership.
- By virtue of their prior occupancy, they assert compelling territorial claims.
- They were self-governing prior to conquest or colonization, and many remain so today (for example, band councils in Canada, tribal governments in the United States, Home Rule in Greenland, Miskito autonomy in Nicaragua).
- Historically, many entered into formal diplomatic or treaty relationships with colonial powers.

To the extent that indigenous peoples meet these criteria, they can assert an international legal personality on par with sovereign nation-states. But not all indigenous peoples can meet these criteria, and those who can often do so in circumscribed fashion. Tribal lands in the United States, for example, are delineated by clearly defined boundaries, but the land is held "in trust" by the federal government. Moreover, in countries where formal treaties with indigenous peoples were signed—and in places like Australia they never were—"government-to-government" relations are typically restricted to the colonizing state or its successor. So it is that in the United States the Supreme Court held in *Cherokee Nation v. Georgia* (1831) that Indian tribes could no longer enter into treaties or agreements with foreign governments, and Congress unilaterally ended the policy of making treaties with Indian tribes in 1871.

A different way to conceptualize sovereignty has been advanced by Stephen Krasner, who identifies four distinct modalities: international legal, Westphalian, domestic, and interdependence (Krasner 1999). In contrast with the theory of statehood promulgated by the Montevideo Convention, whereby entities that satisfy predetermined criteria are regarded as sovereign ipso facto, international legal sovereignty depends on formal recognition by other sovereign states. Westphalian sovereignty entails the right (if not always the ability) to exclude external actors from internal affairs and authority structures, whereas interdependence sovereignty pertains more specifically to the ability to enforce territorial boundaries. Finally, domestic sovereignty consists of the organization and effective exercise of authority within a territory.

Once again, indigenous peoples enjoy many of these prerogatives of sovereignty, as illustrated by the status of Indian tribes in the United States. To be treated as sovereign nations under U.S. law, Indian tribes must first be formally recognized by the federal government; this constitutive act of recognition bears at least some resemblance to the process by which international acts of diplomacy constitute nation-states as legally sovereign.[2] Once recognized, Indian tribes are empowered to exclude nonmembers from their reservations (Pevar 2002: 105), a clear manifestation of interdependence sovereignty. More fundamentally, tribes possess the sovereign authority to form governments and enforce tribal laws. Thus, while Indian tribes do not enjoy Westphalian sovereignty in a strict sense—Congress has plenary power over Indian tribes, giving it the ultimate authority to intervene in tribal affairs or even to extinguish tribal rights—they nevertheless enjoy and exercise other forms of sovereignty as identified by Krasner.

Indigenous peoples clearly possess many attributes of sovereignty and are not unlike stateless nations such as Catalonia, Scotland, Quebec, and Puerto Rico that exercise substantial regional autonomy, or associated states such as Niue and the Cook Islands that are self-governing with respect to internal affairs but voluntarily defer to a "protector" state on external matters such as defense. To be sure, many Indian reservations are larger and more populous than several microstates that currently enjoy complete sovereignty (Deloria 1985: 161–186).

Of course, most indigenous peoples would find it difficult if not impossible to achieve full sovereignty in the form of nation-statehood. Nor do most indigenous activists desire this outcome. Rather, they seek forms of self-determination that can be exercised *within* existing nation-states. Unlike sovereignty, which is an end state, self-determination is an ongoing process whereby peoples "freely determine their political status and freely pursue their economic, social and cultural development."[3] Claims to self-determination include a range of external and internal alternatives, not all of which threaten to dismember existing states. As applied to and claimed by indigenous peoples, self-determination has been equated with everything from sovereign statehood—the ultimate external variety—to municipal-level powers exercised within established states—a relatively weak, even co-opting, internal alternative (Alfredsson 1987; Fleras and Elliot 1992; Sanders 1991). Where along this continuum indigenous peoples fall is an empirical question, as it varies both historically and cross-nationally. Suffice it to say at this point that self-determination is becoming increasingly extricated from its rather close association with overseas decolonization but that it confers at least some degree of internal control over important social institutions such as schools.

Postsecondary Institutions

Sovereignty plays such a central role in my analysis because of its implications for indigenous peoples' control of their own postsecondary institutions. Indeed, political authority has always implied the authority to control higher education (Riddle 1996). During the Middle Ages, sovereignty invested the papacy and its secular counterpart, the Holy Roman Empire, with the authority to establish and control universities. As nation-states became the exclusive loci of legitimate political authority, control over universities was nationalized. I advance a similar argument that links the rise of indigenous postsecondary institutions to the resurgence of indigenous peoples' quasi-sovereign status under international and domestic law.

Defining what exactly constitutes a "postsecondary institution" is complicated by the cross-national and historical scope of my analysis. Its meaning is spatially and temporally contingent, differing across countries and changing over time. Precise definitions therefore await the analyses that follow. In general terms, however, postsecondary institutions vary along two dimensions, degree level and institutional autonomy.

The first dimension, *degree level*, refers to the highest degree or credential awarded by an institution. Based on definitions and classifications established by the International Standard Classification of Education (ISCED) for standardizing cross-national data collection and analyses (UNESCO 1997), I include institutions offering programs at levels 4, 5, or 6. Level 4 institutions provide postsecondary nontertiary programming of up to two years in duration and award certificates such as associate's degrees that prepare students either for admission into level 5 programs or for direct entry into the labor force. Level 5 is defined as the first stage of tertiary education, with programs culminating in a bachelor's degree or its equivalent worldwide. Level 6 programs, representing the second stage of tertiary education, require students to produce original research and lead to advanced research qualifications such as master's degrees or doctorates. Throughout the book, the terms *postsecondary institutions* and *postsecondary education* should be understood to encompass ISCED level 4 and higher.

In addition to an institution's degree level, I classify the extent of its *institutional autonomy* using three categories: independent, affiliated, or integrated (Barnhardt 1991; Hampton 2000). Independent institutions are fully autonomous; they are accredited to award their own degrees. Affiliated institutions are administered "under the academic purview and accreditation umbrella of [a] cooperating institution" (Barnhard 1991: 211) but retain some measure of autonomy. Integrated structures, such as academic departments, are completely subsumed within an encompassing institution. If control over postsecondary education is indeed a prerogative of sovereignty, as Riddle (1993, 1996) argues, then indigenous sovereignty should bear directly on the level of autonomy indigenous postsecondary institutions enjoy.

A THEORY OF INSTITUTIONAL ORIGINS

The resurgence of indigenous sovereignty claims, in combination with the massification of higher education and the destigmatization of minorities, produced conditions amenable to the rise of indigenous postsecondary institutions. These global processes, in turn, are mediated by cross-national differences in the structure of indigenous–state relations and higher education systems. Nation-states act as prisms that bend and refract global processes to produce variation in the emergence of indigenous postsecondary institutions

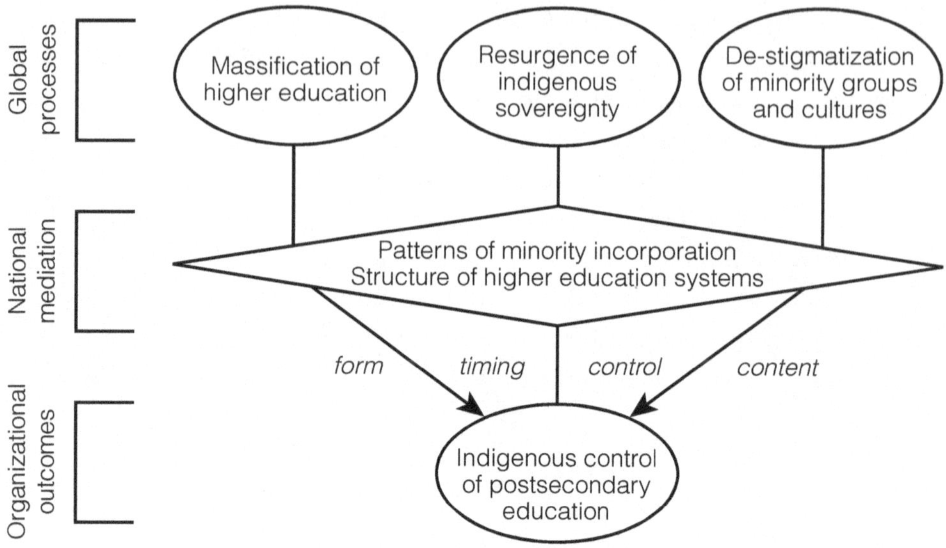

FIGURE I.1. Multilevel processes contributing to the emergence of indigenous postsecondary institutions.

along four dimensions—timing (when was the first one established?), number (how many colleges are there?), control (how autonomous are they?), and form (which organizational structures do they adopt?). Figure I.1 diagrams the contours of this argument.

Separate postsecondary institutions for indigenous peoples emerged within a broader world polity, defined as a global system of social and political actors—individuals, organizations, nation-states, and, I will argue, indigenous peoples—that are constituted by and operate under a shared cultural framework (see Meyer 1980; Meyer et al. 1997a). This "world culture" provides the fundamental building blocks of society. Culture in this sense is not so much a collection of traditions, customs, beliefs, and folkways as it is a system of cognitive templates, organizational blueprints, action scripts, and normative rules that underlie social reality. Culture, in other words, is deeply ontological: It confers status, identity, and rights to social actors; it provides these actors with schemas for making sense of the world; and it sets parameters around what is "proper" or even thinkable at any given historical moment. World culture is therefore constitutive rather than expressive (Meyer, Boli, and Thomas 1987; Jepperson and Swidler 1994; Meyer 1999).[4]

The basic tenets of world culture derive from medieval Christendom. Tracing long-term changes in the trajectory and substance of world culture as it pertains to indigenous peoples is a core task of this book. It was once natural to think of indigenous peoples as savages and to debate whether they had souls. Obviously, such ways of thinking were hardly conducive to the rise of indigenous postsecondary institutions. Neither, for that matter, was the sentiment that indigenous peoples were "uncivilized," which prevailed during the rise of nation-states and the expansion of state-based empires. Only after the deeply transformative events of World War II did notions of indigenous peoples and their rights change in such a way that made indigenous postsecondary institutions possible.

Another source of dynamism in the world polity is rooted in cross-sectional differences among nation-states. The existence of world culture vis-à-vis constitutive subunits, particularly nation-states, is constant at any given point in time, but states exhibit substantial variation with respect to their historical legacies and institutional structures. As world-cultural principles sift through nation-states, they get modified in ways that engender distinctive policies and practices. In this fashion, my analysis explores "the way in which 'common' international events or trends translate into different challenges in different countries as a result of their intersections and interactions with ongoing domestic processes" (Thelen 1999: 389). Although the overall tenor and trajectory of national policies regarding indigenous peoples reflect common world-cultural models, factors such as the conditions of colonization and the institutional configuration of governmental authority produce variation in the formal structure of indigenous–state relations and ultimately in the extent to which indigenous peoples are recognized as sovereign in domestic law. This variation, together with differences in the timing, scope, and structure of postsecondary educational expansion, shaped the emergence of indigenous postsecondary institutions cross-nationally.

My analysis builds on previous work that examines cross-national differences in "incorporation regimes," defined as institutions and policies that structure the integration of migrants into national polities (Brubaker 1992; Soysal 1994; Koopmans and Statham 1999). Yasemin Soysal (1994), for example, shows how the ideology of human rights was funneled by nation-specific institutional configurations and discursive frameworks to produce variation in the incorporation of migrants. By focusing exclusively on patterns of migrant incorporation, however, these studies imply that an integrated and internally consistent set of institutional logics operate within countries, even if those logics differ across countries. In fact, multiple logics of incorporation often coexist in the same country, and the incorporation of indigenous peoples is frequently governed by policy logics that differ greatly from those structuring the incorporation of other minority or immigrant groups. These differences shed light on the vitally important role that indigenous sovereignty plays in the emergence of indigenous postsecondary institutions.

The cross-national component of my analysis compares the efforts of indigenous peoples, all with stronger or weaker claims to sovereignty, to establish separate postsecondary institutions. But to isolate the crucial impact of sovereignty on control of separate postsecondary institutions, it is necessary to make comparisons between indigenous peoples with claims to sovereignty and nonindigenous minorities that lack such claims. To this end, I analyze the effect of *intra*national differences in the incorporation of African Americans and American Indians on the origins, purposes, and curricula of tribal and historically black colleges in the United States. On a basic level, the very emergence of tribal colleges is exceptional, as it contradicted a powerful social and legal trend toward racial integration in higher education during the 1960s and 1970s. Another prominent feature that distinguishes tribal from black colleges (and, for that matter, from "mainstream" colleges) is the curriculum: Colleges serving American Indians incorporate culturally distinctive content into the formal curriculum much more extensively than do colleges serving African Americans. My analysis of tribal colleges as organizations demonstrates how political claims rooted in sovereignty empower Indian tribes not only to resist legal pressures that otherwise discourage the establishment of minority-serving colleges but also to defy institutional processes that impel curricular homogeneity or "isomorphism" across schools (DiMaggio and Powell 1983; Meyer and Rowan 1978; Scott 2003).

The Multilevel Process of Institutional Innovation

A complete understanding of the institutional and political dynamics giving rise to indigenous postsecondary institutions requires attention to each of the three levels of analysis just discussed: global, national, and organizational. My analytic framework unifies all three levels of analysis into a coherent empirical and theoretical whole. As formal organizations, indigenous postsecondary institutions are influenced by the structure of national indigenous policies; in turn, nation-states—and indigenous peoples themselves—are embedded in and shaped by the global institutional environment.

A good deal of theoretical and empirical work focuses on the institutional processes that link different levels of analysis to one another. W. Richard Scott (1994: 83), for example, distinguishes between bottom-up "processes by which institutional forms are created or generated" and top-down "processes by which they are reproduced or diffused." In similar fashion, Francisco Ramirez and his colleagues (1997: 739) draw a "theoretical distinction between eras of innovation and contestation and eras of consolidation and institutionalization." This book focuses primarily on the initial emergence and institutionalization of indigenous postsecondary institutions, touching only briefly on their subsequent reproduction and diffusion.

The genesis of new practices or institutions is closely linked to and shaped by the characteristics of innovators and early adopters (Tolbert and Zucker 1983; Baron, Dobbin, and Jennings 1986; Ramirez, Soysal, and Shanahan 1997; Jang 2003). Indeed, the term *adopters* at this stage in the process may be a misnomer; *adapters* is perhaps more appropriate, as it better captures the agency involved in tailoring new practices or forms to local conditions. Once an organizational model or practice is fully institutionalized—that is, once it assumes a taken-for-granted quality—it flows around the world and is adopted irrespective of functional utility or the characteristics of adopters (Strang and Meyer 1993).

For too long, scholars have tended to portray these distinct processes as theoretically opposed. But as Paul DiMaggio explained in a now-classic essay, the emergence, institutionalization, and diffusion of novel organizations constitute different moments in the same overall process:

> The theoretical accomplishments of institutional theory are limited in scope to the diffusion and reproduction of successfully institutionalized organizational forms and practices. Institutional theory tells us relatively little about "institutionalization" as an unfinished process (as opposed to an achieved state). . . . The first step in developing a fuller understanding of the creation, reproduction, and demise of institutions

must transcend the theoretical opposition between political and institutional models and recognize the explanatory tasks to which each kind of model is better suited. (DiMaggio 1988: 12, 16)

Figure I.2 presents a heuristic model that reconciles the "political" and "institutional" aspects of organizational innovation, institutionalization, and diffusion. The first half of the figure is inspired by the causal imagery of methodological individualism and is based on James Coleman's (1986) analysis of Weber's "Protestant Ethic" thesis. In this model, macrolevel norms (for example, Protestant doctrine) influence microlevel actors (individuals and their values), whose relationships and transactions with one another (economic behavior) aggregate back up to produce systemic changes (the emergence of capitalism). Methodological holists, including world polity theorists (Meyer et al. 1997a), turn this imagery on its head by focusing on what might be called, following Peter Berger (1967), a "sacred canopy." This view of the world begins with "externalization," the process by which individuals pour themselves out into the world (Berger 1967; Berger and Luckmann 1966). Over time, the inventions, innovations, customs, and practices that emerge from this outpouring become objectified, institutionalized, and cemented into practice—in Durkheim's terms, they confront people as "social facts." At this point, institutions become available for widespread diffusion and adoption. As depicted in Figure I.2, the whole process consists of five sequential steps:

1. First, world culture defines and constitutes social actors at multiple levels of analysis—states, individuals, indigenous peoples, and so on—by endowing them with identities, purposes, and capacities (Meyer 2000; Meyer and Jepperson 2000; Frank and Meyer 2002). The number of actors that claim legitimate standing in the world system has contracted and expanded over time in ways that directly impact the legal standing of indigenous peoples (see Chapter One).

2. Social actors are, by their very constitution as "actors," innovative and entrepreneurial: They modify world-cultural models and scripts, transpose them to novel situations, and even invent or improvise new ones (Swidler 1986; Friedland and Alford 1991; Sewell 1992).[5]

3. As innovations and inventions become institutionalized, they begin to diffuse. At this stage, innovations are not adopted so much as they are adapted

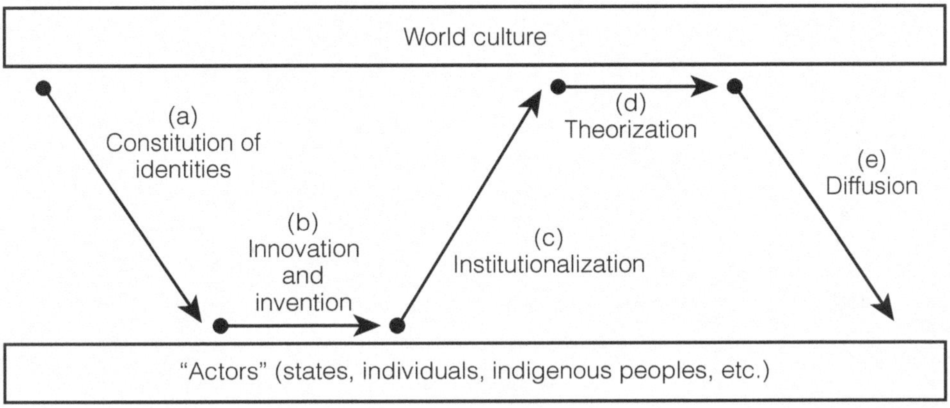

FIGURE I.2. Heuristic model for the analysis of indigenous postsecondary institutions.

to local conditions (as the "prism" imagery of Figure I.1 is intended to convey).

4. Once fully institutionalized, practices or models are incorporated as new elements of world culture, where they undergo theorization: They are made abstract and assume a necessary or functional character (Strang and Meyer 1993).
5. Highly theorized models diffuse around the world in rapid and disembedded fashion.

This general model explains well the development of indigenous postsecondary institutions. Briefly, (a) world culture constitutes indigenous peoples as legitimate actors with claims to self-determination, which supports (b) the establishment of indigenous postsecondary institutions, a microlevel innovation. The precise timing, number, and organizational characteristics of these institutions, however, vary cross-nationally based on the structure of indigenous–state relations and higher education systems. As more indigenous postsecondary institutions were established, they eventually (c) became an institutionalized feature of world culture that is now supported, for example, by the United Nations (see the discussion in Chapter Two). Once institutionalized, an indigenous postsecondary institutional model (d) was made available for widespread adoption and (e) has since diffused throughout the world. The analyses reported herein aim to unpack the long-term and multilevel process by which indigenous postsecondary institutions emerged locally and were institutionalized globally.

NOTES ON METHOD

Understanding the processes operating at each level of analysis—global, national, and organizational—requires different methodological strategies. To explicate the historical, political, and educational contexts that fostered the emergence of indigenous postsecondary institutions, I construct analytical narratives "that respect the specifics of time and place but within a framework that both disciplines the detail and appropriates it for purposes that transcend the particular story" (Levi 1999: 155). These narratives explain changes in the status and standing of indigenous peoples and are anchored in a generalizable account of global-institutional change that can be extended to other empirical cases.

The cross-national analyses situate individual countries within this broader global context. I focus primarily on four countries—Australia, Canada, New Zealand, and the United States—that were among the first in the world to experience the establishment of indigenous postsecondary institutions. Formal comparisons of these cases uncovers striking similarities but also important differences in the status of indigenous peoples and, consequently, in the emergence of indigenous postsecondary institutions.

Consistent with the arguments reviewed previously, general policies toward indigenous peoples in these and other countries reflect broader shifts in world-cultural understandings. This approach follows a whole-to-parts logic that explains the characteristics of lower-level units by reference to systemic properties (Bergeson 1980; Tilly 1984), and is consistent with the "top-down" constitution of actors by a shared world culture.

A deeper comparative analysis reveals historically rooted differences in the status of indigenous peoples and the conditions that gave rise to indigenous postsecondary institutions. These analyses are predicated on a "similar systems" design that aims to explain variation rather than similarities in outcomes. Such a design proceeds as follows: First, cases that vary with respect to the outcome of interest, but that are otherwise as similar as possible in ways theorized to be causally important, are selected for comparison. Then, comparative analysis unearths causal conditions that covary with the outcome. The countries in my analysis are indeed similar in many respects, as each inherited Britain's legal traditions, cultural heritage, and liberal institutions (notwithstanding the French-speaking areas of Canada and the historically Spanish-speaking regions of the United States). My design effectively controls for these characteristics to isolate crucial differences in the ways each country incorporated its indigenous peoples into the mainstream polity. These differences have real and lasting consequences for the legal status of indigenous peoples and the rise of indigenous postsecondary institutions.

In applying a similar-systems design, researchers typically seek to identify necessary and sufficient conditions that explain a qualitative (that is, binary) outcome: In cases where the conditions are present, so too is the outcome; in cases where the conditions are absent, the outcome is absent as well. My approach, consistent with the notion that sovereignty is an ordinal rather than a dummy variable, is more akin to a fuzzy-set view of the world (Ragin 2000), one in which both conditions and outcomes are seen in shades of gray as opposed to black and white. Given that the relative strength of indigenous peoples' sovereignty claims in Australia, Canada, New Zealand, and the United States can be rank ordered, my goal is to determine whether these countries can be similarly ranked on key dimensions regarded as causal.

The organizational-level analyses extend the similar-systems design by comparing the experiences of minority groups within a single country, the United States, to isolate the effect of sovereignty on the development of minority-serving colleges and universities. This component of the book uses comparative-historical methods to inform quantitative analyses of the curriculum offered at black and tribal colleges. I attribute differences in the extent to which minority perspectives are represented in the formal curricula of black and tribal colleges to the contradictory ways that their primary constituents—African Americans and American Indians—were incorporated into the mainstream polity. I use constitutional, juridical, and legislative milestones as lenses through which to examine these inverse patterns of incorporation. The argument again turns on sovereignty: Indian tribes claim a sovereign status, which black Americans never possessed, that supports the establishment of separate institutions and the implementation of culturally distinctive curricular programming.

LOOKING AHEAD

The book is organized into three parts, each corresponding to a sequentially nested level of analysis. Part I focuses on *global* processes. It examines the origins and evolution of indigenous sovereignty claims in international legal discourses and accounts for indigenous peoples' control (or, at least, management) of postsecondary institutions. Chapter One links changes in the international legal standing and normative status of indigenous peoples to broader transformations in the world polity. I argue that the present-day claims of indigenous peoples to self-determination ultimately derive from their recognition as sovereign nations during the sixteenth century. Chapter Two then considers how the changes discussed in Chapter One engendered corresponding changes in the control and purpose of indigenous peoples' education. I argue that the claims of indigenous peoples to self-determination intersected with the postwar "massification" or expansion of higher education to produce the conditions under which indigenous postsecondary institutions first emerged.

Part II analyzes *cross-national* variation in the strength of indigenous sovereignty claims under domestic law and shows how country-specific structures of indigenous–state relations and higher education systems shaped the emergence of indigenous postsecondary institutions. Chapter Three demonstrates that the overall tenor of national policies vis-à-vis indigenous peoples in Australia, Canada, New Zealand, the United States, and elsewhere followed a broadly similar trajectory over time, shaped in common by the global transformations discussed in Chapter One, but also shows that cross-national differences in the political incorporation of indigenous peoples moderates the strength of their sovereignty claims. Chapter Four then explores how these differences, together with variations in the timing, pace, and structure of expansion in each country's postsecondary educational sector, generated distinct patterns in the emergence of indigenous postsecondary institutions.

Part III, which focuses on the United States, isolates sovereignty as the crucial variable giving rise to indigenous postsecondary institutions by comparing the emergence of colleges for an indigenous minority, American Indians, with those for a nonindigenous minority, African Americans. This part of the book considers two *organizational* outcomes—institutional legitimacy and curricular content—with a comparative analysis of tribal and historically black colleges. Chapter Five considers the social, political, and legal circumstances giving rise to colleges and universities that serve American Indians and African Americans. I argue that fundamental differences in the origins, goals, and even the constitutional legitimacy of tribal and black colleges are best understood with reference to the contradictory ways in which American Indians and African Americans were incorporated into the national polity. Chapter Six then presents results from a statistical analysis of tribal and black college curricula. I conclude that tribal sovereignty invests American Indians with the authority not only to charter their own colleges but also to infuse curricula with culturally distinctive content. To conclude the book, Chapter Seven summarizes key findings at each level of analysis, unifies those findings into a coherent theoretical framework, considers some of the challenges currently facing indigenous postsecondary institutions, and speculates about their future.

This introduction has established the conceptual and theoretical foundations on which the remainder of the book rests and also presented the core argument of the book: *Indigenous peoples advance legally and morally compelling claims to political sovereignty that, while not conferring independent statehood, nevertheless support their efforts to establish independent, culturally relevant postsecondary institutions.* To argue that indigenous peoples' control of postsecondary education derives from their sovereignty claims requires an analysis into the origins and content of those claims. That is the task of Chapter One.

PART I

GLOBAL ANALYSIS

CHAPTER ONE

WORLD POLITY TRANSFORMATIONS AND THE STATUS OF INDIGENOUS PEOPLES

States have sovereignty, counties have sovereignty, cities and towns have sovereignty, water districts have sovereignty, school boards have sovereignty. Why shouldn't tribes have total sovereignty? Originally they did.

Vine Deloria Jr. (1969: 144)

SOVEREIGNTY IS A PROPERTY MOST OFTEN attributed to nation-states alone. The idea that indigenous peoples are sovereign not only challenges the core premise of international relations—namely, that sovereignty belongs exclusively to entities organized as nation-states—but also the notion that individuals, understood first as citizens and more recently as humans, are the sole bearers of rights. And yet, indigenous peoples advance morally and legally compelling claims to collective sovereignty, something that distinguishes them from most other racial and ethnic groups. Whereas most historically disadvantaged minorities seek inclusion, understood as the right of individuals to share in the economic rewards and political life of mainstream society, indigenous peoples demand—and increasingly command—the authority to sustain an institutionally and politically separate existence.

The most recent international statement on the rights of indigenous peoples, the U.N. Declaration on the Rights of Indigenous Peoples (UNDRIP), is also the most comprehensive and far-reaching to date. Adopted by the U.N. General Assembly on September 13, 2007, UNDRIP marks the first time that the world community has formally and explicitly recognized the right of indigenous peoples to collective self-determination, defined as "the right to autonomy or self-government in matters relating to their internal and local affairs" (Article 4). Indeed, the declaration is unique among human rights accords in its emphasis on group-based as well as individual rights (Elliott and Boli 2008).

In one respect, one might say that UNDRIP was some three decades in the making, as the earliest drafts began circulating during the late 1970s. But, in another sense, many of the core rights enshrined in the declaration can ultimately be traced to the arrival of Europeans to the New World some 500 years ago. The exceptional quasi-sovereign status of indigenous peoples under international law—*including, crucially, the authority to establish and control independent postsecondary institutions that such a status entails*—is rooted in their treatment as autonomous nations in fifteenth- and sixteenth-century legal discourses. Yet the path from 1492 to 2007 was anything but linear. Several centuries elapsed during which indigenous peoples were denied basic human rights, much less rights as self-determining nations. Although Europeans equivocally recognized (but rarely respected) indigenous peoples' autonomy in the decades following first contact, indigenous sovereignty underwent a centuries-long period of retrenchment before experiencing a renaissance in the post–World War II era. These historical shifts in the standing and status of indigenous peoples reflected broader changes in the world system, understood as a transnational political and cultural polity (Meyer 1980; Meyer et al. 1997a). The analysis of indigenous peoples' rights must therefore begin with the origins and evolution of this "world polity."

THE WORLD POLITY

The modern world polity emerged during the late medieval period with the consolidation, integration, and colonial expansion of the European polity. Its cultural origins, however, are traceable to antiquity.

Cultural Antecedents of the Modern World Polity

The deep historical and cultural foundations of the world polity lie in Hellenic philosophy, Roman jurisprudence, and Judeo-Christian theology. Despite the ecumenical thrust inherent to each mode of thought, all were characterized by a dialectical tension between universalism and particularism. Ancient Greeks acknowledged the universality of *anthropos* as a biological species but drew a rigid social distinction between themselves and *barbaroi*—anyone who couldn't speak Greek (Pagden 1995). Aristotle, moreover, argued that barbarianism was an immutable condition that predestined whole categories of humanity to slavery. This idea persisted well into the sixteenth century, informing debates as to whether indigenous peoples should be regarded as barbarians and therefore as "natural slaves" of the Europeans.

Romans were somewhat more inclusive than their Greek predecessors. To be sure, "provincials" continued to be distinguished from different classes of citizens, but routine procedures existed for incorporating foreigners and even slaves into the *civitas*. Even more expansively, the *jus gentium*—precursor to the modern law of nations—reigned supreme over all humanity regardless of citizenship status. Roman emperors styled themselves "lords of all the world," a title that would later be adopted by Roman Catholic popes who, as Christ's vicars and benefactors of Constantine's apocryphal donation, claimed universal spiritual as well as temporal jurisdiction over the world and its inhabitants (Pagden 1995). At issue here was whether indigenous peoples were subject to or outside of the European law of nations.

Christianity's tremendous capacity for expansion is traceable at least to the Council of Jerusalem in ca. 50 C.E., when early Church leaders decreed that gentiles were allowed to convert directly to the new faith without first circumcising or observing Judaic law. Christians, of course, rarely concealed their contempt for infidels, whether Jews, Moors, or indigenous peoples; indeed, sixteenth-century Europeans debated whether the "savage" indigenes had souls. Still, absent the aggrandizing impulses of Christianity, it is doubtful whether the *European* polity would have become the truly *world* polity it is today.

World Polity Origins and Transformations

Most scholars trace the origins of the world system to the late fifteenth century, when capitalism began to display in earnest its global pretensions (Wallerstein 1974; Nederveen Pieterse 1995). But globalization had important cultural and political implications as well. The "discovery" of indigenous peoples, in addition to providing new economic opportunities for Europeans to exploit, also raised profound religious, moral, and political questions about the nature of the world and the place of Europeans in it.

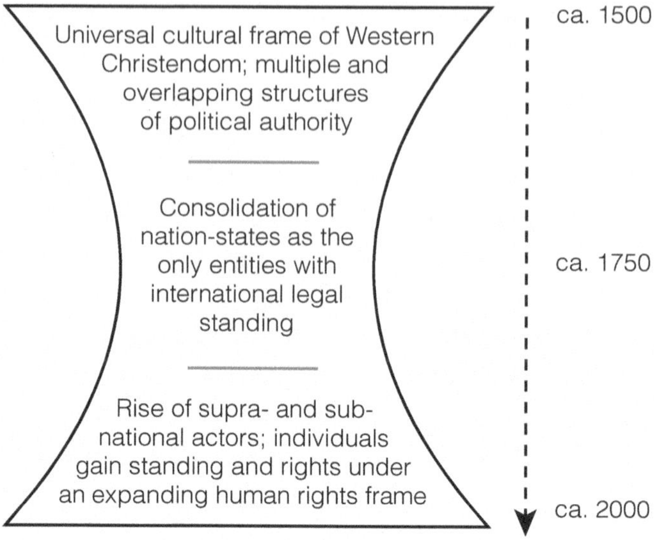

FIGURE 1.1. "Hourglass" development of the world polity, ca. 1500–ca. 2000.

The history of the world polity can be divided into three approximate periods (1500–1750, 1750–1945, 1945–present) during which different world-cultural logics—religious, statist, and "glocal" or postnational—prevailed.[1] These logics, defined as "set[s] of material and symbolic constructions" that are "symbolically grounded, organizationally structured, politically defended, and technically and materially constrained" (Friedland and Alford 1991: 248–249), have shaped the basic cultural, ontological, and institutional contours of the world polity since its emergence.

To illustrate these shifts in world-cultural logics, Figure 1.1 maps the "hourglass" trajectory of the world polity from approximately 1500 to the present. The diagram portrays historical changes in the polity's constitutive structure: the number of entities with legitimate political, legal, and normative standing. Time is arrayed vertically rather than horizontally to capture the secular—and secularizing—devolution of ultimate sovereignty first from God to states and then from states to individuals and subnational groups (Boli 1989).

Sovereignty in the nascent world polity was, as Perry Anderson (1974) put it, parcelized among an overlapping patchwork of feudal emperors, kings, princes, nobles, and lords who ruled alongside and under the auspices of the Catholic Church. The dual character of the European polity—its cultural, economic, and geographical integration but political fragmentation—made it dynamic and volatile. Diplomacy and warfare were regulated by an eclectic synthesis of Christian theology, Roman law, and humanist philosophies, resulting in a law of nations that was at once supranational and supernatural, existing "above" and prior to secular sovereigns (Williams 1990; Pagden 1995; Thornberry 2002).

The political authority of the Church and the legitimacy of its claims to universal jurisdiction waned dramatically after the Reformation in the early sixteenth century and the Peace of Westphalia in 1648.[2] Territorially and culturally delimited monarchies gradually consolidated power in a centripetal process that siphoned the Church's sovereignty from above and the nobility's authority from below. Eventually, the religious upheaval that linked individual souls directly to God found its political corollary in the notion of citizenship, whereby the holy covenant between God and His elect was replaced by the equally sacrosanct (if still fictive) social contract between individuals and their elected sovereign.

With the decline of divinely ordained dynasties and the rise of a secularized system of states, positivism became the organizing principle of international relations. Just as social contract theorists reduced all meaningful political activity within the state to individuals, the positivist worldview recognized states as the only legitimate actors on the global stage. The desacralized law of nations no longer transcended nations (that is, *supra*national law) but now derived from and existed purely between them (that is, *inter*national law). At about this time, it also became common to imagine that states were homogenous communities (Anderson 1991). In most cases, of course, these imaginings remained little more than delusions until extensive nation-building projects could bring them to fruition (Weber 1976).

In the aftermath of World War II, the ontological structure of the world polity reexpanded to include newly decolonized states (Strang 1990, 1991), nonstate groups (Kingsbury 1992), international organizations (Boli and Thomas 1997, 1999), transnational regimes (Krasner 1982; Donnelly 1986; Meyer, Frank, Hironaka, Schofer, and Tuma 1997b), and individuals with rights and standing independently of state membership (Soysal 1994). Meanwhile, efforts to submerge citizens under a common national identity gave way—in principle if not always in practice—to the celebration of cultural diversity, and the enjoyment of one's native language and culture are now fundamental human rights. This postwar "disenchantment" of the nation-state coincided with a resurgence in supra- and subnational identities.[3] Still, states have more to do than ever before: Education, health care, and social welfare are human rights that states are now expected to make available to citizens and non-citizens alike (Meyer et al. 1997a; Soysal 1994). And, to an unprecedented degree, a regime's external legitimacy is contingent on the (perceived) level of internal legitimacy it enjoys. According to Paul Keal (2003: 1), "The moral standing or legitimacy of particular states is bound up with the extent to which other members of international society perceive them to be protecting the rights of their citizens."

Colonialism in the World Polity

As the world polity contracted structurally during the seventeenth and eighteenth centuries, with national states becoming the sole receptacles of sovereignty, it expanded geographically via colonization. This expansion had tremendous and usually disastrous repercussions for indigenous peoples. Figure 1.2 charts the net number of overseas colonies held by Iberia (Portugal and Spain), the United Kingdom, France, and the United States between 1500 and 2000. Patterns of relative growth and decline were punctuated by three "global" wars identified by Immanuel Wallerstein (1983) as world-systemic watersheds—the Thirty Years' War (1618–48), the Napoleonic Wars (1800–15), and the two world wars (1914–45). These colonial eras corresponded roughly to the periods during which religious, statist, and glocal logics prevailed in the world polity.

Spain and Portugal spearheaded the first wave of Europe's overseas excursions, under papal aegis. The Spanish and Portuguese empires peaked near the turn of the seventeenth century and receded thereafter, in lockstep with the decline of the Habsburgs and the papacy in Europe. Their last vestiges persisted until Napoleon's invasion of Iberia presented revolutionaries in Latin America with the opportunity to wage successful independence movements. British colonial expansion during the seventeenth and eighteenth centuries reinforced its own (and Protestantism's) ascendance to hegemony in the world-system.

The sun began to set on the British Empire after reaching its zenith just prior to World War I, and rapid decolonization after World War II precipitated the incorporation of newly independent and juridically equal nation-states into the family of nations. At the same time, sovereignty was circumscribed by the ideology of human rights (Sikkink 1993; Donnelly 2003). The unabashedly statist world "polity" has become, after World War II, a more inclusive world "society" populated with a variety of nonstate actors, including indigenous peoples.

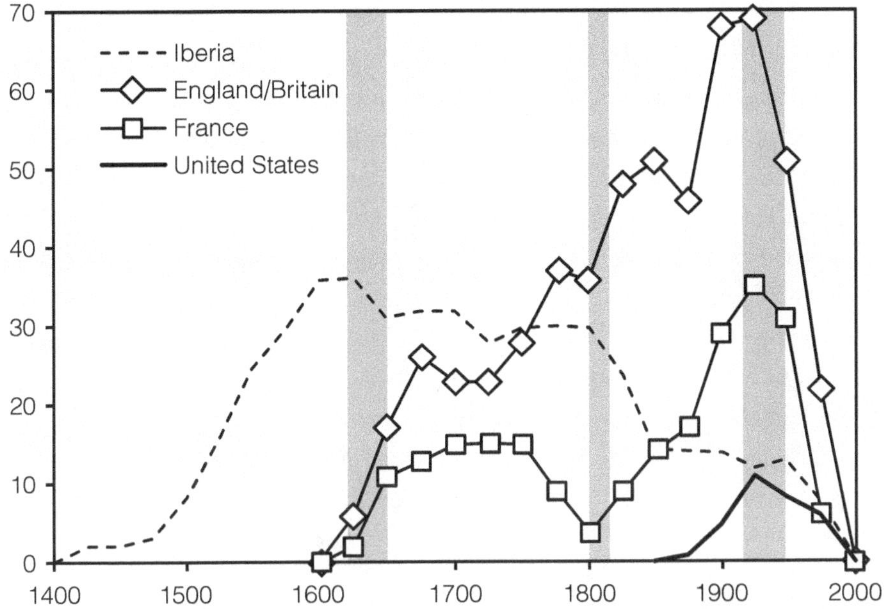

FIGURE 1.2. Net number of Iberian, British, French, and American colonies, 1400–2000.

SOURCE: Strang (1991).

Note: Shaded regions indicate periods of global warfare as identified by Wallerstein (1983): the Thirty Years' War (1618–48), the Napoleonic Wars (1800–15), and the World Wars (1914–45).

INDIGENOUS PEOPLES IN THE WORLD POLITY

Changes in the normative and legal status of indigenous peoples have followed the same hourglass-shaped trajectory as the world polity in general. During the era of first contact, as feudalism waned in Europe, indigenous–colonial relations were couched in the muddled discourses of salvation and sovereignty. The redemption of savage souls justified conquest, but indigenous nations also had natural-law rights that, although frequently violated, were nevertheless clearly articulated by the leading religious and legal scholars of the day. Any pretension of indigenous peoples to sovereignty was quelled by the rise of states, after which dispossession and assimilation became policies du jour. And the contemporary erosion of national sovereignty is producing a global society vaguely reminiscent of the old feudal order, a transformation that has incubated the reemergence of indigenous peoples' claims to sovereignty under the rubric of self-determination.

Religious Logic: Salvation and Sovereignty

Fifteenth-century Spaniards viewed their trans-Atlantic colonial excursions as the next installment of a long and venerated history of expansion that included Joshua's conquest of Canaan (Donelan 1984; McSloy 1996), Rome's colonization of the Iberian peninsula (Lupher 2003), the medieval Crusades (Williams 1990), and the *Reconquista* of Spain from the Moors. Drawing from a variety of religious and civil sources, legal scholars sometimes acknowledged the inherent sovereignty of indigenous nations and at other times vested ultimate title to their lands in Spain. Meanwhile, theologians debated the nature of the *Indios*, conceptualizing them alternately as rational humans or savage barbarians, little better than peasants (Vitoria [1557] 1917: 127–128).

Shortly after Columbus's fortuitous landfall in the New World, Spain dispatched envoys to Rome for papal validation of his "discovery." Authorization was given in 1493 by Pope Alexander VI, himself a Spaniard, in the bull *Inter caetera*. Alexander's bull granted sovereignty over most of the Americas to Spain on the condition that the Spaniards convert the native inhabitants to Christianity. Over the next two centuries, Spain grounded its territorial claims to the New World exclusively in the papal bull.

Despite having received the imprimatur of Christ's worldly representative, the Spanish Crown remained curiously obsessed with justifying its presence in the New World (Hanke 1959). In 1512, King Ferdinand sought the advice of Dominican theologian Matías de Paz and civil jurist Juan Lopez de Palacios Rubios, who concluded that "the Indians had complete rights of personal liberty and ownership but that the king was entitled to rule over them because the Pope had universal temporal and spiritual lordship and had granted him this right" (Donelan 1984: 83). *Dominium*, or ownership rights, resided in the Indians, but *imperium*—ultimate sovereignty—was vested in the Spanish monarch by virtue of the papal donation.

With its legal claims to America so validated, Spain and the papacy turned their attention to the normative and legal status of the continent's native inhabitants. The Laws of Burgos, enacted in 1513, provided for the Indians' conversion to Christianity, and the New Laws of 1542 manumitted all but a small number of Indian slaves by making them direct subjects of the Spanish Crown. In the interim, Pope Paul III had declared in *Sublimis Deus* (1537) that "the Indians are truly men and . . . are by no means to be deprived of their liberty or the possession of their property, even though they be outside the faith of Jesus Christ" (Washburn 1995: 13). However, the inability of kings and popes to enforce their edicts in the New World produced a great deal of decoupling between policies that solemnly recognized and practices that ruthlessly violated the rights of Indians to personhood and property.

To determine once and for all whether the natives were rational human beings and therefore capable of peaceful conversion to the Catholic faith, Charles V commissioned a series of debates, held at Valladolid in 1550–1551 (Hanke 1959). These debates pitted a disciple of Aquinas against a student of Aristotle: Bartolomé de las Casas, a Dominican friar whom Charles designated "Protector of the Indians," argued that the Indians were human beings in spite of their infidelity, whereas Juan Ginés de Sepúlveda, royal historian and chaplain, regarded them as natural slaves of the "civilized" Spanish. The issues debated at Valladolid closely paralleled the aforementioned question of gentile convertibility posed at the Council of Jerusalem some 1500 years earlier. Unlike at Jerusalem, however, the Valladolid debates did not produce a clear victor (Pagden 2001: 69). Las Casas nevertheless remained an outspoken champion of Indian rights, and his tract, *Brevísima relación de la destrucción de las Indias* [*A Short Account of the Destruction of the Indies*], published in 1552, provided a vivid description and excoriating critique of Spanish atrocities perpetrated on the Indians.

The revival of antiquity law and classical philosophy during the Renaissance also shaped official policies toward the Indians. In a series of influential lectures delivered in 1532 and published posthumously in 1557, Francisco de Vitoria, widely acclaimed as the "father" of modern international law, combined Catholic theology, Roman jurisprudence, and Aristotelian philosophy into a synthetic discourse on the rights of indigenous peoples (Thornberry 2002). As with Las Casas, Vitoria affirmed the Indians' inherent rationality; as a consequence, Vitoria argued, they were not only capable of peaceable conversion, but also true owners of the land they inhabited. "This is clear," Vitoria concluded,

> because there is a certain method in their affairs, for *they have polities which are orderly arranged and they have definite marriage and magistrates, overlords, laws, and workshops, and a system of exchange*, all of which call for the use of reason; they also have a kind of religion. Further, they make no error in matters which are self-evident to others; this is witness to their use of reason. ([1557] 1917: 127, emphasis added)

In the very same lecture, Vitoria presaged the trusteeship doctrine of the nineteenth century by suggesting that the natives were unfit to govern themselves:

> Although the aborigines in question are not wholly unintelligent, yet they are little short of that condition, and are so unfit to found or administer a lawful State up to the standard required by human and civil claims. Accordingly *they have no proper laws or magistrates, and are not even capable of controlling their family affairs*. . . . It might, therefore, be maintained that in their own interests the sovereigns of Spain might undertake the administration of their country. ([1557] 1917: 161–162, emphasis added)

The marriages, magistrates, and laws of the Indians were "definite" but apparently not "proper," at least as adjudged by Europeans.[4]

Vitoria's position on papal authority was similarly inconsistent. Although he explicitly denied papal jurisdiction over the New World and its inhabitants in purely *temporal* matters, Vitoria insinuated the pope's ultimate authority—and consequently, his authority to confer jurisdiction to Spain—in a rhetorical sleight of hand that linked worldly to spiritual affairs, over which the pope's sovereignty was regarded as supreme:

> As it is the Pope's concern to bestow especial care on the propagation of the Gospel over the whole world, he can entrust it to the Spaniards to the exclusion of all others, if the sovereigns of Spain could render more effective help in the spread of the Gospel in those parts; and not only could the Pope forbid others to preach, but also to trade there, if this would further the propagation of Christianity, *for he can order temporal matters in the manner which is most helpful to spiritual matters*. ([1557] 1917: 156–157, emphasis added)

Vitoria further justified Spain's colonial claims by elaborating the conditions under which Europeans might deprive the natives of their rights by waging "just wars" against them. Europeans entered the Americas with natural-law rights to travel, trade, and teach the Gospel. These rights applied to all nations equally and could be legitimately upheld by force. War against indigenous peoples was therefore justified by their lack of fidelity to Eurocentric conceptions regarding the duties of sovereigns. The initial presumption of indigenous sovereignty, albeit wholly within a theoretical and legal framework imposed by Europeans, had given colonial powers the pretext under which they could subsequently violate it.

The contradictions and ambiguities in Vitoria's landmark lectures made them decidedly versatile, providing ample room for a shift in policies that summarily denied the sovereignty of indigenous nations. Nevertheless, it was the nascent world system's contradictory character—its political fragmentation and expansive, even universalistic, religious cosmology—that made it broad enough in both structural and cultural terms to accommodate the existence of indigenous polities as distinct and autonomous polities. As nation-states grew more powerful, however, the political autonomy of indigenous nations correspondingly eroded.

Statist Logic: Dispossession and Assimilation

Predictably, the English and French refused to acknowledge the legitimacy of the papal bulls of donation to Spain,[5] although they found much in Spanish colonial discourses to borrow and exploit. In fact, Spanish thinkers unwittingly provided the intellectual fodder for England's colonial expansion. The English translation of Las Casas's *Brevísima relación*, known simply as *The Spanish Cruelties*, spawned the notorious "Black Legend" that exaggerated Spanish atrocities in the New World and fueled anti-Catholic propaganda in England. The failure of Spain to live up to its own standards of justice had strengthened England's imperial ambitions.

The Enlightenment also produced new secular rationalizations for England's displacement of Spain in the New World. The very same rationalizations also justified the expropriation of indigenous peoples' land and sovereignty. As summarized in Table 1.1, social contract theories originating in Britain were imported into international law in ways that simultaneously dispossessed indigenous peoples and challenged the legitimacy of religious—and by direct implication, Spain's—justifications for conquest. Consider, first, Thomas Hobbes's theory of society as expounded in *Leviathan*, originally published in 1651. Hobbes maintained that self-preservation is a paramount natural right of all individuals; indeed, protection of life and property is what ultimately compelled people to quit the state of nature and install an all-powerful ruler or government. To underscore that the lawless state of nature was an empirical condition and not merely a convenient metaphor, Hobbes ([1651] 1988: 65) pointed to the "savages" in America who, "except the government of small Families . . . have no government at all."

TABLE 1.1.
Justifying colonization during the statist era.

Type of justification	Dispossessing Indians	Challenging Spanish claims
Political (Hobbes)	Europeans possess natural-law rights to travel, trade, and preach among Indians, and more generally to self-preservation; if Indian polities could not afford Europeans "adequate" protection, then order could be imposed.	Spain illegitimately conquered organized polities (that is, Aztecs and Incas) under the pretext of religious salvation; England and France colonized lands occupied by "wandering" tribes living in a disorganized state of nature.
Economic (Locke)	There is a natural-law obligation to cultivate the land; nonsedentary indigenous peoples occupied more land than was necessary for sustenance and hence had no legal title, consistent with the legal doctrine of *terra nullius*.	Spain was the most fertile but worst-cultivated land in Europe; the Church owns—and wastes—too much property; other countries such as Britain, "too closely pent up at home," could legitimately colonize new lands.

Vitoria had argued that natural law, in addition to protecting an individual's right to self-preservation, also invested Europeans with the right to sojourn among the natives in America. If indigenous polities were unable or unwilling to protect those Europeans who exercised their natural-law right to travel in the New World, the Hobbesian argument justified the imposition of a government powerful enough to do so. Europeans alone, of course, calibrated the yardstick against which protection would be measured. "The test of civilization," says Paul Keal (2003: 104), "was whether there was a sufficient degree of political organization to allow European settlers to live in much the same degree of personal safety that they enjoyed in their countries of origin." Extending this rationale a bit further, international legal theorists later declared that only "civilized" nations—that is, nations that had reached levels of cultural, political, and economic development on par with European polities—enjoyed full membership in the international community (for example, see Westlake 1894; Hall 1909; Hyde 1922; Lindley 1926; Oppenheim 1928).

The Hobbesian logic was also used to impugn Spanish colonization in the Americas. Although many Catholic theologians had justified conquest based on the presumed need to redeem Indians' wayward souls and punish their violations of natural and divine law, Swiss diplomat Emmerich de Vattel argued in *The Law of Nations* that those ambitious Europeans [that is, Spaniards] who attacked the American nations, and subjected them to their greedy dominion, in order, as they pretended, to civilize them, and cause them to be instructed in the true religion,—those usurpers, I say, grounded themselves on a pretext equally unjust and ridiculous. . . . *[M]en derive the right of punishment solely from their right to provide for their own safety*, and consequently they cannot claim it except against those by whom they have been injured. (Vattel [1758] 1883: 137, emphasis added)

Moreover, the Incas and Aztecs had been "*indios policías* who lived under identifiable governance structures" as opposed to the *indios salvajes* of North America who presumably lived in a state of nature (Abernethy 2000: 193), a presumption that also weakened Spain's position under international law:

Though the conquest of the civilized empires of Peru and Mexico was a notorious usurpation, the establishment of many colonies on the continent of North America might, on their confining themselves within just bounds, be extremely lawful. The people of those expansive tracts rather ranged through than inhabited them. (Vattel [1758] 1883: 36)

On both accounts, the Spanish colonial enterprise was illegitimate. Spain violated natural law and the law of nations by attacking organized polities for reasons other than defense and self-preservation.

The colonization of North America, on the other hand, was perfectly legitimate because indigenous peoples on that capacious continent occupied more land than they needed to sustain their (presumably) nomadic lifestyles. This portion of Vattel's argument embeds a distinctly Lockean approach to dispossession, grounded in an economic rather than a political rationale. According to Locke's ([1690] 1960: 17) labor theory of property, "Every man has a *property* in his own *person*. . . . Whatsoever, then, he removes out of the state that nature hath provided and left it in, he hath mixed his labour with it, and joined to it something that is his own, and therefore makes it his property." But men could not legitimately claim more land than they could reasonably cultivate. This reasoning, coupled with the erroneous assumption that few if any indigenous peoples in the Americas cultivated the soil, justified colonization:

The [indigenous] Americans . . . are rich in land and poor in all the comforts of life; whom nature, having furnished as liberally as any other people with the materials of plenty, i.e., a fruitful soil, apt to produce in abundance what might serve for food,

> raiment, and delight; yet, for want of improving it by labour, have not one hundredth part of the conveniences we enjoy. . . . [T]here are still great tracts of ground to be found, which the inhabitants thereof, not having joined with the rest of mankind in the consent of the use of their common money, lie waste. . . . Thus, in the beginning, all the world was America. . . . (Locke [1690] 1960: 25–29)

England, less concerned with conquest and the salvation of souls than with commerce and the cultivation of land (Pagden 1995; Abernethy 2000), tended to base its colonial claims in these terms.

Locke's labor theory of property figured prominently in theories of colonization under international law. Turning again to Vattel: "Every nation is . . . obliged by the law of nature to cultivate the land that has fallen to its share; and it has no right to enlarge its boundaries . . . but in proportion as the land in its possession is incapable of furnishing it with necessaries" ([1758] 1883: 34). Based on this obligation to cultivate the earth—indeed, the entire Earth—in the most efficient manner possible, Vattel denied Indian nations' title to the New World:

> There is another celebrated question, to which the discovery of the New World has principally given rise. It is asked whether a nation may lawfully take possession of some part of a vast country, in which there are none but erratic nations whose scanty population is incapable of occupying the whole? [. . .] Nations cannot exclusively appropriate to themselves more land than they have occasion for, or more than they are able to settle and cultivate. [Indians'] unsettled habitation in those immense regions cannot be accounted a true and legal possession; and the people of Europe, *too closely pent up at home*, finding land of which the savages stood in no particular need, and of which they make no actual and consistent use, were lawfully entitled to take possession of it, and settle it with colonies. (Vattel [1758] 1883: 99–100, emphasis added)

One cannot help but think that Vattel had England in mind as he wrote about "the people of Europe, too closely pent up at home." England, after all, had exhausted its ability to expand "at home" with the incorporation of Wales and Scotland. "Spain," on the other hand, "is the most fertile and the worst cultivated country in Europe. The church there possesses too much land . . ." (Vattel [1758] 1883: 35). Because the Church prevented Spaniards from cultivating their own land to its fullest and most efficient capacity, the Spanish crown had no right to colonize the land of others. Thus, Vattel's interpretation of Locke simultaneously denied the sovereignty of Indian nations and articulated a decisive transition from religious to statist rhetoric in the international legal discourses of colonization.

The Lockean and Hobbesian streams of thought converged in the principle of *terra nullius*—literally, "vacant land"—which itself had precedent in Roman law. Accordingly, "land occupied by migratory or semi-sedentary peoples [was classified] as *terra nullius* . . . mean[ing] that proprietary rights could only exist within the framework of law enacted by an organized state; the land of prestate people without such law was therefore legally vacant" (Green and Dickason 1989: 235). In regions so defined as vacant, simple "discovery" vested an inchoate title to the land, which could be subsequently perfected (that is, transformed into a full title) by displays of effective occupation. This principle contradicted Vitoria's explicit rejection of the discovery doctrine based on his conclusion that the Indians had been true owners at the time of first contact with Europeans (Vitoria [1557] 1917: 138–139).

Even nations such as the United States whose sovereignty was grounded in discovery recognized the dubiousness of their claims. In 1823, the U.S. Supreme Court argued that "however extravagant the pretension of converting the discovery of an inhabited country into conquest may appear; if the principle has been asserted in the first instance, and afterwards sustained; if a country has been acquired and held under it; if the property of the great mass of the community originates in it, it becomes the law of the land, and cannot be questioned" (*Johnson v. McIntosh* 1823: 591). Discovery, therefore, was not a principled legal doctrine but rather a fait accompli imposed by judicial fiat. This nicety did not, however, prevent Britain from grounding its late-eighteenth-century colonization of Australia exclusively in the legally vacuous pretext that the continent was vacant.

These varied strategies for depriving indigenous peoples of their international legal status and claims to land—the state of nature, property in labor, *terra nullius*, and discovery—amounted to little more than legal fictions and historical revisions (Werther 1992; Reynolds 1996). Still, three decisions rendered by international tribunals during the interwar years indicate the staying power of these fictions:

- In 1926, the Cayuga Indians of New York sought to defend their treaty rights by appealing to the Anglo-United States Arbitral Tribunal (*Cayuga*

Indians [Great Britain] v. United States 1926). The tribunal held that Indian tribes "[are] not a legal unit of international law . . . [and have] never been so regarded. . . . So far as the Indian tribe exists as a legal unit, it is by virtue of the domestic law of the sovereign nation within whose territory the tribe occupies the land, and so far only as that law recognizes it" (Green and Dickason 1989: 84).

- Similarly, the Permanent Court of Arbitration ruled in *Island of Palmas* (1928) that "contracts between a State or a Company . . . and native princes or chiefs . . . are not, in the international law sense, treaties or conventions capable of creating rights and obligations such as may, in international law, arise out of treaties." (Green and Dickason 1989: 94)[6]
- In 1933, the Permanent Court of International Justice arbitrated a dispute between Norway and Denmark over control of Greenland. The court asserted in *Legal Status of Eastern Greenland* (1933) that the island had been *terra nullius* at the time of European settlement, ignoring the obvious presence of native Inuit peoples.

Clearly, indigenous peoples had little hope of gaining international standing during the statist era.

But this did not prevent them from trying. Indigenous peoples continued relentlessly but unsuccessfully to address their grievances to an international audience. One celebrated attempt came in 1923, when Deskaheh, a chief of the Cayuga Nation, traveled to Geneva to argue the case for indigenous sovereignty before the League of Nations. Although his petition to address the League found support among the Dutch, Irish, Panamanian, Persian, and Estonian delegations, Deskaheh's grievances were ultimately dismissed as an internal affair of the Canadian government.

In sum, social contract theories and the positivist turn in international law reconfigured the world polity around individuals and states, effectively "squeezing out" indigenous nations as corporate entities with autonomous legal standing (Anaya 2004; Thornberry 2002). In the decades following World War II, indigenous peoples reemerged as legitimate, self-determining subjects of international law (Barsh 1986, 1994), thus challenging entrenched world-cultural principles that located sovereignty exclusively in nation-states and defined individual citizens as the only rights bearers.

Glocal Logic: Indigenous Self-Determination

Recognition of indigenous peoples' right to collective self-determination occurred incrementally. During the early postwar years, attempts were made to submerge the rights of indigenous peoples entirely within the newly ascendant human rights framework that emphasized integration and equality rather than self-determination and sovereignty. The first official enumeration of indigenous peoples' rights, the International Labor Organization's (ILO) Convention No. 107 of 1957 "Concerning the Protection and Integration of Indigenous and Other Tribal and Semi-Tribal Populations in Independent Countries," recommended the full political integration and cultural assimilation of indigenous minorities, as individuals, into mainstream polities and societies.

Although integration and the extension of equal rights were welcomed by most minority groups, such policies were at odds with the prevailing desires among many indigenous peoples for increased autonomy and recognition of their collective rights to self-government. In advancing their claims, "Forth World" indigenous peoples instead drew extensively from the "Third World" rhetoric of decolonization and self-determination (Roy and Alfredsson 1987; Cairns 2003), at first with limited success. Self-determination had become too tightly coupled with sovereign statehood, and states, fearing violations of their territorial integrity, were reluctant to extend the principle to internally colonized indigenous groups. Consequently, the United Nations limited the right of self-determination to overseas colonies. The "saltwater thesis" articulated in the Declaration on the Granting of Independence to Colonial Countries and Peoples (1960) restricted the right of self-determination to dependencies geographically separated from their metropole by, for example, a "saltwater" ocean. Even the ILO's Convention No. 169 "Concerning Indigenous and Tribal Peoples in Independent Countries," adopted in 1989 to revise the overtly assimilationist agenda of its predecessor, includes the proviso that "the term 'peoples' . . . shall not be construed as having any implications as regards to the rights which may attach to the term under international law" (Article 1[3])—that is, the right of peoples to self-determination.

Recent developments seem to have softened if not entirely reversed these sentiments. As noted, the UNDRIP adopted in 2007 explicitly and unambiguously acknowledges that "indigenous peoples have the right to self-determination" (Article 3), but it also clarifies that "nothing in this Declaration may be interpreted as implying for any State, people, group or person any right to engage in any activity or to perform any act contrary to the Charter of the United Nations or construed as authorizing or encouraging any action which would dismember or impair, totally or in part, the territorial integrity or political unity of sovereign and independent States" (Article 46[1]). In this way, the right of indigenous peoples to self-determination has been reconciled with an international system that remains centered, for now at least, on sovereign nation-states.

Indigenous peoples' participation in international affairs increased sharply during the late twentieth century. In 1977, the International Indian Treaty Council became the first international indigenous organization to participate formally in the United Nations, and in 1982 the Union on International Associations began to keep track of indigenous-focused international organizations, the number of which grew from only nine in 1983 to 149 in 2001 (Union of International Associations 1983, 2001). Also in 1982, the Working Group on Indigenous Populations was established within the U.N. Economic and Social Council to advance the rights of indigenous peoples. In 1993, the U.N. General Assembly declared 1994–2005 the International Decade of the World's Indigenous People; a Second International Decade (2005–2014) was proclaimed in 2004. As part of the first Decade's activities, the United Nations inaugurated the Permanent Forum on Indigenous Issues in 2000, making it the first official U.N. body dedicated to indigenous peoples and their issues. That distinctly indigenous concerns are being addressed independently of other national, ethnic, religious, and linguistic minorities is noteworthy, as it signifies that indigenous peoples possess characteristics, problems, and claims that distinguish them from "minorities" in general. Indeed, these developments indicate that indigenous peoples have resurfaced as sui generis political entities whose rights cannot be wholly subsumed under the rubric of human rights.

This is not to say that indigenous peoples completely eschew human rights. Article 2 of UNDRIP reads: "Indigenous peoples and individuals are free and equal to all other peoples and individuals and have the right to be free from any kind of discrimination, in the exercise of their rights, in particular that based on their indigenous origin or identity." Indigenous claims, however, are neither limited to nor exhausted by individualistic human rights guarantees. Article 5 stipulates that "indigenous peoples have the right to maintain and strengthen their distinct political, legal, economic, social and cultural institutions, while retaining their rights to participate fully, if they so choose, in the political, economic, social and cultural life of the State." Indigenous *people*, as individuals, have the right to negotiate the "terms of inclusion" into mainstream society (Olneck 1993; Ramirez 2006), whereas indigenous *peoples*, as quasi-sovereign nations, can negotiate the conditions of their exclusion. In this respect, indigenous peoples occupy what might be called a "human rights–plus" position internationally that complements their "citizens–plus" status within states (Cairns 2000).[7]

Indigenous peoples mobilize human rights discourses differently from most other minority groups. Appeals to human rights are made not only to protect the rights of indigenous peoples in the here and now but also to challenge the legal sophistries and ethnocentric justifications that Europeans historically used to dispossess them of land and sovereignty. Chief among these was the notion that indigenous peoples were simply too uncivilized to exercise dominium (ownership) or imperium (sovereignty). Nation-states are beginning to revise their positions toward indigenous peoples accordingly, as when the Supreme Court of Canada applied contemporary human rights standards to evaluate the government's historical treatment of First Nations in the landmark *Calder v. Attorney-General of British Columbia* (1973: 169) ruling:

> The assessment and interpretation of the historical documents and enactments tendered in evidence must be approached in the light of present-day research and knowledge disregarding ancient concepts formulated when understanding of the customs and culture of our original people was rudimentary and incomplete and when they were thought to be wholly without cohesion, laws or culture, in effect a subhuman species.

In this fashion, contemporary standards of propriety, scrubbed of all pretensions to racial, cultural, or political superiority, retrospectively undermine the precepts on which Canada, the United States, Australia, New Zealand, and other countries were established and thereby strengthen the claims of indigenous peoples to original sovereignty.

Much progress has also been made in international law to rectify injustices perpetrated during the statist era. The International Court of Justice, for example, repudiated the *terra nullius* doctrine as a principle of international law in its *Western Sahara* opinion of 1975. Australia followed suit in 1992 when the High Court ruled in *Mabo v. Queensland* that *terra nullius* no longer had force in domestic law. Similarly, the *Palmas* decision, which deprived treaties signed with indigenous peoples of their international legal standing, has been modified if not completely abandoned. The preamble of UNDRIP declares that "treaties, agreements and constructive arrangements between States and indigenous peoples are, in some situations, matters of international concern, interest, responsibility and character." These developments represent a profound and fundamental shift in the way international law contemplates the relationship between indigenous peoples and states.

THE CHANGING STATUS OF INDIGENOUS PEOPLES

Accounting for Global-Institutional Change

To explain these international shifts in the status and standing of indigenous peoples, I develop an account of global-institutional change that builds on established notions of dynamism in the world polity. I begin with the basic premise that the culture underlying the world polity is dynamic rather than static, inconsistent rather than integrated, and polysemic rather than definitive (Meyer et al. 1997a; Lechner and Boli 2005; Sewell 1992). Given these qualities, actors situated in different levels of the world system—including nation-states, individuals, and, as I have argued, indigenous peoples—can deploy various (and sometimes contradictory) elements of world culture in the pursuit of their divergent interests. In this sense, world culture serves as "a 'tool kit' or repertoire from which actors select differing pieces for constructing lines of action" (Swidler 1986: 277).

Two mechanisms, *selective appropriation* and *exposure*, are operative. First, actors selectively appropriate elements of world culture, which, by virtue of its polysemy, can support a variety of claims (Sewell 1992). Appropriation may occur horizontally by status "equals" (for example, one state against another) or vertically by "subordinates" (for example, domestic social movement activists against the state). Horizontal appropriation generally takes the form of ideological contestation among competing states, whereby contenders adopt world-cultural precepts, including those espoused by the prevailing "hegemon," to challenge existing power structures and ideological edifices.[8] Conversely, vertical appropriation has affinities with what social movement scholars describe as "framing" (Snow, Rochford, Worden, and Benford 1986; Benford and Snow 2000), the process by which activists strategically mobilize, interpret, and disseminate information to gain support from potential allies or extract concessions from powerful actors.

Second, my use of exposure takes ideas about impression management (Goffman 1959, 1963) and the logic of confidence (Meyer and Rowan 1977) and recasts them at the global level of analysis. It occurs when vertically or horizontally positioned challengers attempt to discredit and displace a hegemonic power by exposing gaps between its stated principles and actual practices. Exposure may fail to produce hegemonic replacement, but it nonetheless compels the existing hegemon to alter or justify its behavior. Although conceptually distinct, appropriation and exposure frequently operate in tandem, with challengers drawing on the hegemon's own stated values or principles to highlight its failure to live up to them.

Explaining Changes in the Status of Indigenous Peoples

At least three instances of "horizontal" appropriation and exposure have contributed to changes in the status of indigenous peoples. During the transition from a nascent world polity grounded in religious logics to a predominantly statist polity, England challenged Spanish hegemony in the New World by appropriating Las Casas's indictment in *A Short Account* to lay bare the dissonance between Spain's colonial policies and practices. Catholic rhetoric in Europe affirmed the personal liberty and collective property rights of indigenous peoples, while across the Atlantic *conquistadores* mercilessly enslaved them and expropriated their lands. English propagandists, some of them Catholic recusants (Williams 1990), deftly adopted the Church's own disingenuous platitudes to assault Spain's papally sanctioned presence in the Americas.

England also appropriated Spanish legal discourses of conquest. "Stripped of some Catholic inflections," writes Patrick Thornberry (2002: 70), "the Spanish natural law discourses furnished an influential repository of source material to justify other conquering enterprises, including the English." The earliest letters patent issued by the English and French crowns to their respective explorers largely mimicked the papal bulls of donation (Williams 1990). And Vitoria's contention that Spain could legitimately administer the natives' affairs for them was later reformulated by Britain and its North American settler derivatives to justify their treatment of Indians as "wards" of the state.[9]

A second case of appropriation and exposure challenged British colonial hegemony in North America during the late eighteenth century. In addition to Locke's obvious and profound influence on the American colonists' notions of "life, liberty, and the pursuit of happiness," his labor theory of property also found expression in their attitudes toward indigenous peoples. During the American Revolution, Lockean principles were mobilized to contest the legitimacy of British colonial policies; after independence was won, Locke's ideas were again invoked to establish American supremacy over the indigenous population. First, American colonists rejected Britain's Royal Proclamation of 1763, which reserved the territories west of the Appalachians for Indians and prohibited colonists from settling there, because it violated Locke's injunction to cultivate the "wasteland" of America (Howard 2003: 45). Likewise, in *Johnson v. McIntosh* (1823: 590), Chief Justice John Marshall argued that "the tribes of Indians inhabiting this country were fierce savages . . . whose subsistence was drawn chiefly from the forest. To leave them in possession of their country, was to leave the country a wilderness." For Marshall as for Locke, cultivated agriculture conveyed title in land; absent that, the best Indians could hope for were rights of occupancy.

A third example of hegemonic competition occurred during the Cold War, but this time it resulted in the improvement of indigenous peoples' status. In an effort to win allies among the newly independent countries of Africa and Asia, Soviet propaganda criticized persistent discrimination and segregation in the United States, a country whose liberal rhetoric hypocritically extolled the equality of all individuals. Soviets presented themselves to the world—and especially the nonwhite Third World—as a multinational federation that not only promoted real (that is, economic) equality but that also supported collective self-determination through the establishment of constituent republics, autonomous areas, and separate administrative regions for national minorities and indigenous peoples (Hele 1994). The Soviet Union actively promoted indigenous peoples' rights in the United Nations and referenced those rights to criticize the United States and other Western countries for their treatment of indigenous peoples (Sanders 1989). John Skrentny (2002) argues that this geopolitical power play was instrumental in catalyzing a "minority rights revolution" in the United States: By framing racism as a national security issue in the fight against communism, minority rights elicited bipartisan support in the highest levels of government.

These mechanisms of appropriation and exposure can also be activated vertically. Civil rights activists in the United States, for example, referenced overseas decolonization to buttress their own claims for equality. Martin Luther

King Jr. made the point forcefully in his "Letter from Birmingham Jail": "We have waited for more than 340 years for our constitutional and God-given rights. The nations of Asia and Africa are moving with jetlike speed toward gaining political independence, but we still creep at horse-and-buggy pace toward gaining a cup of coffee at a lunch counter." But whereas civil rights activists alluded to decolonization to advance a moral critique of racism—if black-skinned Africans could assume control over their own nation-states, why couldn't blacks in the United States simply attend the same schools and enjoy the same rights as white Americans?—indigenous peoples referenced decolonization to support their own demands for political self-determination (Cairns 2003). If colonies in Asia and Africa can achieve *external* independence, why can't indigenous peoples, who themselves were colonized centuries ago, assume more responsibility over their *internal* affairs? Indigenous peoples therefore rejected a civil rights frame emphasizing inclusion in favor of a self-determination frame advocating greater autonomy.

Although indigenous peoples and other disadvantaged racial or ethnic groups make fundamentally different claims, they both engage in selective appropriation and exposure by taking aim at "a democratic state's legitimacy as a principled and law-abiding polity" (Werther 1992: 34). In their struggle for inclusion, nonindigenous minorities invoke the social contract (as instantiated, for example, by the U.S. Constitution) to expose the failure of liberal states to grant them equal rights. In this way, racial and ethnic minorities convert the state's own rhetoric into "weapons of the weak" (Scott 1985). Their avenues of recourse under international law remain limited to claims grounded in human rights, which inhere in individuals rather than groups and apply equally to everyone.[10] Alternatively, indigenous peoples derive their claims not from the social contract or human rights norms, but from their historical sovereignty as recognized under the law of nations:

> a successful assertion of aboriginal status generates a strong case for self-determination and group rights within the modern democratic state precisely because it is not grounded in liberal conceptions of rights that flow from uniform citizenship. Rather, it references sequentially a legitimate international law position of original national sovereignty according to early European law. (Werther 1992: 8)

Indigenous peoples' claims to sovereignty are so compelling not because they regarded themselves as sovereign prior to contact with Europeans—indeed, precontact indigenous societies did not contemplate the concept of sovereignty per se (Boldt and Long 1984)—but rather because Europeans regarded indigenous peoples as sovereign *on their own terms*.[11] The U.S. Supreme Court acknowledged as much in 1832, with its seminal ruling in *Worcester v. Georgia* (1832: 559–560):

> The constitution, by declaring treaties already made . . . to be the supreme law of the land, has adopted and sanctioned the previous treaties with the Indian nations, and consequently admits their rank among those powers who are capable of making treaties. The words "treaty" and "nation" are words of our own language, selected in our diplomatic and legislative proceedings, by ourselves, having each a definite and well understood meaning. We have applied them to Indians, as we have applied them to the other nations of the earth. They are applied to all in the same sense.

So where European colonizers historically imposed their own understandings of international law in ways that justified the dispossession of indigenous peoples, contemporary indigenous peoples now selectively co-opt elements of the very same legal discourses to bolster their modern self-determination claims.

But the question still remains: Why have states, always and everywhere jealous of their sovereignty, begun to recognize the collective rights of indigenous peoples to self-determination? Part of the answer is that states are more vulnerable to indigenous peoples' challenges now than ever before. The "denationalization" of the state after World War II (Sassen 2006), the concomitant ascendance of human rights norms, and the appearance of new nonstate actors on the world stage had a twofold effect. On the one hand, it opened up ontological space for the reemergence of indigenous peoples as legitimate international actors. On the other hand, it created ideological space for the successful rearticulation of indigenous peoples' claims to sovereignty and nationhood. Demands by indigenous peoples for sovereignty are in no way new; they have been advanced for decades, even centuries. It was therefore not the fundamental claims that changed but rather the conditions under which those claims became efficacious. In other words, domestic and transnational opportunity structures changed in ways that rendered the indigenous sovereignty frame more resonant (McAdam 1996; Snow et al. 1986; Morgan 2004).

Contextualizing and Conceptualizing Indigenous Sovereignty

If international law has indeed come full circle in this manner, perhaps it is because the international system has itself come to resemble a bygone era. In thinking about the nature of indigenous peoples' status under international law, it may behoove us to escape what Hedley Bull ([1977] 2002: 258) described as the "tyranny of existing concepts and practices" by reviving bygone conceptions of sovereignty. Bull was the first to posit that today's international society has much in common with the medieval political and cultural order (see also Friedrichs 2001; Kobrin 1998; Mathews 1997). Regional integration and internal fragmentation are eroding state sovereignty from above and below. Authority structures and loyalties are once again layered, as they were in medieval times; supra- and subnational entities have supplemented national states as loci of sovereignty and identity.[12] These transformations were triggered by multilateral wars and facilitated by advances in technology. Just as the Thirty Years' War (1618–48) precipitated the shift away from feudalism, the World Wars (1914–45) began to close the door on exclusively state-centric understandings of global politics. And much as the printing press helped to foster the rise of sovereign states (Anderson 1991), the Internet plays a most important role in linking subnational groups with each other and with the global community. These ontological and structural changes have crystallized around new cultural frameworks. Whereas Christianity provided a common frame of reference in the fragmented feudal order, human rights norms provide normative and ideological cohesion in the contemporary world polity. It is within this context that indigenous claims to sovereignty reemerged.

Despite these profound changes in the constitutive, political, and normative ordering of the world system, international law remains somewhat beholden to the conceptual and lexical scaffolding of sovereign statehood, making it difficult to contemplate indigenous sovereignty in ways that render it acceptable to and exercisable within existing states. A concept found in the Peace of Westphalia in 1648—which, ironically, is widely cited as laying the foundations of exclusive state sovereignty—specified precisely the kind of nested sovereignty I am proposing: namely, *Landeshoheit*, a form of territorially based autonomy that is exercised within the confines of a superordinate political authority (*Oberhoheit*). In the Peace of Westphalia, *Landeshoheit* referred to the autonomy (as opposed to the absolute sovereignty) of electors, princes, and city-states vis-à-vis the Holy Roman Empire (Osiander 2001). In varying degrees, indigenous peoples exercise something akin to this *imperium in imperio* within their respective states today.[13]

CONCLUSION

Indigenous rights discourses have evolved in dialectical fashion over the past five centuries, thanks in no small part to the efforts of indigenous peoples to turn the colonial ideologies of conquest back on their colonizers. Indigenous peoples have been, to paraphrase Roger Friedland and Robert Alford (1991), extremely "artful" in their use of international law: They have deftly appropriated key elements from their colonizers' own legal and normative frameworks, abstracted those elements from their original context, and transposed them to novel situations for different purposes. So it is that a facile recognition of indigenous sovereignty at the time of first contact between indigenous peoples and Europeans became a morally compelling argument for indigenous self-determination in the contemporary era.

Indeed, world culture plants the seeds of its own transformation by constituting social actors and providing the raw material from which they draw, often in rather creative (and disruptive) ways. To be sure, world-cultural change is not wholly endogenous; "unsettled" periods (Swidler 1986) such that existed in the years between, during, and immediately following global wars provide the conditions for advancing new understandings of social reality, interpreting extant understandings in innovative ways or resuscitating old understandings in new settings. Seen in a new light, Eurocentric views of indigenous peoples' rights and responsibilities as articulated in the sixteenth-century law of nations provided the basis for indigenous rights claims in the contemporary human rights era. The next chapter considers how these changes have shaped the nature, purposes, and control of indigenous education.

CHAPTER TWO

INDIGENOUS EDUCATION IN GLOBAL AND HISTORICAL PERSPECTIVE

Hutia te kauri i te itinga ano ka taea [If you want to pull up a kauri tree, you must do it when it is little].

Maori proverb, quoted in Barrington and Beaglehole (1974: 116)

A great general has said that the only good Indian is a dead one. . . . In a sense, I agree with the sentiment, but only in this: that all the Indian there is in the race should be dead. Kill the Indian in him and save the man.

Capt. Richard H. Pratt, 1892, quoted in Wilkinson and Biggs (1977: 143)

WHETHER ONE PREFERS THE METAPHOR OF uprooting or murder, the prevailing opinion among European colonists and their descendents, until recently, was that indigenous cultures and identities should be obliterated. Education was a weapon of choice for this endeavor. Thus did U.S. Army Captain Richard Pratt lay down his gun in the fight against American Indians in order to establish the first boarding school for Indian children in 1879. Spiritual, cultural, and linguistic death replaced corporeal death as policy goals, and schools served as one of the primary grave diggers.

The intentions were often good, as Pratt's adage makes clear. Pratt and others like him fervently believed that assimilation "saved" the uncivilized Indians from themselves. This faith in the transformative power of education was infectious. After studying the educational policies and practices of its neighbor to the south, the Canadian government also adopted the boarding school model for indigenous youth (Barman, Hébert, and McCaskill 1986; Stonechild 2006). The experience for Aboriginal peoples at these boarding schools was so negative that a government website chronicling their history begins with this warning:

> The Web site deals with topics that may cause trauma invoked by memories of past abuse. The Government of Canada recognizes the need for safety measures to minimize the risk associated with triggering.
>
> A National Indian Residential School Crisis Line has been set up to provide support for former Residential School students. You can access emotional and crisis referral services. You can also get information on how to get other health supports from the Government of Canada. (Canada 2010a)

This story, unfortunately, was repeated around the world. Indigenous peoples everywhere were forced into European-style education systems, with the goal of replacing their languages, traditions, and cultures with the colonizer's "civilized" way of life.

But just as the use of education to assimilate indigenous peoples was remarkably uniform across countries, so too has been the recent and sudden shift toward policies that support indigenous peoples' control over education. Sovereignty authorizes collectively organized groups such as nation-states to provide for, manage, or otherwise regulate the education of their members. It therefore follows that the contemporary resurgence in the sovereign status of indigenous peoples under international law should be accompanied by increased indigenous control over their own educational institutions. This is exactly what we find: The unique claims of indigenous peoples (relative to other minority groups) to historical sovereignty account for the recent worldwide emergence of indigenous postsecondary institutions. If colonial education systems were designed to achieve the metaphorical death of indigenous societies and cultures, as Captain Pratt once hoped, the emergence of indigenous postsecondary institutions constitutes a rebirth of sorts.

The basic argument is that schools, over and above their presumed role in imparting skills or knowledge to students, also induct people into bounded religious, cultural, or political communities (Boli, Ramirez, and Meyer 1985; Ramirez and Boli 1987b; Soysal and Strang 1989; Meyer, Ramirez, and Soysal 1992b). Schools are incorporative institutions par excellence, and those established for indigenous peoples have been no exception. But which communities students are incorporated into depends on where sovereignty—and, hence, control of schools—is located.

THE UNIVERSITY AND POLITICAL AUTHORITY

The rise of indigenous postsecondary institutions can ultimately be traced to the founding of the very first universities in thirteenth-century Europe. In her analysis of the emergence and worldwide expansion of universities, Phyllis Riddle (1993, 1996) concluded that changes in the number, nature, and control of universities reflect shifts over time in the locus of sovereignty in the world system. I adapt Riddle's general framework by linking changes in the purpose and control of indigenous peoples' education to structural, political, and cultural transformations in the wider global polity. Global patterns of university expansion, changes in the international status and standing of indigenous peoples, and shifts in the purpose and control of indigenous peoples' education are not adventitious: *All reflect the same underlying global processes.*

Riddle's (1996: 43–44) theory of growth and decline in the number of universities worldwide is simply stated: "From their beginning, universities have been associated with political authority, and control over the university follows the center of political authority. . . . Changes in the pattern of university foundings and failures throughout the world . . . correspond to changes in the pattern of political authority." She delineates three periods in the development of universities worldwide—1200 to 1800, 1800 to 1950, and 1950 to 1985—that "correspond to differences in perceptions of the relationship between political authority, education, and society" (Riddle 1996: 45). Not coincidentally, these periods also overlap substantially with the eras during which different political and cultural logics—religious, statist, and glocal—prevailed in the world polity.

The University's Religious Foundations

The modern university has deep roots in Christianity (Frank and Meyer 2007). True to the name, early universities were indeed universal in character—"catholic" in both the religious and worldly senses. They served as carriers of universal spiritual truths, attracted students from throughout Christendom, and were chartered by popes and emperors who claimed jurisdiction over the entire globe. Indeed, the acquisition of a papal or imperial charter became a de facto requirement for universities in medieval Europe, a precursor to the modern practice of accreditation (Riddle 1993). Control over the production and dissemination of knowledge reinforced the authority of political elites—knowledge, the aphorism goes, is power—but sovereignty also conferred the authority to sanction knowledge as legitimate.

Universities as we know them today owe their existence to what Rodney Stark (2005) calls the "rational theology" of Christianity. According to Stark, the distinctly rationalistic nature of Christian theology can be attributed to the fact that the founder of Christianity, Jesus, left no written record of his divine vision. Unlike with Islam and Judaism, whose sacred texts are understood by their followers to have been written or communicated directly by God and must therefore be accepted uncritically as literal truth, Christian theologians have been forced to debate and deduce God's plan (Stark 2005: 9). This search for truth fomented the modern university, which sprang out of the thirteenth-century synthesis of Christian doctrine and humanist thought.

In contrast with the empire that ruled over central Europe at the time, Christian humanism was both holy and Roman, with a heavy dose of Hellenism mixed in as well. It was premised on the belief that there is a rational order to the cosmos while "maintain[ing] fidelity to the concept of a transcendental purpose for natural society" (Williams 1983: 57). Christian humanism posited humanity's ability to discover the laws that governed nature and society. God had set the universe into motion, but He had also given humans the capacity to reason and hence to understand the ramifications of His divine will. Reflecting this way of thinking, the German mathematician and astronomer Johannes Kepler (1571–1630) once remarked that "I was merely thinking God's thoughts after him."

The advent of colonization in the sixteenth century marks the first wave of worldwide university expansion, as institutions of higher learning were transplanted from Europe to the New World. The first university outside of Europe was established in Santo Domingo, present-day Dominican Republic, in 1538. "Theology was emphasized" in this and other colonial universities "because Dominicans and Jesuits had been instrumental in [their] founding . . . and were interested in training clergy to meet the spiritual needs in the colonies, including the conversion of non-Christians to Christianity" (Riddle 1989: 93). The role that early colonial universities played in the propagation of Christianity will receive more attention shortly. At this point, it is important to note that universities in the New World were mirror images of their counterparts in Europe (Altbach 1998; Perkin 2006), and eventually succumbed to the same secularizing impulses that transformed the very nature of the university as an institution.

The Statist Turn in University Expansion

If "official church theology enjoyed a secure base in the many and growing universities" of the late Middle Ages (Stark 2005: 8), it follows that challenges to the Church should also reverberate down to universities. This is indeed what happened. The Protestant Reformation transformed the nature of sovereignty, knowledge, and by extension the university along two related dimensions. The first such dimension was political. As newly ascendant states began to supplant the sovereign authority of the Church, control over universities was gradually nationalized. Competition among states propelled university expansion. To establish institutions of higher learning simultaneously signaled and conferred authority, prestige, and autonomy. "The very act of founding a university," says Riddle (1989: 37), "was a statement of sovereignty and legitimacy, expressing local control over the authority of institutional knowledge." States established universities to assert their independence vis-à-vis the Church, and to enhance their prestige vis-à-vis other states.[1]

The second change, in part a consequence of the first, was epistemological. As states wrested sovereign control from the Church, they undermined the Church's monopoly over knowledge. Universities established and controlled by states served less as conveyers of religious canon and more as purveyors of national cultures. As Eric Hobsbawm put it, "the progress of schools and universities measures that of nationalism, just as schools and especially universities became its most conscious champions" (Anderson 1991: 71). Martin Trow (1970: 2) further elaborates that "the heart of the traditional university is its commitment to the transmission of the high culture, the possession of which has been thought to make men truly civilized." After the Reformation, this high culture was increasingly writ in national vernaculars as opposed to Church Latin. At the same time, what it meant to be "civilized" came much closer to the original Latin—*civilis*, of or relating to citizens—than it had under the Church, when civility entailed faith in the Christian God. Education, in other words, no longer cultivated souls so much as it created citizens.

Yet another epistemological transformation, in some ways more fundamental than the first, occurred over the course of the seventeenth and eighteenth centuries. The Enlightenment transformed the very nature of knowledge and, hence, the university's function. The study of nature, politics, and society became less metaphysical and more scientific (Frank and Gabler 2006). The secular humanism of the philosophes stripped natural law of its divine connotations and wrote God out of earthly affairs (for example, as with Deism). Consequently, the purpose of the modern "reformed" university was "the creation of new knowledge through 'pure' scholarship and basic scientific research" (Trow 1970: 2).

"Glocalizing" Universities

The contemporary era that began at the close of World War II has witnessed the gradual erosion of raw nation-state authority and the attendant consolidation, intensification, and expansion of world society, all of which implicates higher education. "With [the] supranational political authority" of popes and emperors, "the supranational claims of the university were emphasized. With the rise of national political authority, the emphasis was on national claims. This suggests that a decline in the political authority of the nation-state would result in a renewed emphasis on supranational claims" (Riddle 1996: 52). As national boundaries become more permeable, inter- and supranational higher education ventures correspondingly become more common. Riddle (1996) attributes the emergence of pan-national universities such as the University of the West Indies, the Arabian Gulf University, and the United Nations University to the postwar decline of nation-state sovereignty.

Apart from these isolated examples, the regionalization of higher education (Altbach 1998) has not been widespread, at least with respect to transnational control of universities. Still, efforts at international cooperation and coordination are increasingly commonplace. The Bologna Declaration of 1999, which aims to create a standardized European higher education system, epitomizes this process. I focus, conversely, on the opposite but simultaneous trend: the devolution of control over higher education to subnational minority groups. Although I focus on policies that devolve control to indigenous peoples, other "national" minorities around the world, each exercising some degree of autonomy vis-à-vis their respective nation-states, are also beneficiaries of educational devolution. This trend is most pronounced in Europe, developing pari passu with European integration. Spain's 1978 constitutional reforms, for example, granted substantial political autonomy, including jurisdiction over universities, to regional governments in Catalonia and the Basque Autonomous Community. Similarly, in the United Kingdom, the Scotland Act of 1998 devolved control over universities in Scotland to the newly established Scottish Parliament.[2] And in the former Soviet Union, various "autonomous" republics and oblasts, whose boundaries were drawn to coincide with ethnic divisions, now have their own ministries of education and schools (Graney 1999). These opposing tendencies of transnationalization and devolution are part of a singular process of globalization that redistributes educational authority—along with political authority more generally—above and below the nation-state (Nederveen Pieterse 1995; Davies and Guppy 1997; Astiz, Wiseman, and Baker 2002). As the absolute sovereignty of the nation-state weakens, it becomes easier for subnational regions or minority groups to assert their own sovereignty claims. Such claims invariably entail some form of educational devolution.

With the piecemeal transfer of control over universities away from centralized states, the nature and purposes of higher education have again changed. Today, access to higher education is a matter not only of national progress (sovereignty) but also of individual justice (human rights). Members of previously marginalized groups such as minorities and women have gained entry to universities (Trow 2006); at the same time, the perspectives and worldviews of these groups are increasingly represented in university curricula. The relationship between the decentralization of education and the inclusion of marginalized sensibilities into the academy is direct, as David Corson (1999: 8) has acknowledged with respect to indigenous peoples: "A key feature of today's world is a trend away from centralization and toward diversity and devolution of control. In this new world, many more voices are being raised, including the voices of those who were once dispossessed."

Summary

Worldwide patterns in the consolidation and expansion of higher education follow the same religious–statist–glocal trajectory as the world polity at large (see Chapter One). The earliest universities were universal in all respects. They were chartered by supranational authorities, embodied universal knowledge, and recruited students from throughout Christendom. With the rise of states to power, universities were nationalized and "territorialized" (Soysal 1994). By and large, students did not venture across national frontiers to attend universities, which, as national institutions, were accredited by state authorities and served the cultural, economic, and military needs of the nation. After the Second World War, universities began to reassume their transnational character, spawning what Philip Altbach (1998: 147–159) has called the "new internationalism" in higher education. Students and scholars once again traverse national frontiers with relative ease, expanded access has transformed higher education into a "mass" and even a "universal" enterprise (Trow 2006), and knowledge has taken on a renewed universalistic posture, inasmuch as science is the study of general and immutable laws (Gabler and Frank 2005). At the same time, education is becoming more localized, catering to the needs and desires of subnational groups such as women, minorities, and indigenous peoples.

HISTORICAL PATTERNS IN THE EDUCATION OF INDIGENOUS PEOPLES

Historical patterns in the (higher) education of indigenous peoples have closely tracked changes in higher education more generally, as both have been shaped in common by wider political and institutional processes. For example, Thomas Thompson's (1978: 168–176) delineation of American Indian education into periods of evangelical control (1568–1873), federal control (1873–1964), and Indian control (1964–present) overlaps substantially with Riddle's stages of university expansion and corresponds more generally to the eras during which religious, statist, and glocal logics prevailed in the world polity. This periodization is not unique to the United States but characterizes the development of indigenous education elsewhere in the world was well.

Immediately following the arrival of Europeans to the New World, when sovereignty belonged to pope and emperor, education was a civilizing project designed to Christianize infidel savages and redeem wayward souls. When papal and imperial sovereignty gave way to a secularized system of states, compulsory mass education systems arose to produce rights-bearing and duty-bound citizens (Marshall 1948; Bendix [1964] 1996; Ramirez and Rubinson 1979; Boli et al. 1985; Ramirez and Boli 1987a; Boli 1989). In creating members of "imagined" national communities (Anderson 1991), school systems managed, directed, or controlled by nation-states sought to expunge the political and cultural vestiges of "primordial" indigenous communities. Most recently, indigenous peoples the world over have regained sovereign control of their own educational destinies, using schools to revitalize indigenous cultures and communities.

Education for Salvation, ca. 1500–1750

> Go ye therefore, and teach all nations, baptizing them in the name of the Father, and of the Son, and of the Holy Ghost.
>
> *Matthew 28:19*

"Spreading the Roman Catholic faith," writes David Abernethy (2000: 215), "was an integral part of Spain's imperial project and a primary justification for it." Although early supporters of the imperial project agreed that infidel souls should be saved, people were of two minds regarding proper methods. Some, like Juan Ginés de Sepúlveda, maintained that the brutish Indians were incapable of understanding that conversion to Catholicism was in their best interest and would therefore need to be brought forcibly into the flock. Others, including Bartolomé de las Casas and Francisco de Vitoria, argued that Indians had the use of reason, which made possible their peaceful conversion. Indians, according to Las Casas ([1542] 1992: 10),

> are innocent and pure in mind and have a lively intelligence, all of which makes them particularly receptive to learning and understanding the truths of our Catholic faith and to being instructed in virtue; indeed, God has invested them with fewer impediments in this regard than any other people on earth. Once they begin to learn of the Christian faith they become so keen to know more . . . that the missionaries who instruct them do truly have to be men of exceptional patience and forbearance.

This view won the day in official policies (if not always in colonial practices), and education therefore became a principal component of the colonial and missionary enterprise.

The earliest attempts by Europeans to educate indigenous peoples occurred within the context of Spain's *encomienda* system in the Americas, whereby "the Spanish crown gave or 'commended' Indians to Spaniards, who became encomenderos, and this grant gave the Spaniards the right to exact labor or tribute from the Indians. In return, the encomenderos were obliged to provide religious instruction for their Indians and to protect them" (Hanke 1949: 19). The Laws of Burgos, promulgated in 1512, cemented this arrangement cemented into practice. Article IX reads:

> Also, we order and command that whoever has fifty Indians or more in encomienda shall be obliged to have a boy (the one he considers most able) taught to read and write, and the things of our Faith, so that he may later teach the said Indians, because the Indians will more readily accept what he says than when the Spaniards and settlers tell them.

Although *encomenderos* were required by law to instruct their subjects, in practice this rarely happened. Consequently, in 1542, a royal decree transferred responsibility over Indian education to Catholic friars (Reyhner and Eder 2004). Friars had already demonstrated their success in teaching indigenous peoples. Six years earlier, in 1536, the Franciscans had established the Colegio de Santa Cruz de Tlatelolco near present-day Mexico City to teach Latin, theology, medicine, philosophy, and rhetoric to the sons of Indian nobility (León-Portilla and Shorris 2001). Languages of instruction included Náhuatl, Spanish, and Latin. In 1570, Philip III "declared Náhuatl the official language of New Spain's Indians and ordered that the University of Mexico," the colony's flagship university, "establish a chair of Náhuatl and that all clerics should learn it" (Reyhner and Eder 2004: 19). Philip's order, issued to aid in proselytization, modified a 1550 decree by Charles V that all Indians learn only Castilian Spanish. It was believed, on the one hand, that Indians would receive the Gospel much more readily in their mother tongue; on the other hand, many Spaniards simply doubted the capacity of Indians to learn a "civilized" language. By 1595, however, the college was in ruins (Reyhner and Eder 2004: 18).

Religious instruction was also central to the British and French colonial endeavors in North America. In 1568, the French Society of Jesuits became the first group to bring European education to Indians in North America. Their school, established in Havana, served natives transplanted from Florida (Oppelt 1990). Farther north, Bishop George Berkeley (1685–1753)

> call[ed] for the creation of a college for "propagating the gospel and civil life among the savage nations of America" on the grounds that this had been "the principal motive which induced the crown to send the first English Colonies thither." Such a college would, he hoped, "remove the reproach we [the English] have so long lain under, that we fall far short of our neighbours of the Romish communion in zeal in propagating religion, as we surpass them in the soundness and purity of it." (Pagden 1995: 35)

In this way, competition between Protestants in North America and Catholics in Latin America propelled the expansion of Indian education.

The religious character and motives of indigenous education were apparent in North America, Australia, New Zealand, and beyond. The first universities established in the United States included a mission to educate American Indians (Szasz 1988; Oppelt 1990). The 1650 charter of Harvard University, America's oldest university (established in 1636), provided for "the education of the English and Indian youth of this Country in knowledge and godliness" (Oppelt 1990: 2). Five years later, in 1655, the Indian College at Harvard was erected. An Indian college charged with converting American Indians to Christianity was also established at the nation's second-oldest institution of higher education, William and Mary College, in 1700. Dartmouth College, founded in 1769, became the first American college chartered with the sole purpose of educating Indians. According to its first charter, Dartmouth was committed to the "education and instruction of youth of the Indian tribes in this Land in reading, writing and all parts of Learning which will appear necessary and expedient for civilizing the Christianized Children of Pagans" (Oppelt 1990: 5). The college's Latin motto, *Vox Clamantis in Deserto* ("the voice of one crying in the wilderness"), encapsulates its deeply religious mission. In 1775, the Continental Congress appropriated $500 for the education of American Indians at Dartmouth (Reyhner and Eder 2004: 33). Congress expanded its support of religious instruction for Indians in 1819 by authorizing annual subsidies of up to $10,000 for churches under the Civilization Fund Act.

In Canada as in the United States, religious missions began operating schools for indigenous students in the mid-1600s (Canada 1996a: 434), but an extensive system of state-sponsored religious schools emerged only in the early 1800s. The first higher education institution for Indian students in Canada, Emmanuel College, was established in 1879 "to train Indians to become Anglican catechists, teachers, and interpreters" (Stonechild 2006: 27). "Formal education" at Emmanuel College and elsewhere "was, without apology, assimilationist. The primary purpose of formal education was to indoctrinate Aboriginal people into a Christian, European worldview, thereby 'civilizing' them" (Canada 1996a: 434).

Colonizers came much later to Australia than they did to North America but brought with them the same commitment to Christianize indigenous peoples through education. The first school for Aboriginal children, the Parramatta Native Institution, was established in New South Wales in 1814 "to civilise, educate and foster habits of industry and decency in the Aborigines" (Kidd 2006: 8). Higher education played a lesser role in Australia than it did in North America, given the policy of systematically removing children from their families while very young—in some cases at the time of birth—and placing them in dormitories. This policy was designed to "encourag[e] the conversion of the children to Christianity and distanc[e] them from their Indigenous lifestyle" (National Inquiry into the Separation of Aboriginal and Torres Strait Islander Children from Their Families 1997: part 2, ch. 2). Lack of higher education for Aboriginal peoples also reflected the prevailing belief that advanced study was superfluous to the ultimate goal of assimilation. This view was articulated by the Commissioner of Native Affairs for Western Australia, A. O. Neville, in 1937:

> If the coloured people of this country are to be absorbed into the general community they must be thoroughly fit and educated at least to the extent of the three R's. If they can read, write and count, and know what wages they should get, and how to enter into an agreement with an employer, that is all that should be necessary. (Australia 1937: 11)

To promote assimilation, Neville emphasized that Aboriginal children must be removed from their families by the age of six, adding that it is "useless to wait until they are twelve or thirteen years of age" (p. 11).

Missionaries first arrived in New Zealand from Australia in 1814 and opened a school for Maori children two years later. For the next half-century, mission day schools promoted literacy in the Maori language, and by 1827 missionaries had translated the Gospels into Maori. New Zealand's colonial government began subsidizing mission schools in 1847 but on the condition that instruction was provided exclusively in English (Simon and Smith 2001: 159–160). Although most schools for Maori children taught a limited manual and agricultural curriculum, one institution, Te Aute College, prepared students to attend university and produced a number of Maori university graduates during the late 1800s (Waitangi Tribunal 1998).

These diverse educational ventures throughout North America and Australasia were unified by their ultimate failures. Indian College at Harvard enrolled only five students before literally crumbling to the ground in 1698, while Dartmouth never became a predominantly Indian school despite its mission. In Canada, Emmanuel College endured for nearly half a century before closing in 1823 due to lack of government support and funding (Stonechild 2006: 29), while the school at Parramatta for Aboriginal peoples in Australia closed in 1829 after only fifteen years in operation (Flood 2006: 56). Maori education in New Zealand experienced a different kind of failure. Te Aute College did not close—indeed, it remains open today—but it eventually succumbed to government pressure and replaced the academic curriculum with an agricultural course of study.

Notwithstanding these setbacks, the underlying religious foundations and purpose of indigenous peoples' education did not fade easily; in fact, it persisted well into the nineteenth century. Nor was it confined to first-wave settler colonies in the Americas and Australasia. The General Act of the Berlin Conference in 1885, which regulated the colonization of Africa, committed the imperial powers of Europe to "instructing the natives and bringing home to them the blessings of civilization" (Article 6). Although civilization was a project spearheaded by Christian missionaries, the General Act also recognized the importance of scientists and explorers by extending "especial protection" to them. Beginning in the mid- to late eighteenth century, however, religious motives played an increasingly minor role in the education of indigenous peoples. Nationalistic purposes emerged in their stead, and education became a tool for incorporating and assimilating indigenous peoples into national polities and cultures.

Education for Subjugation, ca. 1750–1960

> Tradition is the Enemy of Progress.
>
> *Motto of a boarding school for American Indians (Washburn 1995: 218)*

With the decline of Christianity as a hegemonic force in global politics and colonial projects, indigenous education became a secular project designed to integrate indigenous people, as individuals, into national communities. Indigenous education was tailored to satisfy the twin nation- and state-building imperatives of cultural assimilation and political incorporation, converting "uncivilized" savages into civilized members of national polities.[3] Use of indigenous languages was suppressed, often violently, in favor of national languages. Even the Spanish monarchy, which had previously championed bilingual education, outlawed the use of native languages in 1795 (Reyhner and Eder 2004: 24).

This shift from religious to statist logics in indigenous peoples' education occurred worldwide. In the United States, Congress repealed missionary subsidies of Indian education in 1873 amid allegations that government support of religious schools violated the constitutional separation of church and state. Direct and sustained federal involvement in the provision of Indian education began in 1879, when Captain Richard Pratt established Carlisle Indian School as the first government-supported off-reservation Indian school. Unlike the task of proselytization, which could be legitimately transacted in any language, the ideology of assimilation required the use of national rather than indigenous languages. To this end, the commissioner of Indian Affairs prohibited the use of Indian languages in schools in 1887 (Prucha 2000: 173). A few years later, in 1891, Congress mandated compulsory school attendance for Indian children (Reyhner and Eder 2004: 89). To facilitate the "mainstreaming" of Indian students, the Johnson-O'Malley Act of 1934 authorized the secretary of the interior to contract with state governments for the education of Indians, an arrangement made necessary because most Indians—at least, those living on reservations—did not pay the state and local taxes that fund public education.

At about the same time that the U.S. government assumed control over Indian education from churches, responsibility for the education of Indians on reserves in Canada passed to the federal government under the first Indian Act of 1876. An amendment to the Indian Act in 1920 made school attendance compulsory for Indian children (Persson 1986: 151). Although it was rare for indigenous students to pursue higher education, those who did automatically became "enfranchised"—they lost their Indian status and hence their right to live on reserves (Henderson 1995: 255).

The Indian Act was amended yet again in 1951 to promote the absorption of Indians into mainstream school systems by allowing the federal government to contract out Indian education to provincial schools, the Canadian equivalent of the Johnson-O'Malley Act in the United States. Some fifteen years later, the *Survey of Contemporary Indians of Canada* (the so-called Hawthorn Report) advocated continued educational integration as the most effective way to achieve equality between Indians and non-Indians in Canada. This policy came to a head in 1969, when the federal government articulated its plan to relinquish control over Indian education by unilaterally transferring responsibility for reservation schools to the provinces. Also in 1969, the federal government assumed control over Indian residential schools from religious denominations and began closing them.

Unlike in the United States and Canada, where indigenous education fell under the jurisdiction of each country's respective federal government (despite repeated efforts to relinquish some of this responsibility to state and provincial governments), the individual state governments of Australia exercised sole responsibility over Aboriginal education for more than 150 years. The education of Aboriginal children was largely regulated through each state's "protection" statutes that governed all aspects of aboriginal life, including marriage, childrearing, residence, employment, education, and alcohol use (Armitage 1995: 34; Perry 1996: 186–187). Victoria enacted the Aborigines Protection Act, the first of its kind, in 1869 (Armitage 1995: 18), followed by Western Australia (1886), Queensland (1901), New South Wales (1909), South Australia (1910), and the Northern Territory (1910). Assimilation was the avowed goal of these statutes. As late as 1961, a conference of federal and state ministers responsible for "native welfare" produced a policy stating that "a major instrument of assimilation is education of aboriginal children" (Hasluck 1961: 4).

In Australia, assimilation and miscegenation were fused into a single policy aimed at expunging the Aboriginal "race" on the continent. An individual's assimilability was thought to be inversely proportionate to the amount of Aboriginal blood coursing through his or her veins, such that "people of 'part' descent [were] more likely to be receptive to the moral uplift of training for citizenship" than people of full Aboriginal descent (Peterson and Sanders 1998: 11). Unlike in the United States, where the distinction between whites and blacks was "absolute, essential, and refractory," miscegenation was encouraged in Australia as a way to absorb black Aboriginals into society (Wolfe 2001: 885). On the assumption, held by no less than Tocqueville ([1835] 2000: 399), that "the half-blood forms the natural link between civilization and barbarism," the

Australian government hoped to "whiten" the Aboriginal population through successive generations of intermarriage.

Responsibility for Maori education fell exclusively to mission schools until 1867, when a national system of state-controlled primary schools for Maori students was established under the supervision of the Native Department. Thus began a century-long era of segregated public education in New Zealand.[4] In 1931, a memorandum penned by Director of Education T. B. Strong expressed the fundamental purpose of Native schools: "In the system of native education in New Zealand, we should provide fully a type of education that will lead the lad to become a good farmer, and the girl a good farmer's wife" (Simon and Smith 2001: 114). Maori boys were to be transformed into individual agriculturalists, while Maori girls were relegated to the role of housewives. The government, less enthusiastic about Maori language fluency than the missionaries had been, also recommended that Maori no longer be used in the classroom. Once again, T. B. Strong articulated the rationale when he claimed that "the Maori language has no literature and consequently . . . the abandonment of the native tongue inflicts no loss upon the Maori" (Simon and Smith 2001: 167). An amendment to the Native Schools Act in 1871 permitted instruction in English only (Armitage 1995: 155).

The Native schools system, as it came to be called, emerged ten years before the Education Act of 1877 created a free, secular, state-funded, and compulsory system of primary schools and a central Department of Education. Maori students were exempted from the compulsory attendance provision of that act until 1894 (Barrington and Beaglehole 1974: 139) but were nevertheless entitled, as citizens, to attend mainstream schools. By 1909, more Maori students were enrolled in mainstream schools than in the government's Native schools (Simon and Smith 2001: 172). The dual educational system persisted until 1969, when all remaining Maori schools were finally closed. To pave the way for integration, a quota system had been introduced in 1940 to facilitate the entry of Maori students into teacher-training colleges (Simeon 1998), and in 1955 provision was made to transfer the administration of Maori schools to local education boards if a majority of parents favored integration (Barrington 1991: 317).

The preceding discussion demonstrates that indigenous education policies were broadly similar and also changed in parallel ways cross-nationally, reflecting global trends that shifted responsibility over indigenous peoples from churches to nation-states. States, no less than churches, sought to assimilate indigenous students, but where churches had tolerated (and often encouraged) the use of indigenous languages as indispensible to the civilizing project, nation-states universally prohibited their use.

International policies promulgated toward the end of the statist era began to recognize the right of minority groups to maintain separate educational institutions, but they did so in a very limited manner. In 1935, the Permanent Court of International Justice issued an advisory opinion upholding the right of "nationals belonging to racial, linguistic or religious minorities . . . to maintain, manage and control at their own expense or to establish in the future charitable, religious and social institutions, schools and other educational establishments, with the right to use their own language and to exercise their religion freely therein" (*Minority Schools in Albania* 1935: 20). Notice, however, that this was an exclusively passive right; it merely prohibited states from interfering with the efforts of minorities to establish, at their own expense, independent schools. Nothing in the decision imposed on states an affirmative duty to allocate resources for minority education. In fact, the primary objective was not to preserve and transmit minority cultures but rather to foster the eventual integration of minority groups into mainstream national societies. Minority schools were a means to an end, not an end in themselves. Quoting again from the opinion: "Equality in law precludes discrimination of any kind; whereas equality in fact may involve the necessity of different treatment in order to attain a result which establishes an equilibrium between different situations" (*Minority Schools in Albania* 1935: 17). In this regard, *Minority Schools in Albania* presaged contemporary affirmative action policies. As with affirmative action, the implication was that separate schools would no longer be needed once "true" equality between the minority and majority populations was achieved (Kymlicka 2001: 192).

Thus, international law during the statist era viewed education primarily as a vehicle for integrating and assimilating minorities. The International Labor Organization's (ILO) Indigenous and Tribal Populations Convention (No. 107) of 1957 exemplifies this logic with respect to indigenous peoples. Article 21 of the convention reads that "measures shall be taken to ensure that members of the [indigenous] populations concerned have the opportunity to acquire education at all levels on an equal footing with the rest of the national community," and Article 23(b) mandates that "provision shall be made for the progressive transition from the mother tongue or the vernacular language to the national language or one of the official languages of the country." Article 24 admonishes signatories to impart "general knowledge and skills that will help [indigenous] children to become integrated into the national community." Interpreted relative to prevailing sensibilities, these policies were quite progressive, insofar as they regarded indigenous peoples as fundamentally "educable" and were motivated by the liberal ideals of equality and nondiscrimination. It was also commonly believed that integrating indigenous peoples into mainstream educational systems would lead inexorably to social and economic advancement. Yet such sentiments, articulated very late in the statist era, were destined to be short lived.

Education for Self-Determination, ca. 1960–Present

> We share a vision of Indigenous Peoples of the world united in the collective synergy of self-determination through control of higher education. We are committed to building partnerships that restore and retain indigenous spirituality, cultures and languages, homelands, social systems, economic systems and self-determination.
>
> *World Indigenous Nations Higher Education Consortium (2005)*

Ideas about indigenous education changed dramatically after World War II. Consistent with the redistribution of sovereign authority above and below nation-states, the education of indigenous peoples has been shaped by the twofold processes of devolution and transnationalization. Control over indigenous education has devolved increasingly downward from states to indigenous peoples. At the same time, international discourses have also become much more prevalent and have often reinforced educational devolution. I consider each process in turn, beginning with the impact of globalization on indigenous higher education.

Top-down developments The right of indigenous peoples to control their own educational institutions follows directly from recent developments in international law. In 1989, the ILO issued the Convention (No. 169) Concerning Indigenous and Tribal Peoples in Independent Countries, which revised the paternalistic and assimilationist tone of its predecessor, Convention No. 107. The revised convention admonishes governments to "recognize the right of [indigenous] peoples to establish their own educational institutions and facilities" (Article 27[3]). It also declares that indigenous children should "be taught to read and write in their own indigenous language" (Article 28[1]). The convention does not simply regurgitate multicultural rhetoric by calling for the increased representation of indigenous cultures alongside other minority perspectives in "common" schools but instead encourages the establishment of "uncommon" schools catering exclusively to indigenous peoples and their traditions (Feinberg 1998).

Indigenous higher education became institutionalized in global discourse during the 1990s. As part of the International Decade of the World's Indigenous People (1995–2004), the United Nations recommended that member governments "establish and support indigenous schools and university-level institutions" (United Nations 1996: ¶ 57). In 1999, participants at the Workshop on Higher Education and Indigenous Peoples in San José, Costa Rica, concluded that "the United Nations should consider sponsoring and supporting the establishment of an international indigenous university, which could take the form of a consortium of existing indigenous institutes of higher education and serve as a parent institution for new centres of indigenous higher education in the world" (United Nations 1999: ¶ 14). The San José document further recommended that "States should support the establishment of educational institutions run by indigenous peoples and should finance them adequately" (United Nations 1999: ¶ 10). Article 14 of the UNDRIP (2007) converts this recommendation for states into a right of indigenous peoples:

1. Indigenous peoples have the right to establish and control their educational systems and institutions providing education in their own languages, in a manner appropriate to their cultural methods of teaching and learning.

2. Indigenous individuals, particularly children, have the right to all levels and forms of education of the State without discrimination.

3. States shall, in conjunction with indigenous peoples, take effective measures, in order for indigenous individuals, particularly children, including those living outside their communities, to have access, when possible, to an education in their own culture and provided in their own language.

These rights, especially the clause requiring states to "take effective measures" in support of indigenous education, go beyond the rights of nonindigenous cultural, religious, and linguistic minorities. The right of indigenous peoples to establish and attend culturally relevant schools is *positive*—it obligates states to support indigenous schools—whereas the corresponding minority right tends to be *negative*. This crucial difference is apparent in Article 2(4) of the Declaration on the Rights of Persons Belonging to National or Ethnic, Religious or Linguistic Minorities (United Nations 1992), which provides only that "Persons belonging to minorities have the right to establish and maintain their own associations" (Article 2[4]). The comparison with indigenous peoples is striking for several reasons:

- First, the right is not specific to education, although "associations" could be construed broadly to encompass minority-controlled schools;
- Second, it is an individual rather than group right, accruing to "persons" belong to minorities rather than to "peoples" or minority groups per se; and
- Third, it does not imply a claim to state support of minority associations.

With respect to obligations regarding the study of minorities, the declaration requires only that states "take measures in the field of education [that] encourage knowledge of the history, traditions, language and culture of the minorities existing within their territory." Otherwise, the declaration does not concern itself with the study of particular minority groups. Quite the contrary, it provides that "persons belonging to minorities should have adequate opportunities to gain knowledge of the society as a whole" (Article 4[4]).

Other minority and human rights discourses are similarly limited. The Convention against Discrimination in Education, promulgated by UNESCO in 1960, calls for the integration of women and minorities into existing schools rather than the establishment of separate institutions (United Nations 1960). Article 4(a), for instance, seeks to "make higher education equally accessible to all on the basis of individual capacity." More generally, Article 27 of the International Covenant on Civil and Political Rights (United Nations 1966) reads:

> In those States in which ethnic, religious or linguistic minorities exist, persons belonging to such minorities *shall not be denied* the right, in community with other members of their group, to enjoy their own culture, to profess and practice their own religious, or to use their own language. [Emphasis added]

Negative rights of this sort ("shall not be denied") provide a much weaker basis on which to establish independent schools than do the positive rights available to indigenous peoples. The rights of minorities are based on the principle of nondiscrimination; those of indigenous peoples are rooted in self-determination.[5] Notice, however, that Article 14 of UNDRIP supports both the right of indigenous *individuals* to attend "mainstream" schools without discrimination and also the right of indigenous *peoples* to establish separate indigenous-controlled schools—it is anchored, in other words, in both the human rights of indigenous people and the quasi-sovereign status of indigenous peoples.

Because indigeneity confers powerful claims to legal, material, and cultural resources—including the right of indigenous peoples to attend their own state-supported postsecondary institutions—it is a highly contested identity, one that many states are not prepared to recognize. The Japanese government refused to acknowledge the indigenous status of the Ainu until 2008, referring to them instead as "minorities" with much weaker rights claims under international law. Likewise, the governments of Cambodia and Thailand prefer the terms "highlanders" or "hill people" to "indigenous peoples" (Miller 2003: 34). Even "the Basques of the Bay of Biscay or the Welsh of Great Britain," who exercise a significant degree of autonomy, "are not considered indigenous, although 'they are certainly as indigenous, technically speaking, as the Saamis of northern Scandinavia or the Jivaro people of the Amazon basin'" (Miller 2003: 37). As indigeneity becomes associated with more rights and resource claims, however, it seems likely that nonindigenous and "equivocally" indigenous minority groups will seek to adopt the label for themselves.

Bottom-up activities These "top-down" international developments fomented changes in national policies that supported the efforts of indigenous peoples to establish their own postsecondary institutions. Beginning in the 1970s, the Commonwealth government in Australia embarked on an ambitious plan to right the historical wrongs of Aboriginal education. The Royal Commission into Aboriginal Deaths in Custody (1987–1991), which concluded that a lack of educational opportunities was partly to blame for the disproportionately high incarceration rates among Aboriginal peoples, culminated in 1990 with the National Aboriginal and Torres Strait Islander Education Policy, a joint initiative adopted by the Commonwealth, state, and territorial governments "to achieve broad equality between Aboriginal people and other Australians in access, participation and outcomes in all forms of education" (Australia 2000: 19). More recently, in 2004, the Indigenous Higher Education Advisory Council was established to "ensure that higher education policy in Australia is informed by Indigenous perspectives," and to redress "the educational disadvantage experienced by Indigenous people" (Office of Aboriginal and Torres Strait Islander Affairs 2003).

The policy shift in Canada was much more abrupt, focusing not only on indigenous peoples' *access to* but also on *control of* postsecondary education. In 1970, as part of the federal government's plan to integrate indigenous students into provincial schools, Blue Quills School in Alberta, a residential school for Indians, was slated for immediate closure. A battle over the fate of Blue Quills became "the first direct confrontation in Canada over Indians' control of education" (Persson 1986: 150). Indians residing on the Blue Quills reserve wanted the school to remain open, and in July 1970 some 300 activists commenced a month-long sit-in (Bashford and Heinzerling 1987: 126; Persson 1986: 165–166). The Department of Indian Affairs agreed the following September to transfer control of the school to the Blue Quills Native Education Council, thereby making Blue Quills the first school in Canada administered by Indians.

The Blue Quills affair ignited a movement in Canada to institutionalize Indian control of Indian education. A policy paper bearing that name—*Indian Control of Indian Education*—was drafted by the National Indian Brotherhood, an organization representing Indian leaders from each province, and submitted it to the Department of Indian Affairs in 1972. The government adopted *Indian Control* as the foundation of its official Indian education policy several months later.

The massive report issued by the Royal Commission of Aboriginal Peoples in 1996 (Canada 1996a) continues to endorse "Aboriginal" control of "Aboriginal" education, including postsecondary education. It lauds indigenous-controlled ventures like Blue Quills (Canada 1996a: 517–522), which has grown since the 1970s to include postsecondary programming. The Royal Commission also proposed the establishment of an Aboriginal Peoples' International University "as a twenty-first century mechanism to promote traditional knowledge and scholarship, undertake applied research related to Aboriginal self-government, and disseminate information necessary to the achievement of broad Aboriginal development goals" (Canada 1996a: 530). By "international," the Commission referred to the different First Nations within Canada.

In the United States, the era of Indian control over education began in 1964, when President Lyndon Johnson first signaled the end of the federal government's policy of "terminating" Indian tribes. In 1969, the Special Subcommittee on Indian Education chaired by Edward Kennedy issued its report, *Indian Education: A National Tragedy, A National Challenge*. The report lamented the deplorable state of Indian education and recommended increased Indian control. The federal government made good on this recommendation—and put its money where its mouth was—first for primary and secondary education in 1972 and 1975, with the Indian Education and Indian Education Assistance Acts, respectively, and then for higher education in 1978, with the Tribally Controlled Community College Act. These acts increased funding for Indian-controlled educational ventures at all levels.

Finally, in New Zealand, the government's decision in 1969 to eliminate the system of separate Maori and mainstream schools may have aligned the country with racial equality norms that began percolating after World War II, but it chafed against the desire among many young Maori for independent culturally relevant education. The heady days of social movement activism during the late 1970s, during which Maori asserted their land, treaty, and cultural rights, culminated in 1982 with the establishment of the first *kohanga reo* ("language nest"), a Maori-immersion preschool. The first *kura kaupapa*, or Maori-language primary school, was founded in 1985, followed by *whare kura*—Maori secondary schools—ten years later. The first *wananga*, or Maori postsecondary institution, was established in 1981, although it did not receive statutory recognition until 1993.

Direct or "grassroots" linkages between previous and potential adopters are especially salient early in the development of new institutional forms (Strang and Meyer 1993; Strang and Soule 1998), and this is true for indigenous postsecondary institutions as well. Transnational cooperation has been particularly extensive between American Indians in the United States and the Maori of New Zealand. In 2001, the American Indian Higher Education Consortium (AIHEC), an organization representing tribal colleges in the United States, invited representatives from New Zealand's three *wananga*, Maori-controlled tertiary institutions, to participate in its annual conference. Delegates from two *wananga* attended. In exchange, fifteen associates from tribal colleges visited New Zealand the following year (World Indigenous Nations Higher Education Consortium [WINHEC] 2005). In similar fashion, the First Nations University of Canada "has entered into over twenty-five agreements with Indigenous peoples' institutions in Canada, South and Central America and Asia and signed agreements with academic institutions in Siberia (Russia), Inner Mongolia (China) and Tanzania" (First Nations University of Canada 2005).

As the "first-movers" of an indigenous postsecondary organizational model, American Indian tribes are located at the epicenter of efforts to export it to indigenous peoples around the world. In 2000, the U.S. Agency of International Development, Department of Agriculture, in conjunction with the American Indian Higher Education Consortium, sponsored a conference on the "Globalization of Tribal Colleges and Universities" in Washington, D.C. The proceedings emphasized the need for more international outreach efforts of the kind already initiated by Haskell Indian Nations University in Lawrence, Kansas, which launched a student exchange with Gorno-Altaisk State University in Siberia in 1999 and with Northwest Indian College in Bellingham, Washington, which sent students to Latin America after participating in the 1992 U.N. Earth Summit in Rio de Janeiro. Other tribal colleges are linked through exchanges and partnerships to indigenous peoples in Latin America, Oceania, Europe, and Africa (AIHEC 2000).

In 1987, indigenous educators from around the world convened the first World Indigenous Peoples Conference on Education. The conference, held triennially, has been hosted by indigenous peoples in Australia, Canada, New Zealand, and the United States. During the 2002 meeting, indigenous higher education providers from North America, Oceania, and Scandinavia established the World Indigenous Nations Higher Education Consortium (WINHEC) as a worldwide indigenous accrediting agency. According to WINHEC (2003: 17), "the intent is to judge the performance of Indigenous-serving institutions and programs against standards appropriate to the Indigenous cultural contexts involved." WINHEC exemplifies what Roland Robertson (1992) refers to as the universalization of particularism: Indigeneity, a quintessentially local identity, has become globalized. Through the establishment of WINHEC, indigenous peoples worldwide—from New Zealand, Nicaragua, Norway, and beyond—are developing a common standard by which to evaluate "indigenous" pedagogy and curricula.

MASSIFICATION OF HIGHER EDUCATION

No discussion of indigenous peoples' education in the postwar era would be complete without acknowledging the central role played by the postwar "massification" of higher education. Massification, the dramatic expansion of higher education after World War II, has proceeded along three related dimensions: enrollment growth, curricular diversification, and institutional differentiation. Postsecondary enrollments have expanded both quantitatively and qualitatively in recent decades. In purely quantitative terms, the aggregate number of individuals attending some form of postsecondary education worldwide has grown exponentially in recent decades, from less than 0.2 percent of the world's inhabitants in 1940 to nearly 2 percent in 2000 (Schofer and Meyer 2005; see also Windolf 1992). Qualitatively, the composition of enrollments has changed dramatically, as witnessed by the expanded participation of historically marginalized groups such as women, minorities, and members of the working class in higher education. Increased student diversity, in turn, has produced curricular changes tailored to student preferences. Ethnic and women's studies departments, as well as vocational and professional programs, are becoming increasingly prevalent in contemporary colleges and universities (Olzak and Kangas 2008; Wotipka et al. 2007; Brint 2002). The appearance of new academic programs and curricula pertaining to minority groups and women can be attributed in part to social, political, and legal changes that opened access to higher education for women and minorities (Gumport et al. 1997); social movement activism among these students and their sympathizers (Rojas 2007); and, more generally, to academe's innate logic for incorporating and rationalizing new forms of knowledge (Frank and Gabler 2007).

Much as enrollment expansion has prompted curricular diversification within postsecondary institutions (Blau 1973; Gumport and Snydman 2002), massification also contributed to greater institutional differentiation within the field of postsecondary education as a whole (Clark 1978). New preuniversity institutional forms were created to absorb the massive influx of enrollments. In Australia, the Commonwealth government established a two-tiered system of postsecondary education in 1964, consisting of higher education (that is, universities) on the one hand and vocational and technical education on the other. These sectors were distinguished by their relative emphases on teaching or research, academic or vocational studies, and undergraduate or graduate credentials (UNESCO 1996). The binary system was abolished in 1989, whereupon some colleges were closed or amalgamated and others became branch campuses of established universities. The Australian higher education system now includes thirty-nine universities, four "self-accrediting" institutions (of which the country's only indigenous-controlled postsecondary institution, Batchelor Institute of Indigenous Tertiary Education, is one), and a sector of non-self-accrediting institutions that are not authorized to award degrees.

A similar distinction between universities and nonuniversity institutions exists in New Zealand. Polytechnics were awarded formal postsecondary status in 1964 (Peddie 1992), and Maori-controlled postsecondary institutions, *wananga*, achieved a similar status in 1990. Other postsecondary institutions in New Zealand include colleges of education and private training establishments (PTEs).

In the United States and Canada, community colleges provide nonuniversity and vocational education. Community colleges first emerged in the United States during the early twentieth century, although "two-year colleges were radically transformed in the years between 1960 and 1980" (Brint and Karabel 1991: 337). Not only did the number of community colleges increase during this period, but their primary function changed as well, "from a predominantly transfer-oriented institution into one principally dedicated to the provision of terminal vocational education" (Brint and Karabel 1991: 339). The first public two-year community college in Canada, Lethbridge Junior College, was not established until 1957 (Dennison and Gallagher 1986), and degree-granting colleges remain much less extensive in Canada than in the United States. Instead, as with Australia until 1989, "most provinces [in Canada] have binary systems of postsecondary education with distinct university-degree and non-degree sectors and have no analogue to the junior and community colleges providing university-level instruction in many American states" (Boychuk 2000: 464).

By itself, massification promoted the inclusion of underrepresented groups and their worldviews into "mainstream" postsecondary institutions and curricula. The addition of another variable—indigenous sovereignty claims—has stimulated the development of postsecondary institutions controlled by, and adapted to the specific needs and cultural sensibilities of, indigenous communities. In New Zealand, for example, a distinction has been made between "*matauranga Maori*"—translated roughly as Maori-style education—and Maori studies programs: "Maori studies is located within a western university . . . [and] focuses on studying Maori society from a Pakeha [white/European] perspective, while matauranga Maori is about studying the universe from a Maori perspective" (Waitangi Tribunal 1998: ch. 3). Thus, whereas increased minority enrollments and the concomitant rise of ethnic studies curricula in mainstream postsecondary institutions reflects the ethos of multiculturalism, separate indigenous-controlled and culturally distinctive institutions stem from the principle of sovereignty.

CONCLUSION

Macrohistorical patterns in the control and purpose of indigenous peoples' education are intimately associated with changes in their political and legal status. Responsibility for indigenous education fell to churches in the religious polity, to nation-states in the modern statist polity, and increasingly to indigenous peoples in the postwar "glocalized" polity. As the locus of control transferred from churches to states to indigenous peoples, the overriding purpose of indigenous education also changed. The salvation of indigenous peoples' souls was the primary motivation of education policies developed under the auspices of religious institutions, whereas nation-states used schools to subjugate and assimilate indigenous peoples. Most recently, indigenous peoples have reassumed control of their own educational institutions. Indigenous postsecondary institutions in particular have become indicators as well as instruments of the renewed political, economic, and cultural self-determination of indigenous peoples.

Global–local dialectics take center stage in the transfer of control over education to indigenous peoples. The universal expansion of higher education is responsible, in part, for the development of colleges and universities adapted to the particular identities and aspirations of indigenous peoples. At the same time, the establishment of indigenous postsecondary institutions around the world is part of an international indigenous rights movement that has forged a global "indigenous" identity. It is important to remember that this newly institutionalized global identity reflects the disparate efforts of indigenous peoples to assert, individually, their own cultural and political agendas against their respective nation-states. These efforts—and the responses of states to them—have followed a broadly common trajectory in Australia, Canada, New Zealand, the United States, and elsewhere. Documenting and explaining these similarities, as well as elucidating relevant differences, is the task of the next chapter. Then, in Chapter Four, I trace the emergence of indigenous postsecondary institutions cross-nationally.

PART II

CROSS-NATIONAL ANALYSIS

CHAPTER THREE

INDIGENOUS–STATE RELATIONS IN COMPARATIVE PERSPECTIVE

"Let's integrate!" the shark said to the kahawai, and opened its mouth to swallow the small fish for breakfast.

Maori saying, in Fleras and Elliott (1992: 182)

THE U.N. DECLARATION ON THE RIGHTS OF Indigenous Peoples, adopted in 2007, signaled the beginning of a new era in the relationship between indigenous peoples and the states they inhabit. As recently as 1989, states explicitly denied indigenous peoples the right to self-determination under international law.[1] This is no longer the case: One hundred forty-three states voted to approve the indigenous rights declaration, including its acknowledgment of the right of indigenous peoples to self-determination, while only four voted against it. These four countries—the United States, Canada, Australia, and New Zealand—are the focus of the cross-national analyses in Part II.[2]

Ironically, the same countries that initially rejected the rights of indigenous peoples under international law have in many ways advanced the farthest in recognizing their rights under domestic law. They were also among the first countries in the world to establish postsecondary institutions for indigenous peoples. And although the overall tenor and trajectory of indigenous policies in these countries reflect international understandings and frameworks (as recounted in Chapter One), they nevertheless differ tremendously with respect to the status and rights accorded to indigenous peoples. Indigenous rights are strongest in the United States, where the Supreme Court has affirmed the inherent sovereignty of Indian tribes since 1832.[3] It is weakest in Australia, where as late as 1979 the High Court concluded that "the contention that there is in Australia an aboriginal nation exercising sovereignty, even of a limited kind, is quite impossible in law to maintain" (Reynolds 1989: 95).[4] Canada and New Zealand fall between these two extremes. Given that sovereignty confers the authority to establish schools and universities (as argued in Chapter Two), these cross-national differences bear directly on the emergence of indigenous postsecondary institutions.

Variation in the relative strength of indigenous sovereignty under domestic law is ultimately attributable to historical differences in the political incorporation of indigenous peoples, defined broadly as the formal structure of indigenous–state relations. To be clear, "incorporation" does not necessarily entail integration into the state; in fact, indigenous sovereignty is premised on the *exclusion* of indigenous groups from conventional decision-making structures and political institutions (Kymlicka 1995). Instead, political incorporation refers more generally to the "political relationships that link the group to the larger system, whether those relationships are responsive to group concerns or not" (Cornell 1988: 88). This chapter identifies cross-national similarities and differences in key dimensions of indigenous incorporation and assesses the impact of these similarities and differences on indigenous peoples' sovereignty claims.

POLICY TRAJECTORIES: CROSS-NATIONAL SIMILARITIES

Indigenous incorporation regimes develop and operate within an overarching world-cultural framework that specifies the general status and standing of indigenous peoples. Not surprisingly, then, the broad contours of indigenous policies in the United States, Canada, Australia, and New Zealand have been quite similar over time (see, for example, Armitage 1995; Canada 1996b: 37–40; Cornell 1988; Fleras and Elliott 1992; Havemann 1999).[5] With some exceptions, cross-national patterns in indigenous–state relations may be organized into four sequential periods:

- First contact and *colonization*;
- Cultural *assimilation*, generally spearheaded by Christian missionaries;

- Political *integration* of indigenous peoples as citizens with "equal" rights; and
- *Autonomy*, self-determination, or limited self-government.[6]

Although these periods did not always occur simultaneously in each country—colonization occurred later in Australasia than in North America, for example—the sequencing was nevertheless common to each, giving rise to common patterns of indigenous–state relations along four broad policy areas: indigenous lifestyles, legal status, land, and language.

Lifestyles

Early colonial and state policies regulating the political incorporation of indigenous peoples established the criteria by which "savage" indigenes could be judged "fit" to enter mainstream society. Between 1869 and 1910, for example, all six British colonies on the Australian continent—which, after independence in 1901, became individual states within the Commonwealth of Australia—enacted paternalistic statutes regulating the minutiae of Aboriginal peoples' daily lives. The statutes installed one or more government "protectors" as official caretakers of Aboriginal peoples and reserves. Small farms were established on reserves to train Aboriginals in the rudiments of agriculture; however, once the farms became profitable, they were sold to white settlers (Perry 1996: 187). Significant lifestyle changes—including, most importantly, profession of faith in Christianity—earned Aborigines exemption from the authority of protectors. They "were to be rewarded for their European behaviour by being excluded from the legal class of Aborigines to whom the special provisions of the law applied" (Armitage 1995: 24). The states repealed their protection acts between 1967 and 1972, with the advent of the self-determination period.

In the United States, the Civilization Fund Act of 1819 represented the first concerted government effort to induce lifestyle changes in American Indians. The legislation appropriated yearly subsidies of up to $10,000 to missionary societies for the purpose of "introducing among [Indians] the habits and arts of civilization" (Prucha 2000: 33). To hasten assimilation, the General Allotment Act of 1887 provided the framework for breaking up communally held reservation lands and allotting individual tracts to tribal members, with the goal of transforming Indians into yeoman farmers. Likewise in Canada, the Act for the Gradual Civilization of the Indian Tribes (1857) sought to eliminate all legal distinctions between Indians and non-Indians. The act enfranchised, and allotted 50-acre parcels of land to, Indians who were "over 21, able to read and write either English or French, . . . reasonably well educated, free of debt, and of good moral character as determined by a commission of non-Indian examiners" (Canada 1996b: 271). These non-Indian examiners, in effect the gatekeepers of civilization, were typically missionaries. A decade later, in 1867, Canada enacted the first Indian Act to consolidate legislation regarding Indians and their reserves. Much like the protection acts in Australia, the Indian Act made government officials in Canada the "pharaohs of aboriginal society" with "broad discretionary powers [that] reached into the minutiae of everyday life" (McHugh 2004: 51).

New Zealand's Native Trust Ordinance of 1844 similarly undertook to "civilize" the indigenous Maori population. The ordinance is remarkable for its ostensibly well-intentioned conviction that the Maori were capable of riding the fast track to civilization. The preamble reads,

> Whereas the native people of New Zealand are by natural endowments apt for the acquirement of the arts and habits of civilized life, and are capable of great moral and social advancement; [. . .] And whereas great disasters have fallen upon uncivilized nations on being brought into contact with colonists from the nations of Europe, and in undertaking the colonization of New Zealand Her Majesty's Government have recognized the duty of endeavouring by all practical means to avert the like disasters from the native people of these Islands, which object may best be attained by assimilating as speedily as possible the habits and usages of the native to those of the European population." (Barrington and Beaglehole 1974: 39–40)

The irony is blunt: The Maori had to adopt European habits and mores as quickly as possible to be saved from the very people they were admonished to emulate. Only three years later, the Education Ordinance of 1847 provided for government funding of mission schools in order to "civilis[e] the race" and "individualise property" (Waitangi Tribunal 1998).

As these examples attest, the assimilation of indigenous peoples was generally premised on their conversion to Christianity; indeed, the salvation of infidel souls was the primary justification for colonizing new lands. In addition to their nominal concern for the spiritual well-being of indigenous peoples, however, colonizers and settlers were also anxious to clear tribally held lands for settlement by "converting" indigenous peoples into individual farmers. In three of the examples—the United States, Canada, and New Zealand—individualizing communally held property was central to the civilizing mission. Allotment was rooted in the assumption, best articulated by U.S. Commissioner of Indian Affairs T. Hartley Crawford in 1838, that "common property and civilization cannot co-exist" (Prucha 2000: 73).

Land

Individualizing tribal lands via policies such as allotment was anathema to indigenous cultures, which helps to explain its centrality to assimilationist projects. The unique cultural relationship of indigenous peoples to land distinguished them from their colonizers and continues to distinguish them from most other racial, ethnic, and minority groups. Indigenous peoples conceived of land in deeply spiritual or religious terms and, consequently, lacked any notion that it could be owned or alienated. Moreover, the distinctive temporal or chronological relationship of indigenous peoples to land—their status as prior occupants, from time immemorial—forms the basis of their contemporary claims to self-determination (Macklem 1993).

In an effort to undermine the special relationship of indigenous peoples to land, including the claim to self-determination that prior occupation entails, European colonizers and their derivative settler-states attempted to deny Aboriginal—that is, collective—rights to land ownership. Much as the General Allotment Act in the United States and the Act for the Gradual Civilization of the Indian Tribes in Canada sought to break up tribal land holdings, European state-builders in New Zealand also chipped away at communal ownership. In 1846, the New Zealand Government Act empowered the colonial governor to disallow Maori ownership of unoccupied land, and the Native Lands Acts of 1862 and 1865 established the legal machinery for converting tribal into individual landholdings (Howard 2003; Barrington and Beaglehole 1974). P. G. McHugh (2004: 51) notes that the "individualization of the communal land title was . . . applied with devastating effectiveness in the United States and New Zealand." By 1920, American Indians had lost more than three-quarters of the land they had held in 1871, whereas in Maori landholdings amounted to just 7 percent of the lands they occupied in 1840 (Stuart 1987; Durie 1998). Australia presents the extreme case: It was colonized under the presumption that the continent was *terra nullius*—it denied the very presence of Aboriginal peoples, much less their land rights. Until recently, then, the issue of individualizing indigenous land tenure was legally moot in Australia.

Also at issue was the ultimate source of indigenous land rights, such that they existed. The U.S. Supreme Court first recognized Indian title to land in 1823 but held that it conferred "a mere right of usufruct and habitation, without power of alienation" (*Johnson v. McIntosh* 1823: 569). Citing the opinions of Chief Justice John Marshall in *Johnson* and related cases, the Supreme Courts of New Zealand and Canada confirmed the existence of Aboriginal title in 1847 and 1887, respectively. In New Zealand, *R. v. Symonds* (1847) held that "Native title is entitled to be respected," but the ruling was effectively nullified thirty years later by *Wi Parata v. The Bishop of Wellington* (1877). In Canada, *St. Catherines Milling v. The Queen* (1887) closely followed John Marshall's conceptualization of Aboriginal title in the United States while carefully ignoring his contention that Indian tribes continued to enjoy residual sovereignty (McHugh 2004: 158)

St. Catherines Milling concluded that Indian title to land derives from, and exists at the will of, the Crown. This view prevailed until 1973, when the landmark ruling in *Calder v. Attorney General of British Columbia* formally recognized the independent existence of Aboriginal title. *Calder* itself cited Marshall's decision in *Johnson v. McIntosh* (1823) as the "*locus classicus* of the principles governing aboriginal title" (p. 380). But *Calder* also proved to be tremendously influential in its own right (Nettheim 2007; Williams 2007). Its influence was especially strong in Australia, where the *terra nullius* doctrine held sway until the High Court overturned it in 1992. The ruling in question, *Mabo v. Queensland*, relied heavily on the definition of Aboriginal title as formulated in *Calder*, as well as on relevant case law from the United States and New Zealand. *Mabo* also referred extensively to international law. It cited a 1975 advisory opinion of the International Court of Justice that discredited *terra nullius* as a tenet of international law and held that the International Convention on the Elimination of Racial Discrimination, which Australia had ratified and incorporated into law in 1975, conferred on Aboriginal peoples a right to inhabit their traditional lands.

Thus, national policies regarding indigenous land rights reflect not only common legal and discursive currents in international law but also direct judicial borrowing. Under conditions of uncertainty and ambiguity, organizations often mimic the policies, practices, and structures of other organizations (DiMaggio and Powell 1983), and the same principle applies to nation-states as organizations writ large. Given that modern conceptions of "Aboriginal title" do not fit neatly into conventional understandings of land tenure, it is not surprising that countries have looked to one another for guidance on the matter.

Legal Status

Policies relating to indigenous lifestyles and land were intimately connected to the legal status of indigenous peoples. Changes in the status of indigenes from wards to citizens presupposed their adoption of certain diffuse "European" lifestyle characteristics. Although colonizers were nominally concerned with the spiritual well-being of indigenous peoples, they were also anxious to alter the worldly status of indigenous peoples in ways that denied their original sovereignty and collective claims to land. This agenda required baptism not by water, fire, or the Holy Ghost but by legislative fiat.

As we have seen, adopting individual land tenure qualified indigenes for citizenship and, correspondingly, for the loss of their separate legal status. Citizenship was incrementally extended to indigenous people who owned individually tenured parcels of land or who had served in the military. In 1852, 1885, and 1887, freeholder indigenes in New Zealand, Canada, and the United States, respectively, became eligible to vote (Fleras 1985; Canada 1996b; Wolfley 1990). In 1919, Congress granted citizenship to all honorably discharged American Indians having served in World War I and, in 1924, unilaterally conferred unqualified citizenship—whether they wanted it or not—to all Indians. Military service during the world wars also qualified Indians in Canada to vote in federal elections, but they were not given the franchise unconditionally until 1960. (Individuals of Inuit descent had been enfranchised a decade earlier.) Many Indians in Canada protested when the federal franchise was extended to them (Kymlicka 1995: 228, n. 18). In fact, Alan Cairns (2000) credits international pressure, rather than demands emanating from indigenous peoples within Canada, with the government's decision to grant Indians the right to vote.

After World War II, integrationist measures in the United States and Canada were predicated on the complete disestablishment of tribal structures. These so-called termination policies, first initiated by the U.S. Congress in 1953, provided the mechanisms whereby the federal government could sever ties with, and revoke the special legal status of, Indian tribes by transferring jurisdiction over them to the individual states. Canada followed suit in 1969 with the White Paper (Department of Indian and Northern Affairs [DIAND] 1969), which called for an end to the federal government's administration of

Indian affairs. An opposite trend occurred in Australia, where, unlike the federal systems of the United States and Canada, the constituent states had retained exclusive jurisdiction over Aboriginal peoples. The intent, nevertheless, was similar: In 1962 an act of parliament granted the Commonwealth (federal) franchise to Aboriginals, and in 1967 a referendum to amend the constitution granted the Commonwealth government power to legislate for Aboriginal peoples concurrently with the states. This objective was achieved by deleting exclusionary references to Aboriginal peoples in the national constitution, thereby depriving them of their "special" status.

In New Zealand, the Maori had theoretically achieved legal equality, as British subjects, with *Pakeha* (that is, New Zealanders of European descent) in the Treaty of Waitangi of 1840. Nevertheless, legislation continued to distinguish between Maori and non-Maori citizens until the *Report on Department of Maori Affairs*—also known as the Hunn Report of 1960—recommended that the "differentiation between Maoris and Europeans in statute law should be reviewed at intervals and gradually eliminated" (Armitage 1995: 146). This recommendation was subsequently incorporated into law in 1967.

These postwar integrationist policies, although sweeping, were generally short lived. Each country underwent an abrupt and remarkably simultaneous policy reversal during the 1970s and 1980s in favor of increased indigenous self-determination. President Richard Nixon repudiated the congressional termination policy in 1970, but its revocation didn't become official until 1975, when Congress passed the Indian Self-Determination Act. The Canadian government retracted its own termination policy in 1973, and the national constitution was patriated and amended in 1982 to recognize the "aboriginal and treaty rights" of First Nations peoples. Australia's Commonwealth government, pursuant to its new authority to legislate for Aboriginals, declared in 1972 its intention to "restore to the Aboriginal people of Australia their lost power of self-determination in economic, social and political affairs" (Gardiner-Garden 1999). And in New Zealand, parliament repealed its integrationist legislation in 1973. The Treaty of Waitangi Act, passed two years later in 1975, affirmed the collective treaty rights of Maori.

Language

In addition to colonial and settler policies regarding indigenous lifestyles, land, and legal status, assaults on indigenous cultures invariably targeted indigenous languages. An 1871 amendment to New Zealand's Native Schools Act of 1867 made the use of English mandatory in classrooms (Howard 2003: 191). In 1887, the commissioner of Indian Affairs in the United States likewise prohibited students from speaking American Indian languages in schools (Prucha 2000: 173–175). Similar policies were implemented in Canada and Australia (Armitage 1995).

As the twentieth century drew to a close, New Zealand and the United States reversed their commitment to linguistic assimilation by taking measures to preserve indigenous languages. The Maori Language Act of 1987 went so far as to elevate Maori to the status of official language in New Zealand, equal in all respects to English. Less extensively, the Native American Languages Act of 1990 expressed the intent of the U.S. Congress to "preserve, protect, and promote the rights and freedom of Native Americans to use, practice, and develop Native American languages." Two years later, Congress enacted legislation to authorize funding for that purpose.

Australia and Canada have been somewhat less enthusiastic in their support of indigenous languages. In these countries, indigenous language policies have generally been left to subnational jurisdictions. To date, no legislation at the Commonwealth level in Australia has been committed specifically to preserving or promoting Aboriginal languages, although the state of New South Wales recently launched a comprehensive Aboriginal Languages Policy designed to enable Aboriginal students to study their languages in school. The policy is the first of its kind in Australia. In Canada, where English and French are official languages, indigenous languages enjoy official status only at the territorial level, in the Northwest Territories (since 1984) and Nunavut (since its inception in 1999). As with Australia, the formulation of indigenous language policies in Canada is largely confined to the provincial and territorial governments (Fettes and Norton 2000) despite the federal government's constitutional jurisdiction over Indian peoples.

Other Cases

Similar trends in indigenous–state relations can be seen in other parts of the world, including in countries that differ markedly from Anglo-derived settler states. Two circumpolar cases, Norway and Greenland, are instructive. Both countries were colonized by Denmark: Norway was subsumed within the Danish kingdom for 500 years, and Greenland continues to be a federacy of Denmark, though one with substantial autonomy. Both countries are organized as social-corporatist polities, distinguishing them sharply from the United States, Canada, Australia, and New Zealand, all of which inherited liberal polities from their British colonizers. Norway, furthermore, is distinctive in that the ethnic Norwegian and Saami populations were equally "indigenous" to the country—Saami in the north, and Norwegians in the south. As such, unlike other European metropolises, Norwegians were geographically contiguous with the peoples they colonized, resulting in centuries of sustained contact between them prior to the incorporation of the Saami into Norway. Greenland's status as a "conventional" colony, one that is separated geographically from its colonizer and in which the population remains predominantly indigenous, also distinguishes it from the North American and Australasian cases.

As with the former British colonies, the colonization of northern Scandinavia and Greenland was predicated on the need to "civilize" the indigenous Saami and Inuit peoples by converting them to Christianity. "The first attempt to Christianize the Saami was by the 'Apostle of the North,' Stenfi, in 1050. . . . In 1313, the Norwegian king proclaimed a 20-year tax reduction for the Saami upon conversion to Christianity" (Beach 1994: 173). Such inducements to assimilate would eventually give way to policies of coerced assimilation, especially during the rise of Norwegian nationalism in the late nineteenth and early twentieth centuries. The Land Act of 1902, for example, made fluency in the Norwegian language a condition of land ownership, effectively excluding most Saami.

European contact with native Greenlanders first occurred during the tenth century, but a continuous European presence was not established until the 1700s. Once again, religion was central to the colonial enterprise in Greenland. The first permanent European settlement was established in 1721 by Hans Egede, a Norwegian missionary who was dispatched to minister the descendents of the first Norse settlers who were presumed, falsely, to still live there. When he discovered that Norsemen no longer remained in Greenland, Egede trained his proselytizing efforts on the Inuit peoples. By 1744 the four Gospels had been translated into the newly developed Greenlandic orthography; a quarter-century later, the entire New Testament was available in the indigenous vernacular (Nuttall 1994: 4). The primary goal of education throughout the remainder of the eighteenth and nineteenth centuries remained the Christianization of the indigenous population. According to Darnell and

Hoëm (1996: 112), "the first Western teachers in Greenland, as in the rest of the Far North, were missionaries arrived there first of all to save the souls of the unenlightened."

Assimilationist and integrationist policies were pursued in Norway and Greenland as aggressively as they were in the United States and the "white dominions" of the old British Empire. The Norwegian parliament continued its policy of assimilating Saami during the years leading into and immediately following World War II, and in 1958 the government declined an invitation to sign the ILO Convention (No. 107) on Indigenous and Tribal Populations on the grounds that the document was irrelevant "since there was no tribal populations [*sic*] in the country" (Thuen 1995: 174). As far as the Norwegian government was concerned, Saami integration into mainstream society was a fait accompli by the late 1950s. Integration took an even more dramatic form in Greenland, when in 1953 the colony was incorporated as an integral county of Denmark. With this political transformation, Greenlanders earned two representatives in the Danish parliament.

Policies toward the Inuit in Greenland and the Saami in Norway began to shift during the 1970s and 1980s, reflecting similar trends elsewhere in the world. Thirty-two years after it refused to sign the ILO's convention on the rights of indigenous people, Norway became, in 1990, the first country to ratify the revised Convention No. 169. Norway's eagerness to affirm indigenous peoples' rights in international law followed a series of developments concerning the rights of Saami in domestic law. In 1987, parliament passed the Saami Act "to provide suitable conditions for the Saami people in Norway to safeguard and develop its language, its culture, and its community life." The act further provided for the establishment of a democratically elected Saami assembly that the Norwegian parliament must consult before passing any legislation that affects the Saami. A year later, the Norwegian constitution was amended to protect Saami rights. According to Article 110a, "It is the responsibility of the authorities of the State to create conditions enabling the Saami people to preserve and develop its language, culture and way of life." On the basis of this constitutional amendment, the Saami Language Act of 1992 established Saami and Norwegian as official languages in six northern municipalities, giving Saami the right to communicate with public officials in Saami dialects, to use Saami in judicial proceedings, and to be taught the Saami language.

The policy shift in favor of expanded political and cultural rights for indigenous peoples was even more discontinuous in Greenland, which spent only a quarter-century as an integral county in the Kingdom of Denmark. The Greenland Home Rule Act, passed by the Danish parliament in 1978 and overwhelmingly approved in referendum by Greenlanders the following year, established a Greenlandic parliament and awarded it jurisdiction over most internal affairs. The act also established Greenlandic and Danish as coequal languages in Greenland. After thirty years of home rule, a majority of Greenlanders now advocate independence from Denmark, and a 2008 referendum paved the way for increased autonomy with respect to criminal justice and oil exploration (Lyall 2009).

The examples of Norway and Greenland demonstrate that the tenor and trajectory of policies toward indigenous peoples were similar in very different parts of the world. Whether in North America, Australasia, or Scandinavia, indigenous–state relations followed a broadly similar pattern that reflected larger macrohistorical changes in the world polity and, in some cases, direct judicial and legal borrowing.

The convergence of legislation and jurisprudence regarding indigenous peoples' lifestyles, land, legal status, and languages around common models supports the thesis that domestic policies are shaped by global institutional processes and cross-national mimesis. But nation-states also actively mediate world-cultural models and frameworks to produce variation in specific outcomes. National configurations of indigenous "incorporation regimes" are especially important. Previous research in this vein (Brubaker 1992; Koopmans and Statham 1999; Soysal 1994) focuses exclusively on national policies and structures that mediate the incorporation of migrants. Migrant incorporation regimes tend to be commensurate with—and indeed, usually derive from—the set of institutional logics (Friedland and Alford 1991; Jepperson 2002) that prevail in a given polity. For instance, liberal polities incorporate migrants as individuals, and corporatist polities organize them into interest groups (Soysal 1994; Koopmans and Statham 1999). Conversely, patterns of indigenous incorporation often fail to align with the institutional structures and political logics of the larger polity. In the archetypically liberal polities of the United States and Canada, for example, indigenous peoples were incorporated as corporate groups, and attempts to "individualize" tribes or bands—that is, to reconfigure indigenous–state relations in the liberal image—have failed. These differences, and the reasons for them, require some explication.

INDIGENOUS INCORPORATION REGIMES: CROSS-NATIONAL VARIATION

As the preceding discussion illustrates, Australia, Canada, New Zealand, and the United States are similar on a variety of dimensions. These similarities are perhaps not all that surprising. They were, after all, colonized by the same imperial power—Britain—and inherited Britain's legal traditions, liberal institutions, and cultural heritage (notwithstanding the portions of North America originally colonized by France and Spain). By holding these similarities constant, it is possible to isolate crucial differences in colonial legacies, political cultures, and demographic factors that have produced cross-national variation the strength of indigenous sovereignty claims.

Despite their commonalities, the British settler societies were colonized at different times (the United States and Canada in the early seventeenth century, Australia and New Zealand in the late eighteenth and early nineteenth centuries) and became independent in different eras (the United States in 1783, Canada in 1867, Australia in 1901, and New Zealand in 1907). Three of the countries—Australia, Canada, and New Zealand—still belong to the Commonwealth of Nations. The United States, in contrast, emerged from a revolutionary break with Britain, giving it a markedly different political system from its "loyalist" counterparts (Lipset 1990). And of particular import for this analysis, the relative size of each country's indigenous population differs. According to recent census estimates for each country, indigenous peoples represent nearly 15 percent of the population in New Zealand (Maori), compared with 3.3 percent in Canada (Indian, Inuit, and Metis), 2.5 percent in Australia (Aboriginal and Torres Strait Islanders), and 1.5 percent in the United States (American Indians and Alaska Natives).

These differences have shaped the incorporation of indigenous peoples into their respective nation-states. I focus on four dimensions of incorporation—colonial, relational, administrative, and structural—that, taken together, account for variation in the development, formal recognition, and relative strength of indigenous sovereignty cross-nationally. These dimensions refer, respectively, to competition among European powers during the process of colonization, treaty making between metropoles or their settler derivatives and indigenous nations, the establishment of reserved-land systems for indigenous peoples, and the organization of political sovereignty within a state. It is important to emphasize that these dimensions are not binary variables that indicate the simple presence of absence of colonial competition, treaty making, reservation systems, or federalism. Nor do they exist independently of each other. As I will show, the dimensions of indigenous incorporation range along continua between complete absence and full presence, and tend in practice to covary.

Colonial: Competition Produces Sovereign Recognition

In 1608, the acclaimed English jurist Lord Chief Justice Edward Coke, presiding over *Calvin's Case*, wrote that "all infidels are in law *perpetui inimici*, perpetual enemies . . . for between them, as with devils, whose subjects they be, and the Christian, there is perpetual hostility, and can be no peace" (Williams 1990: 200). Notwithstanding this sentiment, Europeans often deemed it expedient, even necessary, to ally with indigenous peoples. This was true especially when imperial powers competed with one another for power or influence. These relationships contributed, often inadvertently, to the formal recognition of indigenous sovereignty.

David Abernethy (2000) argues that two axes of competition—one between rival metropoles, the other among indigenous peoples themselves—accelerated rates of colonization. The size and number of colonies grew as would-be colonizers sought to expand their landholdings and extend their spheres of influence at the expense of competitors. Europeans also exploited factions among indigenous peoples in a divide-and-conquer strategy. But colonial competition also *benefited* indigenous peoples by enabling them to play one metropole against another. Competition among European colonizers often produced alliances, understood in distinctly nation-to-nation terms, between indigenous peoples and metropolitan states.

Alliances with indigenous peoples assumed many forms. Some were overtly militaristic; others were primarily economic. Whatever the circumstances, when it served their purposes, Europeans treated Indian nations as relative equals. During the Elizabethan era, "Indians were . . . trading partners, converts, and allies in radical Protestantism's rivalry with papist Spain" (Williams 1990: 220). Similar alliances developed when European-based wars between Britain and another Catholic rival, France, spilled into the New World (Cornell 1988).

British and French colonizers regarded the Indian nations of North America first as trading partners and then as military allies (Cornell 1988; Green and Dickason 1989). Such partnerships and alliances compelled metropolitan powers to concede—however hesitantly, perfunctorily, or implicitly—the sovereignty of indigenous nations. The dynamics of sovereign recognition changed when one colonizer was able to establish political supremacy in a region. In 1763, France surrendered its North American colonies to Britain. Thereafter, British hegemony in present-day Canada obviated Britain's need for Indian military alliances against the French, but hostilities in the American colonies (and later with the new American republic) kept the need alive to the south. Wartime alliances with Indian tribes effectively ceased in the United States and Canada after 1815, when relations between the United States and Britain stabilized following the War of 1812 (Allen 1992; Canada 1996b; Fleras and Elliott 1992; Johnson 1991). From that point forward, indigenous peoples in Canada and the United States made the unwelcome and unilaterally imposed transition "from warriors to wards" (Allen 1992).[7]

Another, more dramatic, example of colonial competition leading to the recognition of indigenous sovereignty comes from New Zealand, where Britain briefly acknowledged Maori independence to deflect French territorial claims (Keal 2003; Howard 2003). In 1835, a confederation of Maori tribes issued a declaration of independence announcing the creation of an "Independent State" styled the United Tribes of New Zealand. Article 2 reads:

> All sovereign power and authority within the territories of the United Tribes of New Zealand is hereby declared to reside entirely and exclusively in the hereditary chiefs and heads of tribes in their collective capacity, who also declare that they will not permit any legislative authority separate from themselves in their collective capacity to exist, nor any function of government to be exercised within the said territories, unless by persons appointed by them, and acting under the authority of laws regularly enacted by them in Congress assembled.

The declaration was signed by James Busby, the official British Resident in New Zealand, and a new flag representing the Maori state was approved by the king.

In sum, North America and New Zealand were colonized during periods of intense geopolitical competition, especially between Great Britain and France (but also, in earlier periods, with Spain). Figure 3.1 shows the net number of

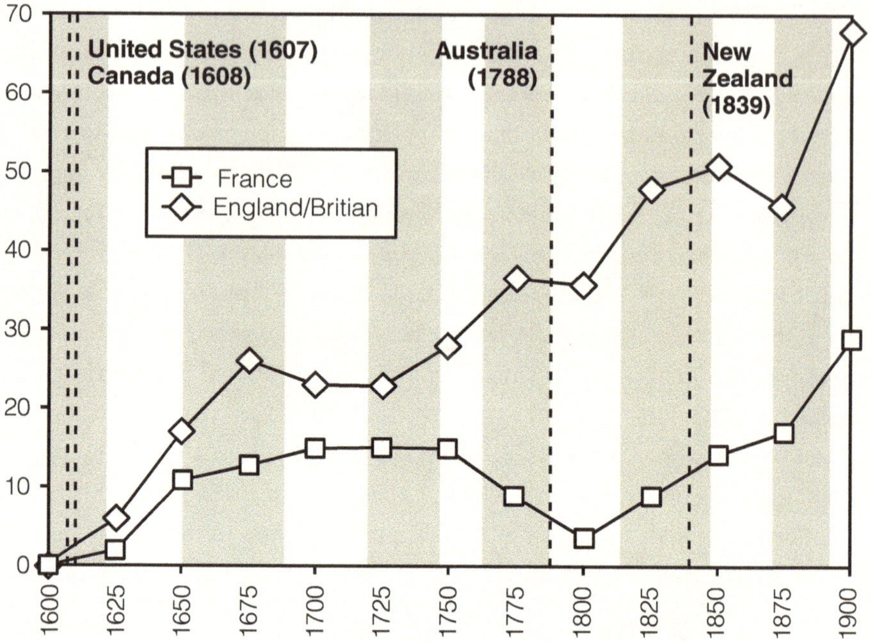

FIGURE 3.1. Net number of colonies held by Great Britain and France, 1600–1900.

SOURCE: Data on colonies comes from Strang (1991).

Note: Periods of stagnation in the world economy, indicated by the shaded regions, taken from Goldstein (1988: 196). These periods are as follows: 1595–1620; 1650–88; 1720–46; 1762–89; 1814–47; 1872–92.

colonies held by Britain and France between 1600 and 1900. When colonies in what are now the United States, Canada, and New Zealand were first established, the British and French empires were both expanding. These colonies, moreover, were founded during periods of stagnation in the global economy (as depicted by the shaded regions in Figure 3.1), during which competition among core powers intensified and peripheral areas were incorporated under direct colonial administration (Chase-Dunn and Rubinson 1977; Boswell 1989).

Of the four countries under consideration, only Australia was colonized without competition from core rivals. When the first settlement in Australia was established in 1788, France was on the brink of revolution, and its empire had reached a nadir. Australia was also colonized at the beginning of a global economic upswing, when Britain enjoyed economic and military hegemony in the world-system. Thus, Australia presents an example where the dominance of one metropolitan power resulted in the outright negation of indigenous sovereignty. Absent competition with colonial rivals, Britain settled Australia under the pretext that it was *terra nullius*—empty land—and therefore belonged to the first "civilized" nation to "discover" and effectively occupy it. This doctrine was upheld by the Privy Council in *Cooper v. Stuart* (1889) and reiterated by Australia's High Court more than eight decades later in *Milirrpum v. Nabalco* (1971), on the assumption that the Aborigines lacked any recognizable legal or political organization. The repercussions have been immense. As a legacy of *terra nullius*, Aboriginal peoples were neither counted in the census nor granted citizenship until the 1960s. The absence of colonial competition in Australia precluded any need to form alliances with Aboriginal peoples and therefore to recognize their sovereignty.[8]

Differences in colonial legacies have impacted the status of indigenous peoples under domestic law in yet other ways. Three countries—Canada, New Zealand, and Australia—maintained extensive political ties with Great Britain after becoming independent, and the British monarch has remained the official head of state in each country. Only in 1982 did Westminster formally relinquish its authority to legislate for Canada. Formal legislative independence was similarly granted to Australia and its individual states, as well as to New Zealand, in 1986. Because of these lasting political relationships, broad conceptions of sovereignty in all three countries have remained more or less faithful to the prevailing British view, which holds that ultimate sovereignty resides in and devolves from the Crown (Macklem 1993: 1316–1317). Such a hierarchical theory of political authority leaves little conceptual room for indigenous sovereignty (Boldt and Long 1984). As a consequence, the Canadian government did not recognize the *inherent* self-government of indigenous peoples until 1995; before then, what powers Aboriginal peoples did hold were expressly *delegated* by and existed at the pleasure of the Crown. Even now, the inherent right to Aboriginal self-government is deemed to operate within Canada's constitutional framework and is subject to the Charter of Rights and Freedoms.

The United States, on the other hand, emerged from the revolutionary break with Britain, giving Americans a unique conception of political authority (Lipset 1990). Contrary to the prevailing British notion of devolved sovereignty, power in the United States is understood as "emanat[ing] upward from the consent of the people" (Macklem 1993: 1316). This idea, that political sovereignty antedates the constitutional state, readily accommodates the inherent sovereignty of indigenous nations. Indeed, this theory of sovereignty regards Indian tribes as extraconstitutional entities that were neither party to nor bound by the U.S. Constitution. The Supreme Court recognized this fact when in ruled in *Cherokee Nation v. Georgia* (1831) that Indian tribes constitute "domestic dependent nations" and continue to exercise a diminished form of original sovereignty. As such, in contrast with the Canadian situation, tribal governments in the United States were historically exempted from the Bill of Rights.

Relational: Treaty Making with Indigenous Nations

Closely related to colonial competition is the relational dimension of indigenous incorporation, where the central question is whether colonial or settler states negotiated formal treaties with indigenous peoples (Craufurd-Lewis 1995). Treaty making was most prevalent in colonies where competition among would-be colonizers was intense, as European governments sought to conclude formal nonaggression pacts or wartime alliances with indigenous nations or to preclude the imperial designs of colonial rivals by staking legal claims to indigenous territory. Indigenous peoples in the United States, Canada, and New Zealand—the countries in which colonial competition led to the sovereign recognition of indigenous nations—signed formal treaties with European colonizers or their derivative states.

Although treaties with indigenous peoples were frequently biased in favor of state or imperial parties, "the fact . . . that treaties were signed, approved, and ratified [at all], is relevant and provides much of the legal armament of indigenous peoples today" (Wiessner 1999: 94). In *Worcester v. Georgia* (1832), the U.S. Supreme Court emphasized the importance of treaties in cementing the relationship between Indian tribes, conceived as quasi-sovereign "nations within a nation," and the federal government of the United States. As far as the Court was concerned, Indian treaties existed on equal footing with treaties concluded between the federal government and foreign nations. It bears repeating a key passage from the highly influential *Worcester* ruling in this context:

> The constitution, by declaring treaties already made, as well as those to be made, to be the supreme law of the land, has adopted and sanctioned the previous treaties with the Indian nations, and consequently admits their rank among those powers who are capable of making treaties. (pp. 559–560)

To paraphrase Durkheim, the substance of a treaty is not as important as the a priori legal foundations and social assumptions that underlie it. Treaties have an international character and are, by definition, entered into by coequal sovereigns. Moreover, the very act of treaty making presumes the prior sovereignty of indigenous peoples, as they cannot surrender land they did not previously own or powers they did not originally possess (Cornell 1988; Fleras and Elliott 1992; Howard 2003). Treaties therefore permit indigenous peoples to frame their relations with states in rather explicit government-to-government or "quasi-diplomatic" terms (McHugh 2004: 191).

In all, Johnson (1991: 648, 666) reports that the U.S. government concluded some 389 treaties with Indian tribes between 1778 and 1868, while in Canada only sixty-seven treaties were negotiated between indigenous peoples and the Crown from 1680 to 1929. The most prominent of the Canadian treaties are the eleven "Numbered Treaties," in which First Nations ceded vast tracts of land comprising over half of present-day Canada. The British Crown concluded only one treaty, the Treaty of Waitangi, with the Maori of New Zealand, and parliament never ratified it (Howard 2003: 184). The Treaty of Waitangi extended full citizenship to Maori individuals, thereby denying their independent and collective nationhood.[9] Some prominent Maori leaders preferred to abide by the terms of the 1835 Maori Declaration of Independence and refused to sign the treaty (Howard 2003: 183).

Of course, treaties with indigenous peoples have not always been honored. The U.S. Congress stopped entering into treaties with Indian tribes in 1871, and in 1903 the Supreme Court ruled in *Lone Wolf v. Hitchcock* that Congress may unilaterally abrogate existing treaties with Indians. Courts in Canada and New Zealand went even further by retrospectively annulling treaties with indigenous peoples. In *R. v. Syliboy* (1929), a Nova Scotia court summarily declared Indian treaty rights unenforceable "because Indians were not independent powers legally capable of concluding a treaty" (Wiessner 1999: 67). Similarly, a New Zealand tribunal argued in *Wi Parata v. Bishop of Wellington* (1877) that "the Treaty of Waitangi lacked binding force in law, precisely because the Maori signatories lacked the authority of sovereign statehood that alone could have made the terms of a treaty with them binding on the Crown and its subsequent judges, officers and subjects" (Keal 2003: 149–150). This ruling simply ignored Britain's formal recognition in 1835 of the Maori's sovereign independence.

The past several decades have witnessed a resurgence in the treaty rights of indigenous peoples. Courts in the United States began to reaffirm Indian treaties during the 1970s. In the well-known and controversial "Boldt decision" of 1974 (that is, *United States v. Washington*), a U.S. federal district court defended the treaty-protected fishing rights of tribes in the Pacific Northwest. Treaty making with First Nations in Canada resumed in 1973, and since then fifteen modern land claims treaties have been negotiated (Indian and Northern Affairs Canada 2008). Section 35(1) of the Constitution Act 1982 proclaims that "the existing aboriginal and treaty rights of the aboriginal peoples of Canada are hereby recognized and affirmed."[10] Subsequently, the Supreme Court of Canada asserted in *R. v. Sioui* (1990) that treaties may not be extinguished without first obtaining consent from the Aboriginal party involved (Johnson 1991: 672; Macklem 2001: 144–145).[11] In New Zealand, the Treaty of Waitangi Act (1975) incorporated the Treaty of Waitangi into domestic law and established the Waitangi Tribunal to adjudicate Maori treaty claims against the Crown; ten years later, the tribunal was granted retrospective jurisdiction extending back to 1840. Nevertheless, a clause in New Zealand's Bill of Rights Act (1990) that would have constitutionalized the Treaty, similar in effect to Canada's section 35(1), was removed from the original draft (McHugh 2004: 418). Moreover, because New Zealand is a unitary state with a unicameral legislature, legislation that is not entrenched constitutionally can be revoked by unsympathetic parliamentary majorities.

Treaties were not signed with Aboriginal peoples in Australia. The British House of Commons Select Committee on Aborigines (1837) refused to enter into treaties with Australian Aborigines because of the belief that they "were so entirely destitute . . . of the rudest forms of civil polity, that their claims, whether as sovereigns or proprietors of the soil, have been entirely disregarded" (Werther 1992: 9). One attempt was made by a private individual to conclude a treaty with indigenous Australians, but the Crown vetoed it (Morse 1988).

Administrative: Reserve versus Nonreserve Systems

The administration of indigenous populations turns on the presence or absence of reserves (or "reservations"), tracts of land set aside for exclusive use by indigenous peoples. Australia, Canada, and the United States have reserve systems; New Zealand, in a conventional sense, does not. I call this dimension "administrative" because reservations and their inhabitants tend to be managed by separate legal codes and bureaucracies that structure the social and political incorporation of indigenous peoples in three ways. First, reservations physically separate indigenous peoples from the majority population. Second, the existence of special regulatory systems for indigenous peoples and their land institutionalizes their distinctive status relative to other groups. Lastly, the administrative edifice imposes bureaucratic "downlinks" that indigenous peoples can later convert into activist "uplinks." Reserve bureaucracies afford indigenous peoples a direct channel of communication with central governments, and separate legal codes give indigenous peoples the wherewithal to prosecute their claims in courts of law (Werther 1992).

Yet another outcome of the physical and legal exclusion of indigenous peoples is that they were not granted citizenship until well after the process of decolonization and state formation, thus reinforcing further their separation from the mainstream polity. Unqualified citizenship was extended to American Indians in 1924, to First Nations in Canada in 1960, and to Australia's Aboriginal peoples in 1967. Conversely, in New Zealand, the indigenous Maori were formally granted equal rights as British subjects under the Treaty of Waitangi in 1840, a strategy designed to co-opt their collective claims to land and sovereignty.

The presence or absence of reserves is important for still another reason: It is an inescapable fact that control of territory is a sine qua non of sovereignty (Meyer 1980). Thus, all else being equal, indigenous peoples on reservations advance stronger claims to sovereignty than do indigenous peoples without a well-defined and legally recognized land base. Of course, all else is rarely equal, and the nature of indigenous title to land, as well as the scope of indigenous jurisdiction on reserves, shapes the extent to which indigenous peoples in reserve-system states are able to advance sovereignty claims.

Given the existence of reserves, courts have been careful to specify the precise nature of indigenous land rights and to formulate justifications for dispossession. The U.S. Supreme Court was at the forefront of these efforts. In *Fletcher v. Peck* (1810: 62) it posed the question, "What is the Indian title?" The answer: "It is a mere occupancy for the purpose of hunting" and does not amount to "a true and legal possession." European explorers, the court continued, had "found the territory in possession of a rude and uncivilized people" and, consequently, "always claimed and exercised the right of conquest over the soil." The *Fletcher* Court based its ruling in the Royal Proclamation of 1763, which had "reserved" lands west of the Appalachian Mountains to the Indians as their "Hunting Grounds." Such language was consistent with the notion that Indian territories ultimately remained *terra nullius* and hence available for eventual colonization. Recall from Chapter One that, according to Locke and Vattel, hunting and gathering were insufficient to stake a legal claim in land; only settled agriculture—mixing one's labor with the land—conferred ownership.

Johnson v. McIntosh (1823: 587–589) further clarified the federal government's position on Indian title by reference to the doctrine of discovery:

> Discovery gave an exclusive right to extinguish the Indian title of occupancy, either by purchase or by conquest. . . . Conquest gives a title which the Courts of the conqueror cannot deny, whatever the private and speculative opinions of individuals may be, respecting the original justice of the claim which has been successfully asserted. . . . It is not for the Courts of this country to question the validity of this title, or to sustain one which is incompatible with it.

By this ruling, the Supreme Court upheld discovery as a fait accompli that, although not grounded in any reasoned legal principles, must nevertheless be acknowledged and accepted.

The Privy Council, then the highest appellate court in Canada, made a similar pronouncement regarding Indian land tenure in 1888. Citing the U.S. Supreme Court's ruling in *Fletcher v. Peck*, the Council held in *St. Catherines Milling and Lumber Co. v. The Queen* (1888: 46) that Indians had a "personal and usufructuary right, dependent on the good will of the Sovereign" to the lands they had traditionally occupied. All Aboriginal rights to land were traced to the Royal Proclamation: Aboriginal title, that is, did not antedate the establishment of British sovereignty in North America. This view held sway until 1973, when the Supreme Court of Canada ruled in *Calder* that Aboriginal title existed prior to colonization. The *Calder* decision represented a turning point in Canada's relationship with First Nations, as it led to the resumption of treaty making and land claims negotiations. Eleven years later, in 1984, *Guerin v. The Queen* established the sui generis nature of Indian title.

In their desire to solve the vexing quagmire of indigenous land rights once and for all, the U.S. and Canadian governments devised a number of plans to abolish reserves. In the first concerted effort to dismantle reservations in the United States, the General Allotment Act of 1887 allotted parcels of communally held tribal lands to individual Indians. As previously noted, "allotted" Indians lost their legal status as members of quasi-sovereign tribal nations and thereby became eligible for U.S. citizenship. The policy of allotment in the United States was repealed by the Wheeler-Howard (Indian Reorganization) Act of 1934, but the damage had already been done: By the 1930s, Indians had lost more than 82 million acres of land (Stuart 1987: 15).

Congress renewed its attempt to disestablish reservations in the 1950s, when it "terminated" the legal status of selected Indian tribes by transferring responsibility over them to individual states. A similar policy in Canada (DIAND 1969) called for the repeal of the Indian Act, which institutionalized a separate legal status for Indians, and the phasing out of federal responsibility for Indians and their reserves. To be sure, the Canadian government had never intended Indian reservations to be a permanent fixture of the legal or physical landscape. "Reserves were meant to be temporary, useful merely to educate and Christianize the Aboriginals and establish agriculture as their primary economic base" (Johnson 1991: 668). Both policies ultimately failed. President Nixon repudiated the termination of Indian tribes in 1970, and the Trudeau government retracted its termination policy in 1973.

Although both the United States and Canada are reserve-system states, the nature of tribal (in the United States) or band (in Canada) authority on reserves differs substantially. In the United States, tribal governments exercise *inherent* sovereignty on reservations: their political authority does not derive from any external source (see, for example, *United States v. Wheeler* 1978). In contrast, band self-government on Canadian reservations is weaker in terms of the nature, source, and scope of indigenous rights. Bands are creatures of the Canadian government; the powers they wield are therefore delegated rather than inherent. And although it is common to applaud the constitutional reforms of 1982 for entrenching the rights of Aboriginal peoples in Canada, the very fact that Aboriginal rights are constitutionalized belies their inherence. If the rights of indigenous peoples truly derive from their original precontact sovereignty, as they are understood to do in the United States, constitutional protection is superfluous. By definition, inherent claims to indigenous sovereignty antedate modern constitutions and therefore do not rely on them for recognition, protection, or confirmation.

I have focused at length on the American and Canadian cases because their administrative systems are the most similar of the countries under consideration and therefore require close attention to decipher the relevant differences between them. But what about the two remaining states, Australia and New Zealand? Recall that Australia was colonized under the legal fiction of *terra nullius*, a fact that leads to the painfully ironic conclusion that reserves were set aside for a population that was deemed, in legal theory at least, not to exist. Australian reservations, according to Richard Perry (1996: 241, 187), "appeared rather late and tentatively" and served primarily as "expedient repositories in which the elders would die away." Thus, until recently, reservations in Australia did not provide the basis from which Aboriginal peoples could advance claims to land rights or self-determination. Aboriginal reserves were instead "total institutions" (Werther 1992: 53), and the relationship between Aboriginals and "protectors" resembled that between inmates and a jail warden (Armitage 1995: 35). Reserves, moreover, were historically administered at the state rather than Commonwealth (that is, federal) level, an arrangement that, for reasons discussed later, further denied Aboriginal sovereignty. Indigenous title to land was not recognized until the High Court's celebrated ruling in *Mabo v. Queensland (No. 2)* in 1992. *Mabo* overturned the *terra nullius* doctrine in regard to land rights, but it stopped short of doing so with respect to sovereignty (Reynolds 1996).

New Zealand presents another unconventional case because it combines elements of reserve- and nonreserve-system administrative regimes. Beginning in 1856, a series of Native (and, after 1947, "Maori") Reserve Acts set aside tracts of land for Maori tribes, although Paul Havemann (1999: 9) notes that "Maori were never segregated formally into reserves." Crown recognition of traditional Maori land ownership "was not based upon nor conceded any inherent Maori authority"; rather, "the purpose of recognizing tribe and *hapu* [subtribe] was to set the legal basis to dissolve it by individualization of title" (McHugh 2004: 185, 266). To this end, the Native Land Act of 1862 established a Native Land Court, presided over by European judges, and empowered it to convert tribal land titles (with ownership grounded in prior occupation) into individual freehold titles (with rights to ownership deriving exclusively from the Crown). As expressed in the preamble of the Native Land Act, the government hoped that the Land Court would "promote the peaceful settlement of the Colony and the advancement and civilization of the Natives" (Gilling 1993: 19).

In this respect, New Zealand rather closely resembles other reserve-system states. Both the United States and Canada created Indian reservations but later moved to allot tracts of land to individual Indian stakeholders as part of a "civilizing" mission. Only a decade after the Treaty of Waitangi was concluded, the Maori lost nearly half of their lands to Europeans (Durie 1998: 119). Common-law Aboriginal title was finally recognized in *Te Weehi v. Regional Fisheries Officer* in 1986, much as the Canadian Supreme Court had done in *Calder* in 1973 (McHugh 2004: 53).

Unlike other reserve systems, however, Maori people were not legally excluded from participation in the mainstream polity. Quite the contrary, the Treaty of Waitangi theoretically conferred full citizenship, as British subjects, to the Maori of New Zealand. As such, the Maori Representation Act of 1867 reserved four Maori seats in the House of Representatives (Fleras 1985).[12] This measure, originally intended as a temporary concession until Maori voters could be integrated into mainstream electoral rolls, had a persistent co-opting effect. Although guaranteed seats in parliament encouraged the illusion that Maori had a voice in national politics, in fact the Maori were severely underrepresented—only four seats were allocated to 60,000 Maori, whereas 250,000 Europeans elected seventy-two representatives (Fleras 1985: 557). The number of Maori seats remained fixed until nationwide electoral reforms in 1993 replaced the first-past-the-post system with proportional representation. Since then, the number of Maori seats has been allocated based on the number of Maori voters registered in specially designated Maori electoral rolls. Several Maori-based political parties have been established to contest these seats. Most recently, in 2004, a former minister of the Labour Party established the Maori Party to advance the cause of Maori land rights. A number of other short-lived Maori political parties, including *Te Tawharau* ("The Shelter") and a feminist Maori party, *Mana Wahine Te Ira Tangata*, were also founded to represent the special interests of New Zealand's indigenous peoples. These parties continue a long tradition of Maori involvement in partisan politics, beginning in 1897 with the formation of the Young Maori Party, whose platform advocated equal treatment for Maori citizens, and in 1928 with the Ratana Political Party, which rejected assimilation (Armitage 1995: 143–145).

Why did New Zealand diverge from a typical reserve-system pattern of excluding indigenous peoples from participation in the mainstream polity? American Indians amount to less than 2 percent of the U.S. population, and First Nations account for approximately 3 percent of all Canadians. Conversely, the Maori represent 15 percent of the population of New Zealand, and, early in the colony's history, in 1840, Maori outnumbered settlers fifty-to-one (Alves

1999: 25). This demographic imbalance posed a credible threat to the fledgling colonial regime, especially in the wake of the "Maori Wars" of the 1860s and the ensuing "King Movement" that advocated Maori sovereignty (McHugh 2004: 265; Alves 1999: 24). Guaranteed parliamentary representation for Maori constituents was implemented to defuse tensions with settlers, and also to give Maori a stake in the system. But, at 15 percent of the population, the Maori comprised a significant voting bloc; consequently, Europeans were careful to institutionalize Maori underrepresentation.

It would seem paradoxical to argue, as I do, that exclusionary policies enhance indigenous self-determination and that policies designed to include indigenous peoples in the mainstream political process actually serve to deny them a voice. Canadian political philosopher Will Kymlicka insists that, even if we consider reforms such as those in New Zealand that make national parliaments more representative of indigenous peoples and their interests, the very fact that they are represented at all may ultimately be counterproductive to their interests: "If anything, the logical consequence of self-government is reduced representation, not increased representation. The right to self-government is a right against the authority of the . . . government, not a right to share in the exercise of that authority" (Kymlicka 1995: 143).

Structural: Federal versus Unitary Systems

If self-government implies the exclusion of indigenous peoples from "mainstream" governmental structures, it nonetheless remains true that some structural arrangements are more conducive to indigenous self-government than others. The structural component of indigenous incorporation regimes concerns the organization of political sovereignty within a state, with a focus on the distinction between federal and unitary systems. If sovereignty is organized federally—that is, if political authority is divided among central and local governments—the relevant question becomes which level of government has competence to legislate for indigenous peoples. In federal systems, indigenous peoples who were treated as sovereign nations during the incipient stages of colonization typically became the responsibility of federal governments, as diplomatic relations almost always fall under exclusive federal purview. Conversely, if the sovereignty of indigenous peoples was ignored or denied, they tended to become the province of subfederal jurisdictions—that is, a purely internal matter. The United States most closely approximates a case of near-exclusive federal jurisdiction; Australia, until 1967, a case of exclusive subnational (that is, state) jurisdiction; and Canada, some combination of federal and provincial jurisdiction. New Zealand is a unitary state.

In the United States, *Worcester v. Georgia* (1832) held that the State of Georgia (and, by extension, any state government) was not authorized to legislate for the Cherokee Nation (or, for that matter, any Indian tribe) within the confines of its own reservation. This ruling was based on the idea that tribes are quasi-sovereign nations under the tutelage of the federal government and was justified by recourse to the international legal theorist Emerich de Vattel, whom we encountered in Chapter One:

> A weak state, in order to provide for its safety, may place itself under the protection of one more powerful, without stripping itself of the right of government, and ceasing to be a state. . . . The Cherokee nation, then, is a distinct community occupying its own territory, with boundaries accurately described, in which the laws of Georgia can have no force, and which the citizens of Georgia have no right to enter, but with the assent of the Cherokees themselves, or in conformity with treaties, and with the acts of congress. The whole intercourse between the United States and this nation, is, by our constitution and laws, vested in the government of the United States. (*Worcester v. Georgia* 1832: 561)

If there were any lingering confusion on the matter, it was dispelled by the Tenth Circuit's conclusion in 1959 that Indian tribes have a legal "status higher than that of states" (*Native American Church v. Navajo Tribal Council* 1959: 134). For this reason, Elazar (1991: 319) has described Indian tribes in the United States as "*de facto* federacies," where *federacy* is defined as an arrangement in which "a larger power [such as the U.S. government] and a smaller polity [such as an Indian tribe] are linked asymmetrically in a federal relationship whereby the latter has greater autonomy than other segments of the former and, in return, has a smaller role in the governance of the larger power" (Elazar 1987: 7).

Unlike the United States, "Canada has no foundation court decision similar to the *Worcester v. Georgia* holding that state law does not apply on an Indian reservation" (Johnson 1991: 698). Section 91(24) of the British North America Act, the act by which Canada was established, gave the federal government jurisdiction—but not necessarily *exclusive* jurisdiction—over Indians and lands reserved to Indians. Parliament has elected on several occasions to transfer some of its responsibilities over Indians to provincial governments, and section 88 of the Indian Act provides that provincial laws of "general application" apply to Indians and non-Indians alike (Long and Boldt 1988; Macklem 2001). Johnson (1991: 699–700) summarizes the key difference between the two countries: "In the United States, the prevailing doctrine is that state laws do not apply in Indian country unless Congress says so, or when the issue is not central to Indian life. In Canada, the opposite theory prevails. Provincial law applies to Indian reserves except when the provincial law is contrary to section 35(1) of the 1982 Constitution Act, contrary to treaty, or contrary to federal law." Consequently, "in Canada, a combination of federal and provincial law smothers tribal governments" (Johnson 1991: 715). This appraisal simply extends a general principle of organizational autonomy to indigenous governance: "The legitimacy of a given organization"—in this case, a tribal or band government—"is negatively affected by the number of different authorities sovereign over it" (Meyer and Scott 1983: 202).

In Australia, states exercised exclusive jurisdiction over Aboriginal peoples within their respective borders until a 1967 referendum gave the Commonwealth government concurrent legislative authority. Section 51(xxvi) of the original Constitution Act (1901) read: "The Parliament shall, subject to this Constitution, have power to make laws for the peace, order and good government of the Commonwealth with respect to: The people of any race, other than the aboriginal race in any State, for whom it is deemed necessary to make special laws." The 1967 referendum simply deleted the exclusionary phrase, "other than the aboriginal race in any State." The referendum also amended the constitution to include Aboriginal peoples in the federal census for the first time.

The relative strength of state governments in Australia has contributed to a greater dependence on international law, especially human rights law, for the protection of Aboriginal rights than is the case in the United States, Canada, and New Zealand, where indigenous rights are more often a matter of constitutional, statutory, or treaty-based law. Given the Commonwealth government's jurisdiction over external and diplomatic affairs, ratifying international human rights instruments gives it leverage vis-à-vis states (Havemann 1999). The International Convention on the Elimination of Racial Discrimination, incorporated into Commonwealth law by the Racial Discrimination Act of 1975, has played an especially prominent role. This reliance on an antidiscrimination convention is also consistent with the historical tendency to deal with Aboriginal peoples in terms of "blood" rather than political status (Wolfe 2001). The Australian case compares starkly with the United States, where the Supreme Court treats American Indians "not as a discrete racial group, but, rather, as members of quasi-sovereign tribal entities" (*Morton v. Mancari* 1974: 554). Even land rights issues in Australia were initially framed in terms of human rights, namely, the "human right to own and inherit property" (*Mabo v. Queensland [No. 1]* 1988; Fleras 1999: 248).

The question, however, still remains: What difference does it make whether subfederal jurisdictions are empowered to legislate for indigenous peoples? As a general rule, the nearer a level of government or constituency to indigenous peoples, the more hostile is its attitudes toward indigenous rights, resources, and sovereignty. As far back as 1763, the Royal Proclamation decreed that only the Crown could negotiate with the Indians, especially when land cessions were at stake, and expressly forbade colonial governments or private persons from doing so without royal assent. It accused the colonists of "great Frauds and Abuses" against the Indians. More than a century later, the U.S. Supreme Court held in *United States v. Kagama* (1886: 383) that "Indian tribes . . . owe no allegiance to the States, and receive from them no protection. Because of the local ill feeling, the people of the States where they are found are often their deadliest enemies." As recently as 1991, Chief Justice McEachern of the Supreme Court of British Columbia invoked Thomas Hobbes to the effect that First Nations peoples in his province never possessed title to land:

> It would not be accurate to assume that . . . [the] pre-contact existence [of aboriginal peoples] in the territory was in the least bit idyllic. [They] had no written language, no horses or wheeled vehicles, slavery and starvation was [*sic*] not uncommon, wars with neighboring peoples were common, and there was no doubt, to quote Hobbes, that aboriginal life in the territory was, at best, "nasty, brutish and short." (*Delgamuukw v. British Columbia* 1991: 126)

McEachern's ruling, in addition to offending the multicultural sensibilities that have come to define modern Canadian society, was also subsequently overturned by the Supreme Court of Canada (*Delgamuukw v. British Columbia* 1997) for its lack of legal merit.

More generally, federalism also matters because of its potential for accommodating indigenous self-determination (Courchene and Powell 1992; Tarr, Williams, and Marko 2004). Federalism is conducive to the idea that sovereignty can be divided and shared with indigenous peoples. First Nations in Canada claim, without much success, to comprise a distinct "third-order" of government alongside the federal and provincial governments. The powers they wield more closely resemble those of municipalities, subordinated to other levels of government (Fleras and Elliott 1992: 71–72). Nevertheless, a new territory with a majority Inuit population, Nunavut, was created in 1999. The arrangement is an example of de facto indigenous self-government: The Inuit are self-governing insofar as they compose a majority in the territory, and can, if they wish, elect governments that serve indigenous interests.[13]

In unitary countries such as New Zealand there is no precedent for dividing sovereignty among multiple jurisdictions. Indeed, as a unitary country with a unicameral parliament and no written constitution, policies in New Zealand are subject to the vicissitudes of partisan politics. In 1989, for example, the standing Labour government embarked on a plan to transfer the provision of Maori services from the central government to local *iwi* (tribes). The policy, although popular among the Maori, was short lived. In 1990, a newly elected government, led by the conservative National Party, curtailed the Labour Party's framework (Fleras and Elliott 1992: 192).

Summary and Analysis

Four dimensions of incorporation—colonial, relational, administrative, and structural—intersect to produce variation in the extent to which indigenous peoples are constituted and recognized in domestic policies as "sovereign" entities. It is tempting, but imprecise, to conceptualize each component as simple dichotomies, such that indigenous peoples (1) were or were not implicated in competition among would-be colonizers; (2) signed or did not sign treaties with European metropoles and their settler derivatives; (3) were segregated on reserves and administered by separate bureaucracies or directly incorporated into mainstream polities; and (4) are members of federal or unitary states, and, if federal states, are the exclusive concern of federal or subfederal governments. Instead, each dimension should be understood as a continuum with qualitative endpoints at full absence and full presence, along which countries are located. Such a framework captures variation in degree rather than differences of kind.

Table 3.1 summarizes cross-national differences in the political incorporation of indigenous peoples. In terms of indigenous sovereignty, *colonial* com-

TABLE 3.1.
Cross-national differences in the political incorporation of indigenous peoples.

	Australia	Canada	New Zealand	United States
Colonial	Colonized exclusively by Britain under the pretext of *terra mullius*	British competition with France and the United States produced a need for Indian military allies until 1815	French colonial pretensions led Britain to recognize Maori sovereignty in 1835	Competition with Britain and Spain contributed to the recognition of Indian tribes as sovereign nations
Relational	No treaties signed with Aboriginal peoples	Dozens of comprehensive treaties signed	One treaty, the Treaty of Waitangi, signed for all Maori	Hundreds of treaties signed, generally with individual tribes
Administrative	Reserves functioned as "total institutions" under the authority of official protectors	Indian bands exercise delegated authority on reserves	Maori were never formally segregated onto reserves, and were extended nominal citizenship at state formation	Indian tribes exercise inherent sovereignty on reservations
Structural	Federal; states had exclusive jurisdiction over Aboriginal peoples until 1967	Federal; federal government has jurisdiction over status Indians, with substantial residual authority enjoyed by provinces	Unitary	Federal; near-exclusive federal jurisdiction over Indian tribes

petition had the most profound ramifications for New Zealand, where French pretensions to the north island resulted in Britain's acknowledgment of a fully sovereign Maori state between 1835 and 1840. In the United States and Canada, two axes of competition—the struggle between France and Britain for control over the North American colonies on the one hand, and the war for independence that pitted Britain against the renegade American colonies on the other—produced nation-to-nation relationships with Indian nations but nothing akin to formal, internationally recognized declarations of independence. In Australia, Britain alone staked colonial claims to the continent, allowing colonizers to ignore the legal existence of Aboriginal peoples *tout court.*

Along the *relational* dimension, the U.S. government negotiated hundreds of treaties with individual tribes, giving rise to quasi-diplomatic government-to-government relationships. In Canada, the practice of signing comprehensive treaties that covered all tribes in a particular geographical area, as opposed to treaties with individual tribes, was much more prevalent, giving any one tribe weaker claims to sovereignty. In New Zealand, the British signed only one treaty, the Treaty of Waitangi, with a confederation of Maori chiefs, and the rights issuing from that treaty are not constitutionally entrenched, as they are in Canada.[14] No treaties with indigenous peoples were ever ratified in or for Australia.

The United States also ranks highly on the *administrative* dimension because Indian tribes exercise a great deal of autonomy, as inherently sovereign nations, on reservations. The delegated sovereignty of band governments on reserves in Canada is much weaker, although a policy adopted by the federal government in 1995 recognized for the first time the inherent nature of indigenous self-government. New Zealand represents a hybrid "crossover" case that combines a weak reserve system with policies designed to incorporate the Maori as individual members into the mainstream polity. Australia has a system of reserves, but Aborigines did not, until recently, enjoy any legally recognizable title to the lands they occupy.

Finally, New Zealand's status as a unitary country places it lowest on the *structural* dimension: The Maori do not comprise a distinct order of government but rather are represented in parliament; moreover, laws regarding Maori self-government and treaty rights are not constitutionally entrenched. In the federal states of the United States, Canada, and Australia, the relative strength of indigenous sovereignty depends on the level of government that has jurisdiction over indigenous peoples. The U.S. federal government commands the most extensive, if not entirely exclusive, jurisdiction over Indian tribes. The administration of Indians and Inuit in Canada falls under federal purview as well, but the provinces are also accorded a substantial degree of authority to legislate for Aboriginal peoples, at least relative to state governments in the United States. In Australia, state governments had exclusive jurisdiction over Aborigines until 1967, when the Commonwealth government assumed concurrent jurisdiction.

These different dimensions of indigenous incorporation regimes often coalesce in practice. Colonial competition led to formal treaty-based alliances with indigenous peoples; in Australia, where Britain went unchallenged for colonial hegemony, no treaties were concluded. In turn, treaties often (but not always) reserved lands for indigenous peoples and codified their rights and powers on reservations. Furthermore, because treaties are instruments of diplomacy between sovereign nations, they tended to be transacted between indigenous groups and central (or federal) governments. Only in Australia, where indigenous peoples were treated not as sovereign nations but as colonial subjects, did subfederal governments enjoy exclusive jurisdiction over indigenous peoples and their affairs.

THE ROLE OF PARTISAN POLITICS

Although the historical legacies of colonization and the institutional structures of indigenous–state relations clearly affect the relative strength of indigenous sovereignty claims, partisan politics play an important role as well. Unlike the enduring historical legacies and durable structural configurations that undergird a polity, partisan support for indigenous rights ebbs and flows with election cycles. Some political parties, particularly those on the left of the ideological spectrum, are more supportive of indigenous peoples' rights than others. The presence or absence of sympathetic allies in government has certainly contributed to sweeping policy changes in support of indigenous self-determination, even if its effect tends to be more catalytic than causal.

A dramatic shift in U.S. Indian policy began in 1968, when President Lyndon Johnson, a liberal Democrat, delivered a special message to Congress that outlined his intention to replace the government's failed bid to terminate Indian tribes with a policy that supported "self-help, self-development, and self-determination" among American Indians (Prucha 2000: 249). Johnson's Republican successor, Richard Nixon, reiterated the government's commitment to Indian self-determination in another special message to Congress in 1970 (Prucha 2000: 256–258). Such bipartisan support indicated that tribal self-determination was an idea whose time had come. In Australia, policies favoring Aboriginal self-determination gained momentum after the election of Gough Whitlam's Labour government in 1972. Canada presents a case in which one government, headed by Prime Minister Pierre Trudeau of the left-leaning Liberal Party, advanced and subsequently retracted a policy to end the special status of Indians.

Partisanship, of course, can also work against indigenous peoples. Robert Muldoon, leader of New Zealand's conservative National Party and prime minister between 1975 and 1984, called for an end to "special privileges" for

Maori and a final settlement of all outstanding claims under the Treaty of Waitangi. Muldoon was succeeded by Labour candidate David Lange, who between 1984 and 1989 saw two key pieces of legislation enacted: the Treaty of Waitangi Amendment Act (1985), permitting retrospective claims under the Treaty of Waitangi, and the Maori Language Act (1987), promoting Maori to the status of official language.

As the example of New Zealand attests, when indigenous rights are not formally "constitutionalized" they fall prey to the pendulum swings of partisan politics. The same holds true in Australia, where "the lack of constitutionally entrenched rights means that reforms may last only as long as the government in office—as the disjuncture between the Keating [Labor] and Howard [Liberal] governments' Aboriginal affairs policies illustrates" (Fletcher 1999: 341). Prime Minister Paul Keating of the Australian Labor Party was instrumental in shepherding the Native Title Act of 1993 through parliament. His successor, John Howard of the center-right Liberal Party, campaigned on a "One Australia" policy that, among other things, sought to deprive Aboriginal peoples of their "special" status and land rights. The return of the Labor Party to power in December 2007 resulted in Prime Minister Kevin Rudd's apology to Aboriginal peoples and, in 2009, the fulfillment of a campaign promise to sign the U.N. Declaration on the Rights of Indigenous Peoples.

These examples demonstrate that significant reforms were initiated or key pieces of legislation enacted by political parties on the left: Democrats in the United States, Liberals in Canada, and Labor governments in Australia and New Zealand. But in the two North American cases, policies supporting indigenous self-determination were implemented independently of partisan politics. The politically conservative Republican Party carried out reforms initiated by Democrats, and the Liberal Party in Canada reversed its own stated goal of abolishing the special legal status of Indians. In New Zealand and Australia, the success of indigenous self-determination policies wavered as governments oscillated between each country's Labor and conservative opposition parties.[15] Through it all, governments were prodded, influenced, and constrained by international law, the expanding discourse of indigenous self-determination, the policies of other governments, and by indigenous peoples themselves. States rarely acknowledged indigenous self-determination of their own volition; indigenous peoples were there to help them along.

SOCIAL MOVEMENT ACTIVISM

The foregoing discussion has focused on structure to the near exclusion of agency. Indigenous peoples, of course, are not merely objects of state action and control. They are also subjects who frequently take matters into their own hands, and direct action has been pivotal in the nearly universal policy shift from integration to self-determination. A focus on social movement activism, which operates outside of established administrative or mainstream political channels, complements the structural analysis.

Perhaps the best-known and most influential examples of indigenous activism came from the Red Power movement in the United States (Cornell 1988; Nagel 1996). The number of American Indian protest events increased dramatically in the mid-1960s. Cornell (1988: 198) acknowledges that "the tactics of Black protest had a powerful influence on Indian thinking." American Indians adapted many of the protest tactics developed by African Americans during the civil rights movement but employed them in the service of different, even contradictory, ends. The sit-in became, in the Pacific Northwest, the fish-in: The former dramatized African Americans' demands for integration, whereas the latter drew attention to the treaty-based rights of Indian tribes. Similarly, the March on Washington in 1963 provided a loose template for the Trail of Broken Treaties in 1972. Occupations also became a tactic of choice among Indian activists, the most famous being the nineteen-month seizure of Alcatraz Island in the San Francisco Bay between November 1968 and June 1971, and the takeover of Bureau of Indian Affairs headquarters in Washington, D.C., in 1972. Protests turned violent during the ten-week standoff between Indian activists and federal agents at Wounded Knee in 1973.

Social movement tactics, says Tarrow (1998), have a modular quality, making them transposable to new contexts. This was certainly the case when American Indians activists borrowed from the repertoire of the African-American civil rights movement, but it is also true of indigenous social movements abroad. In Australia during the mid-1960s, Aboriginal and white students organized "freedom rides" that were modeled after those conducted in the American South during the civil rights movement (Short 2003). In New Zealand, members of Nga Tamatoa, a social movement organization established and led by Maori university students, participated in the Trail of Broken Treaties caravan to Washington, D.C., and subsequently organized their own march on

Wellington—the Land March—in 1975 (Howard 2003: 193). Two years later, in an event reminiscent of Alcatraz, Maori protesters began a 507-day occupation of Bastion Point, an area claimed by Maori under the Treaty of Waitangi. The occupation ended when government officials deployed police and military personnel to evict the activists.

A similar fate befell Mohawk protesters during the standoff at Oka, near Montreal, in 1990. Municipal leaders in Oka sought to expand a golf course onto lands claimed by the Mohawks. The ensuing occupation, lasting seventy-eight days, pitted armed Indian activists against the police and military. Fleras and Elliott (1992: 96) draw the appropriate comparisons between Oka and Wounded Knee—the issues that ignited both events, which involved armed conflict between indigenous protesters and the government, were similar, as was the duration of each standoff—and comparisons with Bastion Point could be made as well. Oka has been called a "watershed in Aboriginal renewal" (Fleras and Elliott 1992: 92–96) that led two provinces, New Brunswick and Quebec, to establish seats for Aboriginal people in their legislatures. The Oka standoff also prompted the Canadian government to establish the Royal Commission on Aboriginal Peoples (Battiste 2000), whose monumental report will shape Canada's policies toward its indigenous peoples for some time to come.

In January 1972, Aboriginal activists in Australia invented a novel protest tactic: Using beach umbrellas and plastic sheeting, they erected a makeshift "Aboriginal Tent Embassy" on the lawns outside the quondam Parliament House in Canberra (Dow 2000; Chesterman and Galligan 1997).[16] The "embassy," established in the wake of the High Court's *Nabalco* decision upholding the *terra nullius* doctrine and the Liberal government's refusal to recognize Aboriginal land rights, dramatized Aboriginal sovereignty—as a sovereign nation, the activists reasoned, Aboriginal peoples should send representatives to the capital. The event's symbolic value was further enhanced by its coincidence with Australia Day, commemorating the arrival of the British to Sydney Cove in 1788. The ramshackle tents remained on the lawns of parliament until July, when police forcibly removed the remaining activists. The tent embassy protests have been reenacted every Australia Day since 1992 and served as a model for similar protests by Saami activists in Norway during the early 1980s (Paine 1985).

CONCLUSION

I have argued that world-cultural models and assumptions supply the master frameworks within which nation-states interact with indigenous peoples. World culture confers ontological standing on nation-states and indigenous peoples, provides states with broad policy prescriptions for dealing with indigenous peoples, and affords indigenous peoples the conceptual tools for asserting their self-determination against states. As I have shown, however, indigenous peoples around the world are not equally successful in advancing their claims to self-determination. Some enjoy "more" sovereignty than others, based largely the distinctive historical and institutional legacies of indigenous–state relations. As I discuss in the next chapter, cross-national variation in the strength and structure of indigenous sovereignty has had profound implications for the establishment of indigenous postsecondary institutions.

CHAPTER FOUR

THE EMERGENCE OF INDIGENOUS POSTSECONDARY INSTITUTIONS

We desire to establish the education of Aboriginal People as a separate issue from Aboriginal education. . . . The former can be undertaken in mainstream institutions by Aboriginal people who wish to access them, by choice. We have no argument with this. However there is still a large clientele within the Aboriginal community who do not want to go, at least initially, to "white fella" institutions where cultural integrity is not honoured.

Federation of Independent Aboriginal Education Providers (Australia 2003b: 21)

FOR HUNDREDS OF YEARS, INDIGENOUS peoples have been forced to attend "white fella" schools. With brutal efficacy, these schools stripped indigenous peoples of their cultures and systematically implanted them with the languages, beliefs, and values of their European colonizers. Indigenous ways of knowing were emphatically not honored but rather were denigrated and targeted for eradication. It is therefore not surprising that indigenous peoples are reluctant to attend mainstream schools. Although wholesale assimilation is no longer a legitimate policy goal, mainstream educational institutions remain culturally alien to indigenous peoples. Attrition rates are high, in part because students report feelings of cultural isolation (Benjamin, Chambers, and Reiterman 1993; Bourke, Burden, and Moore 1996).

Beginning in the 1960s, indigenous peoples began to establish their own postsecondary institutions, ones that valued and valorized indigenous cultures. Indigenous postsecondary institutions, unlike their "white fella" counterparts, were founded explicitly to preserve indigenous cultures. Indigenous postsecondary institutions appeared first in the United States, Canada, New Zealand, and Australia, and then began diffusing around the world. What accounts for the emergence of these institutions?

Previous chapters have examined changes in global conditions that fostered the emergence of indigenous postsecondary institutions. The overarching tenor and trajectory of national policies toward indigenous peoples and their education evolved in similar fashion cross-nationally, in line with broader shifts in world-cultural logics. Over time, primary control over indigenous education transferred first from churches to states and subsequently from states to indigenous peoples. As the parties responsible for indigenous education changed, so too did the ends to which indigenous education was employed. Churches were principally concerned with integrating indigenous "savages" into the community of believers. Missionaries frequently learned and used indigenous languages to accomplish this mandate. It mattered little whether indigenous peoples found their salvation through the medium of English, French, Spanish, Náhuatl, Algonquian, Maori, or a host of other languages, just as long as they were, in the final analysis, saved. Cultural markers such as language became much more important with the transition to state control over indigenous education. The reasons were twofold: Fledgling nation-states sought to consolidate political sovereignty and generate a unified national culture. Indigenous peoples, as sovereign nations in their own right, threatened both aims. Nation-states therefore used education to integrate indigenous peoples into the mainstream culture and polity. These efforts persisted until the 1960s, when, as discussed in Chapter Two, indigenous peoples around the world began to regain control over their own educational destinies.

The devolution of control over indigenous education to indigenous peoples themselves occurred nearly simultaneously around the world and reflected broader policy shifts that reaffirmed the quasi-sovereign status of indigenous peoples. These policy shifts, in combination with the worldwide expansion of higher education from an elite to a mass enterprise (Trow 2006), provided the context within which indigenous postsecondary institutions first emerged. But within this global context, cross-national differences in the history and structure of indigenous–state relations produced distinct patterns in the establishment of indigenous postsecondary institutions. To understand these processes, we need a framework for analyzing how global processes get translated into local realities.

A FRAMEWORK FOR ANALYSIS

The concept of *political opportunity structures* in the social movements literature provides a useful framework for understanding how cross-national differences in indigenous–state relations patterned the emergence of indigenous postsecondary institutions (Kitschelt 1986; Kriesi et al., 1995; McAdam 1996). A political opportunities framework maintains that the timing, form, and outcomes of collective action depend on the institutional structure of political systems and the configuration of power within those systems. Some elements of a country's opportunity structure are relatively durable or "concrete." For example, the degree of governmental centralization and the division of powers within a polity are generally stable and determine the number of access points available to social movement actors. "Variable" opportunities, such as the presence of allies in government, also matter. Social movements are more likely to find success—that is, to have their demands translated into policies and practices—when activists have the support of elected officials or powerful bureaucrats. Success is less likely to the extent that those in power are unsympathetic to a social movement.

In much the same fashion, country-specific patterns in the political incorporation of indigenous peoples—the colonial, relational, administrative, and structural dimensions that structure formal relations between indigenous peoples and states—serve to facilitate or inhibit the establishment of indigenous postsecondary institutions. The political opportunity structures defined by indigenous–state relations produce variation in the number of indigenous postsecondary institutions that are established and the degree of organizational autonomy they enjoy. Other structural factors, such as the timing and pace of postsecondary enrollment expansion and the nature of institutional differentiation in a country's tertiary education sector, also contribute to the emergence, autonomy, and form of indigenous postsecondary institutions. Thus, although global developments explain the absolute timing of indigenous postsecondary institutions—their initial emergence during the 1960s and 1970s in the wake of new world-cultural understandings of indigenous peoples' cultural, political, and educational rights—national opportunity structures anchored in distinct historical, colonial, and political legacies shape the relative timing of their emergence in the United States, Canada, New Zealand, and Australia.

But just what, exactly, are an indigenous postsecondary institutions, and what are some of their attributes? The next section canvasses official definitions of indigenous postsecondary institutions and provides a brief synopsis of their emergence in North America and Australasia. The remainder of the chapter is devoted to an analysis of their emergence and subsequent spread around the world.

INDIGENOUS POSTSECONDARY INSTITUTIONS: AN OVERVIEW

Definitional Differences

Wherever in the world they are located, indigenous postsecondary institutions share a commitment to serving indigenous students and preserving indigenous cultures. Nevertheless, precise definitions as to what constitutes an indigenous postsecondary institution differ across countries. In the United States, indigenous postsecondary institutions take the form of community colleges, technical institutes, and universities established by one or more Indian tribes. A "tribally controlled college or university" is defined by the Tribally Controlled College or University Assistance Act of 1978 (25 USC 1801[a][4]) as "an institution of higher education which is formally controlled, or has been formally sanctioned, or chartered, by the governing body of an Indian tribe or tribes, except that no more than one such institution shall be recognized with respect to any such tribe." Three additional institutions—a technical institute, an art institute, and a university—are chartered and operated by the federal government (either the Bureau of Indian Affairs or Congress).

In New Zealand, Maori-controlled postsecondary institutions or *wananga* are defined by the Education Act of 1989 (section 162[4][b][iv]) as "characterised by teaching and research that maintains, advances, and disseminates knowledge and develops intellectual independence, and assists the application of knowledge regarding ahuatanga Maori (Maori tradition) according to tikanga Maori (Maori custom)." Thus, as with tribal colleges and universities (TCUs) in the United States, *wananga* are defined by law. Unlike the United States, *wananga* constitute a distinct institutional form that distinguishes them from all other "mainstream" institutions in the country. That is, *wananga* are not simply Maori-controlled polytechnics, colleges, or universities but rather comprise something qualitatively different. Also unlike the United States, *wananga* received their official charters as "tertiary education institutions" (TEIs) from the New Zealand government, rather than from their founding tribes or subtribes. Like all other TEIs (including universities, polytechnics, and colleges of education), *wananga* are required to follow standard public sector accountability processes (New Zealand 2000: 4).

Indigenous postsecondary institutions in Canada, in contrast with their counterparts in the United States and New Zealand, are not defined by law; as such, "there is no single definition of the term Aboriginal post-secondary institute" (First Nations Education Steering Committee 2008: 1). There is, however, a government agency that offers an official definition: For the purposes of its *Register of Postsecondary and Adult Education Institutions*, Statistics Canada identifies "Aboriginal providers" as those institutions that are either controlled by one or more of the First Nations or Métis groups, receive at least 25 percent of their funding from one of these groups or from funds that either the federal or a provincial government has set aside for First Nations and Métis programs, are located on a reserve, or whose mission or mandate is to serve First Nations and Métis peoples (Orton 2009). According to this definition, postsecondary institutions can qualify as "Aboriginal" via multiple routes: control, funding, location, or mission. An institution need not be governed by indigenous peoples, for example, so long as its primary mission is to serve indigenous peoples or it receives government funding for that purpose.

Australia differs from the United States, New Zealand, and Canada in that one institution, the Batchelor Institute of Indigenous Tertiary Education, stands alone as the only Aboriginal-controlled higher education institution in the country. The Batchelor Institute was established under the authority of the Northern Territory government to "provide tertiary education relevant to the needs of Aborigines and Torres Strait Islanders" and to "facilitate, encourage, develop and improve study and research, particularly in subjects of relevance to indigenous people" (Article 7, Batchelor Institute of Indigenous Tertiary Education Act of 2005).

Embedded in these definitions are several key aspects of indigenous postsecondary institutions that require further elucidation. At the most basic level, we need to explain why the United States, Canada, and New Zealand have multiple indigenous postsecondary institutions while Australia has only one. We also need to account for differences in institutional autonomy and control, which at the very least hinges on whether indigenous postsecondary institutions were chartered by the state or by indigenous groups themselves. Definitions also point to differences in form. Here the primary distinction is whether mainstream organizational structures are adopted or distinctive institutional forms created. Finally, indigenous postsecondary institutions are defined by law in some countries but not in others, and where it exists this authority is vested in different levels of government.

Patterns of Emergence

The Navajo Nation founded the first indigenous-controlled postsecondary institution in the world, Navajo Community College (since renamed Diné College), in 1968. Of the thirty-five TCUs established since then, all but three—Haskell Indian Nations University, Southwestern Indian Polytechnic Institute, and the Institute of American Indian Arts—were founded and chartered by Indian tribes. (The exceptions, as previously noted, were chartered by the federal government.) The vast majority of these institutions are community colleges awarding vocational certificates and associate's degrees, although they also include three technical schools, one art institute, five colleges accredited to award bachelor's degree, and two colleges accredited to confer master's degrees. Most TCUs are located on Indian reservations; one college, Ilisagvik College, serves indigenous students in Alaska. All but six TCUs are currently accredited by mainstream agencies, and the exceptions are candidates for accreditation.

Tribal colleges and universities are unique among higher education institutions in the United States. Although most resemble mainstream community colleges in their tripartite mission to serve local communities, offer vocational programs, and award transfer degrees, TCUs seek "not to mimic mainstream institutions but to reflect and sustain a unique tribal identity" (Guillory and Ward 2008: 97). As such, TCUs are not only committed to providing American

Indians with access to higher education, but they also strive to protect indigenous languages, traditions, and cultures. Vocational programming, a mainstay of community college curricula, is tailored to local reservation economies.

Eight years after Navajo Community College was founded, the Saskatchewan Indian Federated College, a degree-granting university-college within the University of Regina, was established in Canada. The college, which in 2003 became the First Nations University of Canada (FNU), was until recently administratively and financially independent of but academically integrated within the University of Regina. FNU is the only indigenous-controlled postsecondary institution in Canada recognized by the Association of University and Colleges of Canada, an organization providing de facto accreditation to member institutions. (Formal accreditation does not exist in Canada.) The university awards certificates, diplomas, bachelor's degrees, and master's degrees in a variety of academic, vocational, and professional programs.

FNU was preceded by several smaller ventures and at least one failed effort to provide culturally relevant postsecondary training to indigenous peoples in Canada. Manitou College, established in Quebec in 1973 and modeled after Navajo Community College, was provincially accredited and enrolled up to 130 students before ultimately closing in 1979 due to lack of financial support (Stonechild 2006). More successfully, Blue Quills First Nations School became Canada's first aboriginal-administered school in 1971, after local First Nations communities wrested control over what to that point had been a residential school operated by the federal government. Blue Quills began offering postsecondary courses in concert with the Universities of Alberta, Calgary, and Athabasca in 1975 (Bashford and Heinzerling 1987: 132–133) but did not become an independent college in its own right until 1990. Similarly, the Native Education Centre in Vancouver, B.C., first opened its doors in 1967 and bills itself as British Columbia's largest private Aboriginal college, but it did not incorporate and begin offering postsecondary courses until 1979.

Today, the Aboriginal Institutes' Consortium in Ontario estimates that there are approximately fifty Aboriginal postsecondary institutions in Canada; however, this tally includes adult and community education centers that are not authorized to award degrees. The official *Register of Postsecondary and Adult Education Institutions* compiled by Statistics Canada (2007) lists a dozen indigenous-controlled colleges, institutes, or degree-granting institutions, among which only four—Nicola Valley Institute of Technology (NVIT),

Saskatchewan Indian Institute of Technologies (SIIT), the First Nations University of Canada, and, until its merger with NVIT in 2007, the Institute of Indigenous Governance (IIG)—are authorized under provincial legislation to award degrees (Aboriginal Institutes' Consortium 2005).

Unlike the organizational field of indigenous postsecondary education in the United States, where the tribally controlled community college form predominates, Canada's indigenous postsecondary institutions exhibit a wide variety of institutional forms. The landscape includes public and private institutes, cultural and vocational colleges, adult learning centers, a tribal college, and a federated university college. Moreover, the Canadian institutions target different Aboriginal populations. First Nations University, for example, serves "students of all nations" (First Nations University of Canada 2009) whereas the Gabriel Dumont Institute of Native Studies and Applied Research, established in 1980 as a nonprofit corporation, caters explicitly to Métis and nonstatus Indians (Dorion and Yang 2000).

A very different situation obtains in New Zealand, where the Education Act of 1989 recognized *wananga* as a separate category of Maori-serving postsecondary education providers. Two *wananga* were established prior to this statutory "elevation" to the status of Crown (that is, public) tertiary institutions. The first, Te Wananga o Raukawa (TWoR), opened in 1981 as a joint venture among several tribes (*iwi*) and subtribes (*hapu*) but did not receive formal recognition under the Education Act until 1993. TWoR describes itself as "a reformulation of an ancient institution, the *whare wānanga*" (Te Wananga o Raukawa 2000: 15), a place of higher and spiritual learning in precontact Maori societies. A second *wananga*, Te Wananga o Aotearoa (TWoA), was founded in 1984 as the Waipā Kōkiri Centre (Te Wananga o Aotearoa 1999). It became the first private training establishment (PTE) accredited by the government's New Zealand Qualifications Authority in 1986 and received Crown tertiary status along with TWoR in 1993. Its thirteen campuses served 66,729 students in 2004 (New Zealand 2005c), making it the largest tertiary institution in New Zealand at the time. TWoA enrolled fully 61 percent of Maori students in higher education, and 13 percent of *all* domestic tertiary students. The third and final *wananga*, Te Whare Wananga o Awanuiarangi (TWWoA), opened in 1992 and became a Crown institution in 1997. *Wananga* offer a range of programming, much of it focusing on content relevant to Maori cultures, and award certificates, diplomas, bachelor's degrees, and postgraduate degrees in specialized areas such as education, social work, environmental studies, and Maori studies.

If the state of indigenous postsecondary education in New Zealand differs substantially from that in North America, Australia presents an even more dissimilar case. Where the United States, Canada, and New Zealand are each home to multiple indigenous postsecondary institutions, indigenous-controlled postsecondary education in Australia is confined to only one institution: the Batchelor Institute of Indigenous Tertiary Education (BIITE), located in the extremely remote and sparsely populated "Top End" region of the country. Indigenous-controlled postsecondary education also developed significantly later in Australia than in the other countries. BIITE became "the first ever education institution in Australia offering higher education courses to be owned and controlled by Indigenous Australians" on July 1, 1999, by act of the Northern Territory Legislative Assembly (Batchelor Institute 2005).

BIITE, which aspires to full-fledged university status, had humble origins as an annex of a residential school for Aboriginal students during the mid-1960s. But it was not until 1989 that "the Commonwealth Government—through the Higher Education Funding Act (1988)—recognised Batchelor College as a higher education institution" (Batchelor Institute 2005). The institute was designated an autonomous public "agency" by the government of the Northern Territory in 1995 and passed to indigenous control four years later. Today it "enrolls more Aboriginal and Torres Strait Islander students at the higher education level than any other tertiary institution in Australia" (Batchelor Institute 2005); indeed, it is the only postsecondary institution in the country that restricts admission to indigenous students. BIITE is a dual-sector institution that offers both university-level and vocational courses and "follow[s] a 'both ways' philosophy, with the aim of bringing together 'Indigenous and Western knowledge and academic traditions'" (Australia 2000: 71).

Aside from BIITE, a number of independent adult and vocational education providers for Aboriginal students, referred to as "Independent Indigenous Vocational Education and Training" institutes (Australia 2003b), operate throughout the country. The first independent Aboriginal adult education college in Australia, Tranby Aboriginal College Co-operative for Aborigines Ltd., was established near Sydney in 1957 (Tranby Aboriginal College 2004) but did not become a registered training organization with the authority to award diplomas until 1994. In all, some fourteen indigenous-controlled vocational and adult education institutions receive funding under the Commonwealth government's Indigenous Education Strategic Initiatives Programme (Australia 2005: 57). However, the Department of Education, Science and Training (Australia 2003b: 17) notes that these indigenous institutes "exist at the margin of the system rather than as an integrated part of it." In this respect, they resemble the panoply of non-degree-granting adult learning centers that operate in Canada.

THE RISE OF INDIGENOUS POSTSECONDARY INSTITUTIONS

Indigenous postsecondary institutions exhibit a great deal of cross-national variation with respect to their timing, number, autonomy, and forms. Much of this variation can be accounted for by patterns of indigenous–state relations in general and the relative strength of indigenous peoples' sovereignty claims in particular. In brief, indigenous postsecondary institutions emerged first and enjoy the most autonomy in countries where the claims of indigenous peoples to sovereignty are the strongest. These claims, as I concluded in Chapter Three, are strongest in the United States, weakest in Australia, and intermediate in Canada and New Zealand. Moreover, the number of indigenous postsecondary institutions is roughly proportional to the number of indigenous "entities" (tribes, bands, *iwi*, *hapu*, nations) recognized or constituted as sovereign. And, in most cases, indigenous postsecondary institutions tend to adopt pre-university organizational forms that developed or expanded to accommodate the explosion in tertiary enrollments after World War II.

Timing

Indigenous postsecondary institutions emerged first in countries with a long history of recognizing indigenous sovereignty and decades later in countries that have only recently acknowledged indigenous self-determination. As previously noted, the first such institution appeared in the United States, when the country's second-largest Indian tribe, the Navajo Nation, established Navajo Community (Diné) College in 1968. Canada followed suit with the establishment of Saskatchewan Indian Federated College, known today as the First Nations University of Canada, in 1976. Next was New Zealand, where a confederation of Maori tribes founded Te Wananga o Raukawa in 1981. The government recognized TWoR as an official tertiary education provider a dozen years later. Finally, although Aboriginal Australians have been involved in the provision of adult and vocational education in concert with religious organizations for over fifty years, only in 1999 was the first indigenous-controlled higher education institution, BIITE, formally established in Australia. Thus, the order in which the first indigenous postsecondary institution was established corresponds directly to the relative strength of indigenous sovereignty claims cross-nationally.

The link between the initial emergence of indigenous postsecondary institutions and government recognition of indigenous peoples' cultural and political rights is fairly consistent across countries. Tribal colleges first appeared in the United States in 1968, the same year President Lyndon Johnson repudiated Congress's termination policy in favor of one that supported Indian self-determination. Similarly, the first indigenous postsecondary institution emerged in Canada only three years after the government retracted its integrationist White Paper in 1973 and replaced it with the policy articulated in *Indian Control of Indian Education*. *Wananga* first appeared in New Zealand six years after parliament reaffirmed the Crown's legislative commitment to the Treaty of Waitangi in 1975. And, in Australia, BIITE achieved its current status as an autonomous indigenous-controlled higher education institution six years after Australia first recognized Aboriginal title to land in the Native Title Act of 1993.

Social movement activism was also central to the early innovation and development of indigenous postsecondary institutions. During its occupation of Alcatraz, in 1969, the activist group Indians of All Nations issued a proclamation declaring its intentions for the island. Indian education topped the list:

> A Center for Native American Studies will be developed which will train our young people in the best of our native cultural arts and sciences. . . . Attached to this center will be traveling universities, managed by Indians, which will go to the Indian Reservations in order to learn the traditional values from the people, which are now absent in the Caucasian higher educational system.

Also in the United States, the same activist organization that orchestrated the takeover of Bureau of Indian Affairs headquarters in 1972 and the occupation of Wounded Knee in 1973, the American Indian Movement, established a number of "survival schools" in the 1970s (Nagel 1996: 129). Likewise in New Zealand, an organization formed by Maori students, college graduates, and activists in 1970, Nga Tamatoa, campaigned for Maori-language schools (Howard 2003: 193). Even more directly, sit-in protests at Blue Quills School in Alberta, Canada, also in 1970, were responsible for bringing about Indian control of that school, although it did not become a college until 1990.

Indigenous participation in and control over lower levels of schooling further contributed to the establishment of indigenous postsecondary institutions. In some countries, indigenous postsecondary ventures followed directly from indigenous-controlled primary and secondary endeavors. Formal recognition of *wananga* in New Zealand came after the establishment of Maori-language preschools, *kohanga reo*, in 1982, and primary schools, *kura kaupapa Maori*, in 1985. In the United States, Navajo Community College was founded by the same educational and tribal leaders who established Rough Rock Demonstration School, the first American Indian community-controlled primary school, on the Navajo Reservation (McCarty 2002). Robert A. Roessel Jr., the inaugural director of Rough Rock, also served as the first president of Navajo Community College (Senese 1991; Stein 1992). In Australia, the establishment of independent Aboriginal community schools at the primary and secondary levels throughout the 1970s and 1980s preceded the incorporation of BIITE as a tertiary education provider. And in Canada, Eber Hampton (2000: 216) concluded at the turn of the millennium that "in terms of First Nations control, First Nations university education is where elementary and secondary education was twenty years ago."

Number

As with timing, indigenous sovereignty is one factor that contributes to the number of indigenous postsecondary institutions in each country. Figure 4.1 plots the number of these institutions in the United States, Canada, New Zealand, and Australia.[1] In the United States, the Bureau of Indian Affairs (BIA) supported the establishment of Navajo Community College but wrongly assumed that it would be the only tribally controlled college in the United States. Arguing that one pan-Indian postsecondary institution could sufficiently meet the educational needs of all indigenous Americans, the BIA opposed the establishment of additional tribally controlled colleges and was reluctant to fund them (Stein 1990).

Why, then, have three dozen TCUs been established? As argued in Chapter Two, establishing colleges and universities is a prerogative of sovereignty, and the BIA could not prevent individual tribes, as quasi-sovereign nations, from establishing their own institutions. Each federally recognized Indian tribe therefore

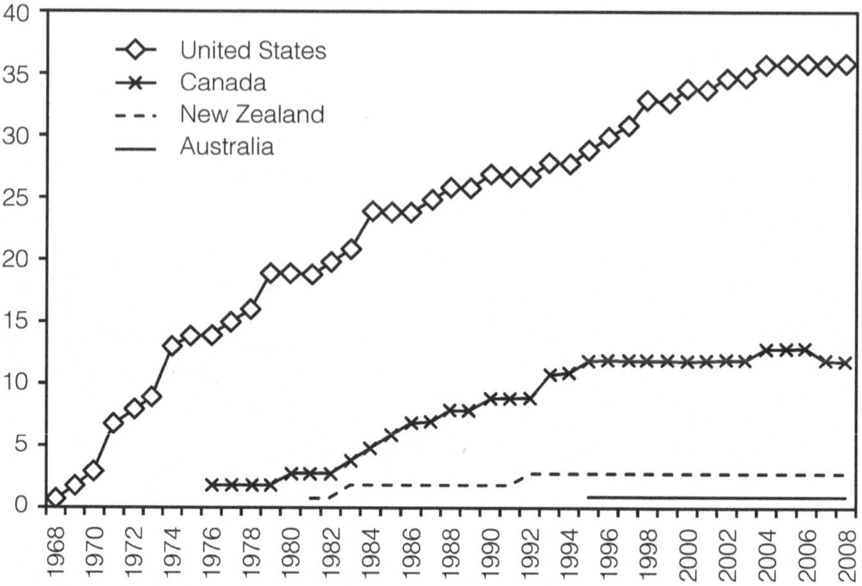

FIGURE 4.1. Number of indigenous postsecondary institutions in the United States, Canada, New Zealand, and Australia.

has the *potential* authority to charter a tribal college. Of course, not all tribes *actually* do so, and many tribes establish colleges jointly with others. For instance, Bay Mills Community College, located in Brimley, Michigan, serves the state's twelve federally recognized tribes, and Northwest Indian College in Bellingham, Washington, caters to Indian peoples throughout the Pacific Northwest.

Absent strong claims to indigenous sovereignty, structural conditions tend to be much more influential in shaping the number of indigenous postsecondary institutions in a country. In Canada, where provincial governments are actively involved in chartering and funding indigenous postsecondary institutions, decentralization engenders a great deal of institutional diversification and proliferation (Ben-David and Zloczower 1962). This helps to account for Canada's estimated fifty Aboriginal postsecondary institutes (Aboriginal Institutes' Consortium 2005). However, because indigenous sovereignty is significantly weaker in Canada than it is in the United States, only twelve of these institutions are regarded by the federal government as formal postsecondary institutions (Statistics Canada 2007), and even fewer—four—are independently authorized to award degrees. A similar argument could be made for Australia, where only one of fourteen indigenous postsecondary institutions—the Batchelor Institute—is accredited as a degree-granting institution. The same principle explains why in New Zealand, where the Maori constitute slightly more than 15 percent of the population, only three *wananga* are formally recognized and constituted as such by the Crown.[2] Firstly, New Zealand is a unitary country, which produces centralized control of higher education and reduces the impetus for institutional proliferation. Secondly, the government signed (via the British Crown) only one treaty with the Maori, so individual *iwi* and *hapu* have weaker claims for establishing their own institutions than, say, individual Indian tribes in the United States that signed treaties with the federal government. Each of the three *wananga* originated as pan-tribal ventures that currently serve Maori students, and indeed *all* New Zealanders, from throughout the country.[3]

To isolate the effects of sovereignty on—or, at least, to make sovereignty a more plausible explanation of—the number of indigenous postsecondary institutions, we must first rule out any possible effect of population size. The assumption is that larger indigenous populations, especially among college-aged groups, would straightforwardly produce more postsecondary institutions, if only because demand for them would be greater. Table 4.1 presents data on the absolute and relative size of indigenous populations cross-nationally for the year 2000, along with official estimates of each country's respective college-aged populations. Using *total* indigenous population counts in Table 4.1, each indigenous postsecondary institution serves, on average, approximately 458,514 Aboriginal people in Australia; 207,466 Maori in New Zealand; 114,125 American Indians in the United States; and 58,738 status Indians in Canada. Consequently, there does not appear to be any systematic relationship between the number of postsecondary institutions serving indigenous students and the size of the indigenous population in a country.

But what if we consider the size of the relevant age group? Indigenous populations tend to be quite youthful. In Canada and Australia, the indigenous population aged fifteen to twenty-four accounts for 9 and 18 percent of the total indigenous population, respectively, while in the United States and New Zealand approximately 12 percent of each country's indigenous population is aged eighteen to twenty-four. Again, there would also appear to be no direct correspondence between the number of indigenous postsecondary institutions in a country and the size of its college-aged indigenous population.[4]

TABLE 4.1.
Indigenous population statistics, ca. 2000.

	Indicators			
Country	*Indigenous population*	*Total population*	*Percent indigenous*	*Indigenous population aged 18–24*
Australia	458,520	19,413,240	2.4%	83,988[a]
Canada	704,851[b]	32,805,041	2.1%	63,883[a]
New Zealand	622,400	4,061,400	15.3%	71,390
United States	4,119,301[c]	295,734,134	1.4%	462,801

[a] Population aged 15–24.
[b] Registered status Indians only.
[c] Includes individuals claiming mixed descent.

SOURCES: Australia (2003c); Canada (2003); New Zealand (2005c); U.S. Census Bureau (2000).

Institutional Autonomy

In addition to timing and number, indigenous sovereignty is intimately related to institutional autonomy. Tribal colleges and universities in the United States enjoy the most autonomy, as most are independently accredited and are chartered directly by Indian tribes acting in their capacity as sovereign nations. Yet this was not always the case. The independence of TCUs was initially compromised on two fronts. First, as with all community colleges, tribally controlled community colleges are subject to the tacit control of employers and universities (Brint and Karabel 1991). Given their focus on vocational education, community colleges are compelled to acknowledge the power of business interests, which, by virtue of their prerogative to hire graduates, are able to define what types of education are viable. Likewise, transfer-oriented community colleges must adapt their curricula to ensure that the degrees they offer will transfer to four-year colleges and universities. Tribal colleges often entered into articulation agreements with mainstream colleges and universities for this purpose.

Funding regimes have also compromised the autonomy of tribal colleges. Community colleges receive a significant portion of their funding from taxes levied by state and local governments. But most TCUs are located on federal trust territory—Indian reservations—that are largely exempt from state and local taxation (Cunningham and Parker 1998). States, moreover, are not obligated to help fund tribal colleges because the provision and administration of Indian services falls under exclusive federal jurisdiction. As such, TCUs find themselves almost wholly dependent on the federal government for funding, most of which is congressionally authorized by the Tribally Controlled College and University Assistance Act of 1978 (TCCUAA).[5] To be eligible for this funding, a TCU must (1) be accredited or a candidate for accreditation making satisfactory progress toward full accreditation; (2) possess a tribal charter; (3) have a predominantly Indian board of directors; and (4) maintain at least 50 percent Indian enrollment (U.S. Department of Education 1998).[6] Despite this source of regular funding—something that indigenous postsecondary institutions in other countries often lack—it has never been adequate. The original act in 1978 approved $4,000 per Indian student, and the 1986 reauthorization increased funding to $5,820 per student (Boyer 1997: 77). In 1989, however, actual appropriations amounted to a dismal $1,900 per Indian student, merely a third of the amount authorized by Congress. Throughout the 1990s, appropriations oscillated around $3,000 per student; in 2002 they reached $3,900, still well below the $6,000 authorized by Congress ("Federal Funding Increases" 1991; Boyer 1997; Guillory and Ward 2008).

Prior to 1980, when funding under the TCCUAA was first distributed, tribal colleges were forced to find alternative means of support. The same is true today for TCUs working to meet conditions for eligibility. Most have done so with money distributed via Title III of the Higher Education Act of 1965, which authorizes funds for developing institutions. Title III funding is not disbursed directly to recipients but is instead funneled through established colleges and universities; consequently, new tribal colleges often enter into bilateral arrangements with mainstream institutions that provide conduits for funding (Oppelt 1990; Stein 1990; Shanley 1993; U.S. Department of Education 1998; Wabaunsee 1998). Such funding arrangements compromise the autonomy of tribal colleges.

The funding regime for indigenous postsecondary institutions in Canada today resembles that in the United States prior to 1980. First Nations postsecondary institutions "have not been afforded authority similar to that of their southern counterparts. Instead, current federal and provincial policies force Aboriginal institutions to partner with 'recognized' mainstream post-secondary institutions in order to access funding and to ensure the credibility and portability of student credentials" (Aboriginal Institutes' Consortium 2005: 9). Indeed, all but four "Aboriginal institutions lack recognition from federal and provincial governments as having the authority to grant certificates, diplomas, and decrees; therefore, the credentials obtained by students attending Aboriginal institutions do not hold the same currency as credentials obtained in mainstream institutions" (Aboriginal Institutes' Consortium 2005: 29). Two institutions—NVIT and IIG—were recognized as independent postsecondary providers under British Columbia's College and Institution Act in 1993 and 1995, respectively, and SIIT is similarly recognized under provincial legislation in Saskatchewan. As previously noted, First Nations University is the only Aboriginal-controlled institution to enjoy membership in the national Association of Universities and Colleges of Canada. FNU was, until recently, also the only indigenous postsecondary institution in Canada to receive ongoing financial support from the federal government. As a university-college federated with the University of Regina, however, FNU is administratively and academically integrated within its "parent" institution. Most other indigenous postsecondary institutions in Canada are classified as colleges and institutes that cannot introduce new programs under their own authority but rather must seek government approval.

FNU's autonomy was substantially curtailed in 2010, when it relinquished control over its finances to the University of Regina. This move came after the governments of Saskatchewan and Canada terminated their funding to FNU in March of that year amid allegations of corruption and financial mismanagement at the institution. Among other things, senior administrators were accused of filing inflated expense reports, taking inappropriate vacation payments, and wrongfully dismissing internal auditors who investigated financial irregularities. The cuts amounted to $12 million, or roughly half of FNU's annual budget. The government of Saskatchewan subsequently restored its annual grant of $5.2 million, albeit under a four-year arrangement that gave the University of Regina the authority to administer and manage these funds. As such, FNU effectively lost its status as an "affiliated" yet semiautonomous institution and became, for all intents and purposes, a fully "integrated" unit within its parent university (Barnhardt 1991; Hampton 2000). In an effort to balance its budget in the wake of these funding cuts, FNU has reduced course offerings, consolidated academic programs, and eliminated forty-six faculty and administrative positions (First Nations University of Canada 2010). Despite these changes, the federal government has yet (as of November 2010) to reinstate its long-term core funding.[7]

The autonomy of Canada's indigenous postsecondary institutions is further eroded by jurisdictional squabbles over which level of government bears ultimate responsibility for the higher education of indigenous peoples. Unlike in the United States, where Indian education clearly falls under the purview of the federal government, the lines separating federal from provincial jurisdiction in Canada are blurred. Three of the four independent First Nations postsecondary institutions were recognized and incorporated under provincial law, and the fourth, FNU, is federated with a provincial university.

Provincial involvement in indigenous peoples' higher education is extensive in Canada because the federal government interprets its responsibility for First Nations education under the Indian Act to include only primary and secondary schooling. Postsecondary education, it claims, falls under the exclusive constitutional purview of the provincial governments (Hampton 2000; Aboriginal Institutes' Consortium 2005; Stonechild 2006; Jenkins 2007). Provincial governments, on the other hand, contend that the provision of postsecondary education to First Nations students is a constitutionally mandated responsibility of the federal government. Even at FNU, Canada's only Aboriginal-controlled university, debates over jurisdiction rage. Saskatchewan allocates "funding to the college on the understanding that operational funding was a federal responsibility," while Ottawa argues that "the federal government could not assume continuing financial responsibility for the administration of a college which, as a post-secondary institution, is clearly the responsibility of the provincial government" (Stonechild 2006: 93–94). Given this reluctance to fund First Nations postsecondary institutions, Stonechild (2006: 124) concludes that "Aboriginal institutions will continue to be forced to partner with mainstream universities and colleges for recognition and additional resources."

In recent years postsecondary education for First Nations in Canada has been framed as a treaty right. Although the Canadian government initially denied that treaties conveyed a right to postsecondary education, the Supreme Court of Canada held in *Greyeyes v. The Queen* (1978) that "Indian post-secondary funding flowed from the treaties" (Stonechild 2006: 85). Several treaties between First Nations and the Crown included promises from the federal government to provide education but often left unclear exactly which levels would be provided. The federal government read ambiguous treaty provisions narrowly to encompass only primary and secondary education, while indigenous peoples have argued that all levels of education should be covered. In conjunction with the Supreme Court's ruling in *Nowegijick v. The Queen* (1983: 30), which held that "treaties and statutes relating to Indians should be liberally construed and doubtful expressions resolved in favour of the Indians," higher education has increasingly been included as part of the government's treaty obligations toward First Nations.

Contemporary negotiations between First Nations and the federal and provincial governments of Canada now include explicit provisions regarding indigenous control of postsecondary education. For example, Article 103 of the Nisga'a Final Agreement Act of 2000 provides that the Nisga'a government is empowered to make laws respecting "the establishment of post-secondary institutions that have the ability to grant degrees, diplomas and certificates," as well as "the determination of the curriculum" and "the accreditation and certification of individuals who teach or research Nisga'a language and culture." As a result, Wilp Wilxo'oskwhl Nisga'a (Nisga'a House of Wisdom) was established in 1993, offering courses in conjunction with the University of Northern British Columbia.

Treaty rights are not essential to the creation and sustenance of indigenous postsecondary institutions in Canada, however, as the case of the Gabriel Dumont Institute of Native Studies and Applied Research demonstrates. Established in 1980, the institute serves Métis—the descendants of mixed Aboriginal–European unions who are not recognized under the Indian Act as belonging to a registered band—and seeks to "promote the renewal and the development of Métis culture through research." It is nevertheless telling that the institute did not receive federal funding for this purpose until 1983, a year after the Constitution Act was amended to protect "aboriginal" as well as "treaty" rights, thereby extending official recognition to Métis peoples.

The preceding discussion suggests that the autonomy of indigenous postsecondary institutions would seem to be negatively affected by the number of different authorities—federal, provincial, and perhaps, indigenous—sovereign over it (Meyer and Scott 1983: 202). Debates in Canada over which level of government has responsibility for indigenous peoples' higher education have created an environment in which funding is precarious and most indigenous postsecondary institutions are forced to partner with mainstream colleges and universities.

Jurisdictional issues also come into play in Australia, but they assume a somewhat different and less contentious form. As with provinces in Canada, states in Australia enjoy jurisdiction over education. The individual states also retained exclusive jurisdiction over Aboriginal affairs until 1967, when the Commonwealth government assumed concurrent powers. Given this division of authority, BIITE's location in the Northern Territory is no accident. The Northern Territory not only has the largest proportion of Aboriginal peoples in the country, but as a territory it also enjoys fewer powers and less autonomy vis-à-vis the Commonwealth government than do states. Recall from Chapter Three that, when it comes to the rights of indigenous peoples, federal governments are typically much more progressive than subfederal jurisdictions are, and educational policy is certainly no exception to this general rule. Even today, Andrew Armitage (1995: 38) reports that "the state authorities remain committed to policies of integration with limited modifications . . . [whereas] the Commonwealth government has encouraged the development of separate institutions for Aboriginal peoples." Precisely because the Commonwealth government plays a larger and more active role in the Northern Territory than it does in the states, Australia's only autonomous, Aboriginal-controlled, self-accrediting indigenous higher education institute was established there.

Indeed, BIITE represents one of only four self-accrediting nonuniversity institutions in Australia with the authority to develop and offer courses. It was also one of only three such institutions to survive the restructuring of Australia's tertiary system in the late 1980s, during which sixty-three institutions were consolidated, amalgamated, or closed in response to a new policy that restricted Commonwealth funding to institutions with at least 2,000 students. BIITE's continued existence in the wake of this restructuring was a remarkable feat, given that it enrolled only 159 students at the time (Goedegebuure and Meek 1991; Harman 1991; Marginson 2006).

Unlike in the United States, Canada, and Australia, the division of sovereignty among multiple levels of government is not an issue in New Zealand, a unitary country. Instead, all three *wananga* were established as independent, privately controlled Maori institutions, and only later did the government recognize them as Crown institutions authorized to award degrees. As such, however, they are beholden entirely to the Crown for funding and certification as degree-granting institutions. Yet when the Crown implemented a new funding regime that discriminated against *wananga*, Maori educators successfully challenged the government by framing their grievances in terms of treaty rights. The problem arose in 1989, when the Education Act abolished capital funding for the establishment, development, and expansion of TEIs and instead began to allocate funding based solely of equivalent full-time student enrollments. Because *wananga* were not formally recognized under the Education Act until 1993, they did not receive start-up capital funding from the government, as had TEIs established prior to the 1989 reforms. Moreover, the very small enrollment base of *wananga*—early on, at least—put them at a marked disadvantage relative to non-Maori tertiary institutions. An advocacy group representing *wananga* filed a claim in the Waitangi Tribunal, the statutory body charged with settling Maori claims under the Treaty of Waitangi, in 1993, alleging that the per capita funding regime discriminated against *wananga* and violated the Crown's treaty commitment to support Maori programs. The Tribunal held that the *wananga* institutional form, as "an ancient process of learning that encompasses te reo [the Maori language] and matauranga Maori [Maori education]" (Waitangi Tribunal 1998: §5.6), is protected under the Treaty of Waitangi. According to the Tribunal, the Maori language and Maori education are "*taonga*" (treasures) that enjoy protection under Article 2 of the treaty, and therefore the government is obligated to fund *wananga* on par with other educational institutions.

Aside from a one-time injection of capital funding for *wananga* that resulted from the Waitangi Tribunal's decision, the shift to per student allocation models created an incentive for institutions to increase enrollments. This incentive helps account for the rapid enrollment explosion at *wananga* in recent years. Figure 4.2 shows that enrollments at *wananga* have grown exponentially, from 440 students in 1994 to 45,500 in 2002. Most of this increase occurred at TWoA and is attributable in part to the increased participation of non-Maori students: The share of Maori students at TWoA decreased from 77 percent of enrollments in 2002 to approximately 45 percent only two years later (Te Wananga o Aotearoa 2009).

By 2003, rapid enrollment growth at TWoA had outstripped the financial management systems in place. Amid accusations of extravagance, wasteful spending, and nepotism (Cohen 2005a; Tahana 2007), the government appointed a Crown manger to restructure the institution. In a controversial proposal, the Ministry of Education called on TWoA to reduce enrollments by revising its mission and programming to focus exclusively on Maori content. Curricular specialization, it was thought, would prompt most non-Maori students to enroll elsewhere and thereby cut the number of students by more than half. TWoA

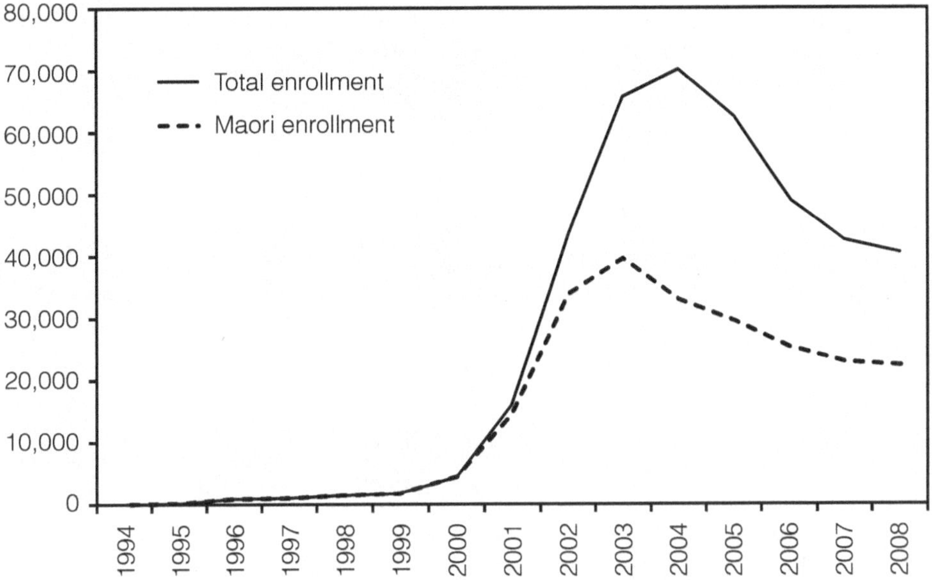

FIGURE 4.2. Combined enrollments at New Zealand's three *wananga*, 1994–2008.

SOURCE: New Zealand (2003, 2008).

countered that it had a treaty-based right to define its own mission, which included a commitment to serve students from any racial or ethnic background, "particularly those who have previously been prevented from participating in tertiary education as a result of various barriers" (Te Wananga o Aotearoa 2009: 10). TWoA further maintained that all its courses were taught using distinctly Maori delivery methods, even in "mainstream" courses devoid of Maori substantive content. (Exactly what this Maori pedagogy or "*āhuatanga Māori*" entails remained ambiguous.) Once again TWoA appealed to the Waitangi Tribunal, alleging that the government had violated its treaty obligations toward the Maori. While the Waitangi Tribunal (2005) acknowledged that the placement of TWoA under temporary financial management had been a legitimate government prerogative, it defended the institution against the government's effort to dictate a change in academic mission. The Tribunal held that *wananga* are accountable to both their founding community (the Maori) and their funding source (the Crown) but that they are ultimately governed by neither and should remain autonomous. It also implored the government to "recognise the wananga's overlapping and at times possibly conflicting duties" to its indigenous and governmental stakeholders.

The preceding discussion has argued that the autonomy of indigenous postsecondary institutions varies as a function of financial stability and independence (Pfeffer and Salancik 1978), which itself depends largely on the political status of indigenous peoples (but also on adherence to mainstream organizational accounting and management practices). In the United States, tribal colleges and universities are established and chartered in most cases by quasi-sovereign Indian tribes, and funding for these ventures flows from the special trust relationship between tribes and the federal government. Financial support for indigenous postsecondary institutions in Canada is more precarious, as provincial and federal officials continue to debate which level of government is ultimately responsible for indigenous peoples' higher education. Most postsecondary institutions for First Nations students have been incorporated by provincial governments, pursuant to their constitutional authority over education, even though the federal government bears responsibility for Indian affairs. As a unitary country, New Zealand has avoided jurisdictional turf wars or "buck passing," but *wananga* have nevertheless had to contend with discriminatory funding practices and government-directed efforts to redefine their academic missions. In both Canada and New Zealand, treaty-based claims have afforded indigenous peoples the means to demand government support or deflect government incursions. Finally, BIITE in Australia enjoys substantial autonomy, but it was won relatively late (in 1999) and self-directed Aboriginal postsecondary education remains confined to only one institution.

Organizational Form

If sovereignty invests indigenous peoples with the authority to establish their own postsecondary institutions (or to have postsecondary institutions established for them), massification shaped the kinds of institutions they have become. As higher education became a mass and increasingly a universal enterprise (Trow 2006), new and specialized nonuniversity organizational forms emerged or expanded to absorb the influx of students (see Chapter Two). In most cases, these organizational forms provided the blueprints for indigenous postsecondary institutions.

Indigenous postsecondary institutions exhibit a greater diversity of forms in some countries than in others, a phenomenon that reflects the degree of

TABLE 4.2.

Cross-national diversity in postsecondary institutional forms.

United States	*Canada (excluding Quebec)*	*Canada (Quebec only)*	*New Zealand*	*Australia*
Doctoral research university	University	Université	University	University (private and public)
Master's (comprehensive) university or college	University college	Collège universitaire	Institute of technology and polytechnic	Technical and further education (TAFE) college
Baccalaureate college	Community college	Collège communautaire	*Wananga*	Private training establishment
Community college	College of applied arts and technology (Ontario only)	Collège d'enseignement général et professionnel (CEGEP)	Private training establishment	
Associate of arts college	College institute of technology and advanced learning (Ontario and Saskatchewan)	Collège d'arts appliqués et de technologie	Specialist college	
Specialized institutions	Provincial institute	Collège professionnel privé		
Postsecondary vocational and technical schools	Private career/ vocational college	Autres établissements spécialisés		
	Other specialized institutions			

SOURCE: UNESCO, World Higher Education Database, www.unesco.org/iau/onlinedatabases/index.html.

institutional diversity in the postsecondary sector more generally. Table 4.2 documents the institutional forms that exist in each country's postsecondary sector. In the United States, for example, most tribal colleges were established as community colleges, although they are continually "upgrading" into four-year colleges and, in a few cases, master's-level universities. A handful of tribal colleges are technical and vocational institutes rather than community colleges. By comparison, First Nations postsecondary institutions in Canada are a heterogeneous lot. They include a university-college (FNU); community colleges such as Red Crow Community College; provincial institutes such as NVIT, IIG, SIIT, and the Gabriel Dumont Institute of Native Studies and Applied Research; and technical institutes such as Saskatchewan Indian Institute of Technologies and Six Nations Polytechnic. And in Quebec, whose education system differs from the rest of Canada, the provincial government recently announced that it will fund a First Nations *collège d'enseignement général et professionnel* (CEGEP, or "college of general and vocational education"), an institution that prepares students for either university studies or direct entry into the workforce. As with most other First Nations postsecondary institutions in Canada, the college will partner with mainstream institutions (in this case, other CEGEPs) for de facto accreditation.

In Australia, BIITE is a "dual sector" institution that offers a mix of vocational and university-grade programs. The institute bridges a binary divide that, until 1989, had segregated vocational and higher education into different institutional sectors and funding streams. Still, some two-thirds of BIITE's approximately 3,000 students are enrolled in vocational and technical education (VTE) programs, so "the majority of [its] funding is as a VTE institution" (Australian Universities Quality Agency 2006: 25). During a recent audit, the Australian Universities Quality Agency (2006) recommended that BIITE not be designated a university, a status to which it aspires.

New Zealand presents an exception from the general rule that indigenous postsecondary institutions adopt mainstream organizational structures that prevail in the nonuniversity tertiary sector. As distinctly Maori higher education institutions, *wananga* constitute a sui generis organizational form and are defined in law alongside universities, polytechnics, and colleges of education. I posit that indigenous postsecondary institutions evolved into a distinctive type of organization in New Zealand but not elsewhere for much the same reason that Quebec maintains its own educational system and institutions, distinct from English-speaking Canada. Quebecois and Maori are both "national" minorities—one is a stateless nation; the other is an indigenous people (Kymlicka and Norman 2000). Both Canada and New Zealand openly acknowledge their bicultural foundations. In Canada, England and France are regarded as founding nations (preceded, of course, by "First Nations"), and

English and French are both official languages. In New Zealand, the country's founding document, the Treaty of Waitangi, was negotiated between Maori chiefs and the British Crown, and the official languages since 1987 are English and Maori. And, just as Quebec is recognized as a distinct society with its own institutions, the Maori are acknowledged collectively as a culturally distinct partner in New Zealand, a "nation within a nation" that is entitled to establish and attend separate educational institutions.

Summary

Table 4.3 summarizes the emergence of indigenous postsecondary institutions along four dimensions: timing, number, autonomy, and form. The initial appearance of these institutions first in the United States and subsequently in Canada, New Zealand, and Australia is consistent with the relative strength of indigenous sovereignty in these countries. The number of indigenous postsecondary institutions in each country would also appear to vary as a function of indigenous sovereignty: The number is greatest in the United States, where sovereignty resides in individual Indian tribes, and lowest in Australia, where Aboriginal sovereignty was never officially acknowledged.

Perhaps more than for timing and number, indigenous sovereignty directly affects institutional autonomy. Indigenous postsecondary institutions are more likely to receive direct government funding—and, as a consequence, enjoy more institutional autonomy—when indigenous peoples are acknowledged as possessing sovereignty. Thus, funding for TCUs in the United States is relatively stable (if still in most cases inadequate), whereas only one institution in Canada, the First Nations University, has historically received regular financial support from the federal government. First Nations in Canada have nevertheless been increasingly successful in framing indigenous-controlled higher education as a treaty right. Treaty negotiations with the Nisga'a in British Columbia, for example, included the explicit right to control postsecondary education. Likewise in New Zealand, the Treaty of Waitangi obligates the government to fund *wananga*. In the United States, the treaty right to education is largely implicit: Treaties created a trust relationship between the federal government and Indian tribes, and the government supports Indian education as part of this trust. Indigenous-controlled higher education came late to Australia (where no treaties with indigenous peoples were signed) and remains limited to an exceptional case, the Batchelor Institute of Indigenous Tertiary Education.

TABLE 4.3.
Patterns in the emergence of indigenous postsecondary institutions.

	Australia	*Canada*	*New Zealand*	*United States*
Timing	Batchelor Institute of Indigenous Tertiary Education recognized as a higher education institution in 1989, designated an autonomous public agency in 1995, and passed to Aboriginal control in 1999	First unsuccessful attempt to establish an indigenous college in 1973; precursor to the First Nations University of Canada established in 1976	Te Wananga o Raukawa opened in 1981; officially recognized as a tertiary education institute in 1993	Navajo Community College established in 1968
Number	1	12	3	36
Autonomy	High after 1999; BIITE is one of four self-accrediting nonuniversity institutions	Low; compromised by lack of stable funding, absence of independent accreditation, and jurisdictional squabbles over responsibility for First Nations education	Medium; government intervention checked by treaty rights; Te Wananga o Aotearoa placed under (and subsequently freed from) Crown management	High; dedicated funding and independent accreditation of colleges chartered directly by quasi-sovereign tribes
Forms	Dual-sector institution (vocational and higher education)	Integrated structures, community colleges, cultural colleges, technical institutes	Sui generis institutions	Community colleges, technical institutes, universities

The institutional forms assumed by indigenous postsecondary institutions are a function not of indigenous sovereignty but of postsecondary massification more generally, with the lone exception of New Zealand. In most cases, indigenous postsecondary institutions simply adopt forms that are prevalent in a country's preuniversity sector. Only in New Zealand, where Maori represent a sizeable percentage of the population and are recognized as a "founding" nation, did a distinctive institutional form, *wananga*, emerge. And, yet, massification has been important not only in shaping the formal structure of indigenous postsecondary institutions but also in expanding the participation

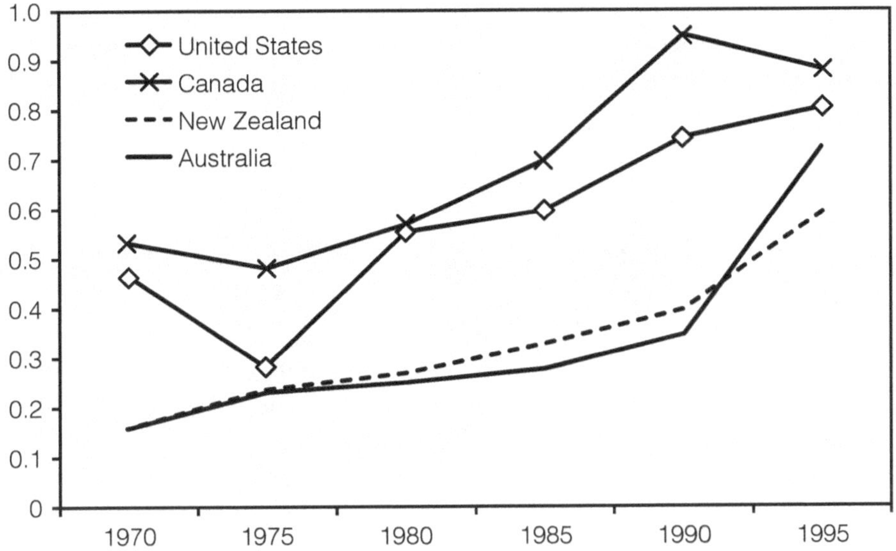

FIGURE 4.3. Cross-national tertiary enrollment ratios, 1970–1995.

SOURCE: UNESCO (1999).

Notes: "A gross enrolment ratio . . . is derived by dividing the total enrolment . . . , regardless of age, by the population of the age group which according to national regulations, should be enrolled at this level. . . . For tertiary education a duration of five years following the end of secondary general education was used for all countries" (UNESCO 1999: II-5). The figure does not include more recent trends because enrollment data collected after 1997, when UNESCO adopted the International Standard Classification of Education, are not comparable with pre-1997 data.

of indigenous peoples in postsecondary education. In this way, postsecondary educational expansion played a catalytic if not a directly causal role in the emergence of indigenous postsecondary institutions.

THE ROLE OF HIGHER EDUCATION MASSIFICATION

Chapter Two discussed how the worldwide expansion of higher education enrollments after World War II produced an environment conducive to the emergence of indigenous postsecondary institutions. Figure 4.3 plots tertiary enrollment ratios for each of the countries in my analysis over time (UNESCO 1999). These ratios convey the number of students enrolled in postsecondary education (regardless of age) as a percentage of the relevant age group. The overall trend between 1970 and 1995 is upward, although the extent of participation varies substantially across countries. Canada and the United States began the period on either side of 50 percent of the relevant age group enrolled but finished at 87 and 80 percent, respectively. The enrollment ratios for Australia and New Zealand hovered between 15 and 20 percent in 1970, much lower in comparison with North America. New Zealand showed steady gains throughout the period, and by 1995 approximately two-thirds of the relevant age group was enrolled in higher education. Rates of expansion were somewhat slower in Australia until 1990, when enrollments doubled, from 35 to 70 percent, in only five years. This sudden spike is due to the transition from a "binary" to a "unified" system of higher education in 1989. Nonuniversity students who previously had not counted under the binary system were now included under the unified system.

One outcome of tertiary massification is the expanded participation of traditionally underrepresented and marginalized groups such as women, the working classes, ethnic minorities, and indigenous peoples. The top panel of Figure 4.4 plots indigenous postsecondary enrollments as a proportion of total enrollments in Australia, Canada, and the United States; the bottom panel charts Maori enrollments in New Zealand. (New Zealand is plotted on a different chart because the scale of Maori participation is much greater, given their relatively large share of the population.) There have been significant gains in indigenous participation over time. In some cases, enrollment growth has been truly phenomenal. In Canada, for instance, the number of Indian students enrolled at colleges and universities grew from only sixty in 1961 to more than 13,000 in 1987, due in large measure to a government assistance program for status Indians and Inuit peoples (Stonechild 2006: 64). Similarly in New Zealand, Maori students accounted for nearly one-quarter of tertiary enrollments in 2004, which is disproportionate to their share of the total population.

Although overall enrollment rates are increasing, indigenous students continue to be segregated horizontally by field of study and vertically by postsecondary sector: They are overrepresented in lower-status disciplines and are concentrated in preuniversity or vocationally oriented institutions.[8] Business and management, social sciences and history, and education accounted for 42 percent of all bachelor's degrees earned by American Indians in 1994 (U.S. Department of Education 1998: ch. 4). Maori postsecondary students in New Zealand are also overrepresented in the social sciences and humanities. Approximately 70 percent of all Maori students enrolled in bachelor's degree

FIGURE 4.4. Indigenous postsecondary enrollments as a percentage of total in Australia, Canada, the United States, and New Zealand.

SOURCES: Australia (2001, 2003a); Canada (2003); U.S. Department of Education (2001); New Zealand (2003); UNESCO (1994, 1998, 1999).

Notes: In Australia, pre-1990 data do not include enrollments in vocational education and training (VET) institutes. Enrollments in Canada include status Indians only.

programs in 2003 studied management and commerce, society and culture, education, or the creative arts (New Zealand 2005b: 79). In Australia, indigenous student enrollments in the vocational sector surpassed nonindigenous participation for the first time in 1996, but Aboriginal students remain grossly underrepresented in the university sector (Australia 2000).

Early massification initiatives focused merely on promoting indigenous peoples' access to mainstream higher education systems, not on fostering indigenous control of independent postsecondary institutions. In 1961, for instance, the Maori Education Foundation Act in New Zealand established the Maori Education Trust to encourage Maori participation in higher education. Such initiatives have been, on one dimension at least, extremely successful. Maori boast the highest rate of tertiary participation of any ethnic group in New Zealand, including whites (New Zealand 2005a). In 1998, 7.4 percent of college-aged Maori were enrolled in tertiary institutions, compared with 8.6 percent for the population at large. By 2003, the rate of Maori participation jumped to 20.2 percent, far outpacing the rate of 13.4 percent for all students (New Zealand 2005b: 77). Much of this expansion occurred within *wananga*.

In Canada, where the original focus was likewise on access rather than control, the Department of Indian and Northern Affairs introduced a financial assistance program for indigenous postsecondary students in 1968. This initiative, known today as the Post-Secondary Student Support Program (Canada 2000), provides financial support for tuition, travel, and living expenses incurred by status Indians and Inuit students. A similar program in Australia, the Aboriginal Participation Initiative established in 1985, provided supplementary funding to encourage the participation of indigenous students in higher education. In 1991 the Australian government renewed its commitment to equity in tertiary education by introducing its "Fair Chance for All" policy, targeting not only Aboriginal people but also economically disadvantaged students, women, people from non-English-speaking backgrounds, and persons with disabilities.

These measures focused primarily on issues of access and participation but largely neglected the issue of indigenous peoples' involvement in the process and control of higher education. A recent report by the Department of Education, Science and Training in Australia concluded that "Aborigines are not pleased with a policy which offers them equality—equality of access, or continuance and of performance in relation to education provided by mainstream providers—when what they seek is authority to design, administer and deliver an education based upon and compatible with the values and purposes of their own society" (Australia 2003b: 11). Recent policies have begun to emphasize indigenous control over the provision of higher education, in recognition of the fact that indigenous peoples are entitled both to participate in mainstream higher education systems (a *human* right) and to establish or manage their own schools (a *sovereign* right).

In New Zealand, for example, the Maori Education Trust was abolished in 1993 and immediately reconstituted with a new mission: to facilitate Maori authority over education. Where the earlier focus had been on the expanded participation of Maori students in mainstream schools, the new emphasis was on Maori control over their own schools (Walker 2005). In Australia, the National Aboriginal and Torres Strait Islander Education Policy, adopted in 1990, promoted increased access as well as greater involvement by indigenous peoples in educational decision making. And in Canada, provincial policies such as Ontario's Aboriginal Post-Secondary Education and Training Strategy of 1991 aimed to "increase the extent and participation of Native people in decisions affecting Native postsecondary education" (Aboriginal Institutes' Consortium 2005: 40).

INDIGENOUS POSTSECONDARY INSTITUTIONS: A GLOBAL PHENOMENON

The emergence of indigenous postsecondary institutions has not been limited to the Anglo-derived settler societies of North America and Australasia, although these countries were and continue to be the leaders with respect to indigenous-controlled higher education. A similar pattern of emergence is observed elsewhere in the world: The establishment of indigenous postsecondary institutions is everywhere preceded by a fundamental shift in government policies toward increased support of indigenous peoples' rights and autonomy. Several examples from two disparate regions—Scandinavia and Latin America—illustrate this pattern.

Perhaps nowhere is the relationship between indigenous sovereignty and control of higher education more explicit than in Greenland. A former colony of Denmark, Greenland achieved home rule in 1979, giving Inuit full jurisdiction over domestic affairs. The Inuit Institute was established four years later. The institute originally offered a two-year curriculum akin to community colleges in the United States, but in 1989 it was reestablished as Ilisimatusarfik—the

University of Greenland—with the authority to award bachelor's and master's degrees. Ilisimatusarfik is recognized as a university within the Danish system, and its credentials are transferable to Nordic countries (Claus Andreasen, Provost of Ilisimatusarfik, personal communication, April 28, 2000). Degrees are offered in public administration, cultural and social history, Greenlandic language and literature, and theology. The university enrolls approximately 100 students (Ilisimatusarfik 2005).

In Norway, the Saami College was founded in 1989 on the heels of legislation that promoted use of the Saami language, incorporated Saami cultural protections into the constitution, and established an advisory Saami assembly. As the world's only Saami higher education institution, Saami College serves Saami from throughout Scandinavia and its degrees are recognized in Norway, Sweden, and Finland. The college trains Saami teachers and journalists, promotes Saami language use, and advocates biodiversity and sustainable development (Saami College 2005). It was originally established as one of ninety-eight regional and vocational colleges in Norway, and despite enrolling only 100 students it survived the restructuring of the nonuniversity postsecondary system into twenty-six university colleges in 1994. In this respect, the experience of Saami College closely resembles that of BIITE in Australia, which survived a similar consolidation in the 1980s. Today, most instruction at the reconstituted Saami University College is transacted exclusively in the Saami language.

Half a world away, the emergence of indigenous postsecondary institutions in Latin America coincided with the mobilization of indigenous social movements during the late twentieth century. These "new" social movements were rooted in ethnic (indigenous) rather than class (peasant) identities, derived inspiration and support from the international community, and contributed to the extension of political and cultural rights to indigenous peoples (Brysk 2000; Yashar 2005). The first indigenous postsecondary institution in Latin America, the University of the Autonomous Regions of the Caribbean Coast of Nicaragua (Universidad de las Regiones Autónomas de la Costa Caribe Nicaragüense), was established in 1995, less than a decade after the Nicaraguan government granted two indigenous regions on the Atlantic coast legal autonomy (Campbell 2006). A second institution, the Bluefields Indian and Caribbean University, also serves indigenous Nicaraguans.

In Mexico, the Autonomous Indigenous University, founded in 1999, seeks "to meld a traditional Western education with an emphasis on knowledge that is particularly relevant in indigenous communities" (Lloyd 2003). This approach is reminiscent of the "both-ways" philosophy expounded by BIITE in Australia. The Autonomous Indigenous University is the first of eight indigenous universities the government plans to build throughout Mexico, including in Chiapas (*Indian Country Today* 2005; Reyes 2005).

Plans to establish an indigenous university in Ecuador were first discussed in 1988 but did not come to fruition until Columbus Day, 2000, when the Intercultural University of Indigenous Peoples and Nationalities (Universidad Intercultural de las Nacionalidades y Pueblos Indígenas) opened its doors to students (Laurie, Andolina, and Radcliffe 2005; Walsh 2002). That same year, the National Intercultural University of the Amazon (Universidad Nacional Intercultural de la Amazonía) was established in Peru, but formal instruction in bilingual education and agriculture did not commence until 2006.

The election of Evo Morales as Bolivia's first indigenous president in 2005 heralded the creation of three new indigenous universities, with courses to be taught in one of three indigenous languages: Aymara, Quechua, and Guarani. The announcement, made in 2008, came in the wake of Morales's promise to "decolonize" the country (Associated Press 2009). The Bolivian example represents an extreme case in which variable opportunity structures—the presence of absence of partisan allies in government—played a directly causal role in the emergence of indigenous postsecondary institutions. By then, indigenous postsecondary institutions had become sufficiently institutionalized globally that a change in political leadership could lead to the rapid establishment of indigenous universities.

One additional example, coming not from Scandinavia or Latin America but from the Russian Federation, indicates the degree to which indigenous postsecondary institutions have become a truly institutionalized feature of the modern world-cultural landscape. Only two years after the fall of the Soviet Union, the government of the Russian Federation established the State Polar Academy in St. Petersburg in 1993, with the "objective of training a new generation of indigenous intellectuals, who will be able to develop their national culture . . ." (United Nations 1999: ¶ 38). In today's world, any country that aspires to democracy and that has an indigenous population is expected to establish indigenous postsecondary institutions or else support the efforts of indigenous peoples to do so.

At least two factors account for the worldwide diffusion of indigenous postsecondary institutions. As with the "first-mover" countries, one factor centers on the strength of indigenous sovereignty claims within countries. Indigenous sovereignty gives impetus to the creation of indigenous postsecondary institutions. Greenland and Nicaragua are paradigmatic in this regard, insofar as the establishment of indigenous universities followed the granting of Inuit home rule in the former and the establishment of two autonomous regions for indigenous peoples in the latter. The second factor has more to do with a country's cultural embeddedness in and associational linkages to the global polity, as both the Russian and Latin American experiences illustrate. Following the collapse of communism, Russia became much more receptive to world-cultural norms, including those which promote indigenous peoples' rights and the establishment of culturally relevant postsecondary institutions for indigenous peoples. In Latin America, the emergence of indigenous colleges and universities was facilitated by the growing participation of Amerindians in global civil society. According to Brysk (2000: 101), "In 1982 only two non-North American indigenous groups attended the UN Working Group [on Indigenous Populations], but by 1999 two-thirds of the participants came from the third world," especially Latin American countries. International fora such as the Working Group provided formal venues where "Fourth Worlders" (indigenous peoples) from the "Third World" could learn how to establish indigenous postsecondary institutions from "First World" indigenous peoples.

As indigenous postsecondary institutions become increasingly institutionalized in global discourses—that is, as they begin to be seen as morally proper, functionally necessary, or even inevitable—we can expect their worldwide diffusion to continue. Several recent developments suggest that the process of institutionalization is well under way. A number of international institutions and experts have issued recommendations for the continued establishment and support of indigenous postsecondary institutions. UNESCO, for example, seeks to "facilitate indigenous people's access to higher education, encourage the establishment of indigenous universities, and develop higher education programmes that incorporate indigenous knowledge and culture" (UNESCO 2003). And only a year after it was established as the first official body with a mandate to advise the United Nations on issues affecting indigenous peoples, the Permanent Forum on Indigenous Issues in 2003 "encourage[d] States, specialized bodies and the United Nations system to consider creating international indigenous universities" (United Nations 2003: 19). This recommendation was followed a year later by a proposal of the Special Rapporteur on the situation of human rights and fundamental freedoms of indigenous people, Rodolfo Stavenhagen, that "States should support . . . [t]he establishment of indigenous universities as well as incentives for non-native students to undertake their studies in such universities" (United Nations 2004: 8).

Another clear signal that institutionalization has arrived was the establishment of the World Indigenous Higher Education Consortium (WINHEC) in 2002. Indigenous educators first proposed the idea of a higher education consortium in 1993, and WINHEC was officially launched nine years later by indigenous stakeholders from Australia, Canada, New Zealand, Norway, and the United States. Among other things, WINHEC serves as "an accreditation body for indigenous education initiatives and systems that identify common criteria, practices and principles by which Indigenous Peoples live" (WINHEC 2003: 3).[9] The example of WINHEC shows that the process of institutionalizing indigenous postsecondary institutions occurs not only in venues traditionally dominated by states, such as the United Nations, but also in grassroots organizations established by indigenous peoples themselves.

CONCLUSION

Although the legal and normative principles giving rise to indigenous postsecondary institutions derive ultimately from world-cultural rights discourses, the translation of those global principles into local realties remains the primary domain of nation-states. Nation-specific colonial legacies, political traditions, and institutional structures produced variation in the potency and efficacy of indigenous peoples' sovereignty claims under domestic law. In turn, the relative strength and salience of indigenous sovereignty, together with the worldwide massification of higher education, patterned the emergence indigenous postsecondary institutions.

The analyses in Part II have treated sovereignty as an ordinal variable, with countries ranked based on the extent to which they recognize the sovereignty of their indigenous populations. When considering the Anglo-derived settler states of North America and Australasia, the United States would place at or near the top of an indigenous sovereignty scale, while Australia would fall somewhere near the bottom. These differences are attributable to a variety of historical, colonial, and political factors that ultimately shaped the emergence of indigenous postsecondary institutions. Navajo Community College, established in 1968, was the first indigenous-controlled postsecondary institution in the world, while the Batchelor Institute of Indigenous Tertiary Education did not pass into Aboriginal control until 1999.

For all their differences, American Indians and Aboriginal Australians are both "indigenous" and therefore possess claims to sovereignty, however weak, under domestic and international law. To pinpoint the crucial impact of sovereignty on the emergence of indigenous postsecondary institutions, we must now treat it as a binary variable that distinguishes indigenous minorities with sovereignty claims from nonindigenous minorities with no such claims. That is the task of Part III, which shifts focus to tribal colleges and universities in the United States and compares them with historically black colleges and universities. Sovereignty, I argue, not only gives indigenous peoples the authority to establish and control separate colleges; it also gives them the leverage with which to transform mainstream institutional and curricular models. The argument will once again focus on patterns of minority-group incorporation, albeit at a different level of analysis. Whereas Part II explored how differences in the political incorporation of indigenous peoples shaped the emergence of indigenous postsecondary institutions cross-nationally, Part III considers the effect of internal differences in the incorporation of two minority groups in the United States, African Americans and American Indians, on the origins, legitimacy, and curricular composition of tribal and black colleges.

PART III

ORGANIZATIONAL ANALYSIS

CHAPTER FIVE

MINORITY-SERVING COLLEGES IN THE UNITED STATES

The white man forbade the black to enter his own social and economic system and at the same time force-fed the Indian what he was denying the black.

Vine Deloria (1969: 173)

WHEN IT WAS FOUNDED IN 1968, NAVAJO Community College in Tsaile, Arizona, became not only the first tribally controlled college in the United States but also the first indigenous postsecondary institution in the world.[1] Since then, some three dozen tribal colleges and universities (TCUs) have been established on or near Indian reservations throughout the country. But although TCUs were the first postsecondary institutions in the world established by and for indigenous peoples, they were not the first postsecondary institutions in the United States with an explicit mission to serve minority students. Colleges and universities for African American students, known today as historically black colleges and universities (HBCUs), antedated TCUs by more than a century. The nation's first HBCU, Cheyney University of Pennsylvania, was founded as the Institute for Colored Youth by a Quaker philanthropist in 1837. The last HBCU was established in 1964, when the Louisiana Legislature chartered the Southern University at Shreveport just weeks before President Lyndon Johnson signed the Civil Rights Act into law. There are currently 105 HBCUs still in operation throughout the southern and mid-Atlantic United States, down from 112 in 1964.

These inverse patterns of institutional emergence and development pose an interesting paradox. What accounts for the rise and expansion of separate colleges for American Indians when similar institutions for African Americans are no longer established and, as I will show, when those that remain face threats to their continued survival? Once again, sovereignty is the crucial variable that explains the establishment of TCUs: Tribal sovereignty legitimizes the existence of separate, racially identifiable institutions in a legal and political environment otherwise intent on promoting racial integration. American Indians (or more precisely, Indian tribes) claim a quasi-sovereign status that African Americans lack, and this fundamental difference has tremendous ramifications for the ability to establish and sustain separate minority-serving institutions in the post–civil rights era.

Recent years have witnessed a flurry of scholarship on minority-serving colleges and universities in the United States, not only TCUs and HBCUs but also Hispanic- and Asian-serving institutions (see, for example, Merisotis and O'Brien 1998; Gasman, Baez, and Turner 2008). Although this work has taken great strides in spotlighting institutions that for too long have existed on the periphery of both education systems and research agendas, it remains fundamentally limited by a tendency to treat institutions for different minority groups in isolation. My task, to isolate the effect of sovereignty on the rise of postsecondary institutions for indigenous peoples, necessitates a direct comparison with similar institutions for minority groups that lack sovereignty claims. Thus, whereas previous chapters examined the effect of *cross*-national differences in the incorporation of indigenous peoples—all with some claim to sovereignty—on the emergence of indigenous postsecondary institutions in their respective countries, this chapter analyzes the effect of *intra*national differences in the incorporation of American Indians and African Americans on the establishment of TCUs and HBCUs in the United States. To this end, I trade cross-country comparisons for comparisons of organizations within the same country.

AN OVERVIEW OF TRIBAL AND BLACK COLLEGES

TCUs and HBCUs, together with other minority-serving colleges and universities,[2] are unified by a commitment to educating historically disadvantaged students who remain grossly underrepresented among postsecondary enrollees and graduates. Despite this shared commitment, tribally controlled and

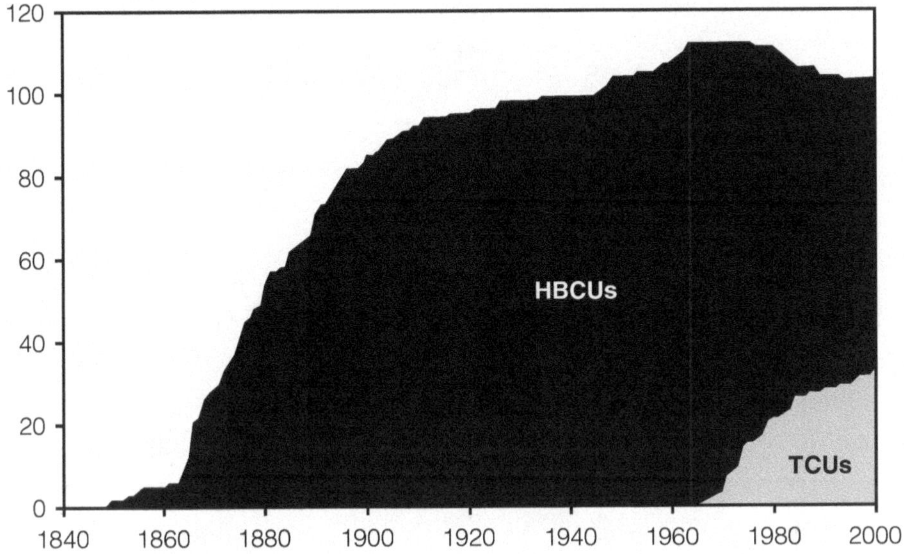

FIGURE 5.1. Cumulative number of historically black and tribal colleges, 1840–2000.

Note: HBCUs = Historically black colleges and universities; TCUs = Tribal colleges and universities.

historically black institutions differ tremendously with respect to their origins, development, and missions. Figure 5.1 illustrates differences in the emergence and development of HBCUs and TCUs. The establishment of HBCUs spanned the period between 1837 and 1964, emerging first in the northern United States and expanding rapidly in the postbellum South under conditions of legalized segregation after the Civil War. Few HBCUs were established directly by the constituents and communities they served. Although black churches founded a handful of colleges for African American students, most private HBCUs owe their existence to northern philanthropists, industrialists, and missionaries (Anderson 1988; Gasman 2008). State governments also established separate and ostensibly equal colleges for black students, to prevent newly emancipated slaves from attending white institutions.

HBCUs acquired their designation as "historical" institutions in 1965, when the Higher Education Act defined them as colleges and universities that were "established prior to [the Civil Rights Act of] 1964, whose principal mission was, and is, the education of black Americans." The policy shift from segregation to integration accounts for the "flat line" and gradual decline in the number of black colleges after 1964, as HBCUs that closed or merged with other institutions were not replaced. The forty public and forty-nine private four-year HBCUs still in operation, together with a small two-year sector composed of eleven public and five private colleges, account for 16 percent of African American enrollments in postsecondary education but award one in four bachelor's degrees earned by black students.

It has been suggested in recent years that HBCUs may be wasteful relics—or worse, illegal vestiges—of a bygone era, one in which African Americans were not permitted to attend "mainstream" colleges and universities. Citing the landmark *Brown v. Board of Education* (1954) decision that declared separate schools for black and white children to be inherently unequal, the Supreme Court ruled in 1992 that the existence of three historically black and five predominantly white colleges and universities in Mississippi was traceable to the former segregated system of higher education. This ruling, handed down in *United States v. Fordice* (1992: 724), suggested that "closure of one or more institutions would decrease the discriminatory effects of the present system." More recently, in 2009, Mississippi Governor Haley Barbour recommended that the state's three historically black universities—Alcorn State, Mississippi Valley State, and Jackson State—be consolidated into one institution as a cost-saving measure. The proposal, tellingly, left the state's predominantly white universities intact (Jaschik 2009).[3] Also in 2009, a Georgia state legislator suggested that the state's public black colleges be merged with neighboring majority-white institutions "both in the interest of cost savings and in the hope of remedying . . . an 'unconstitutional' system of continuing segregation in higher education" (Stripling 2009).

Such proposals threaten to reduce the number of HBCUs even further. Integration mandates have already altered the enrollment composition of many HBCUs, such that a growing number of historically black institutions are no longer predominantly black. Enrollments at public HBCUs, in particular, have felt the impact of federal injunctions that ordered the desegregation of state-controlled higher education systems. The share of African American students at these institutions declined from 83 percent in 1976 to 78 percent in 2001 (Provasnik, Shafer, and Snyder 2004). By contrast, private HBCUs are shielded from integration mandates and enrolled a slightly larger share of African American students in 2001 (93 percent) than they did in 1976 (92 percent).

Unlike HBCUs, which emerged as segregated institutions, TCUs were founded in the wake of policies that reaffirmed the right of Indian tribes to self-government. A shift in federal Indian policy from assimilation to self-determination invested Indian tribes with the authority to charter their own colleges. Six TCUs were established during the "first wave" of expansion between 1968 and 1972 (Stein 1992). The number of TCUs stood at twenty-nine by the time the *Fordice* ruling impugned the legitimacy of public HBCUs in 1992. Currently, thirty-six TCUs enroll approximately 10 percent of the 127,000 American Indian and Alaska Native students in higher education. Most TCUs originated as community colleges, although six have since expanded into four-year colleges and two—Sinte Gleska University and Oglala Lakota College, both in South Dakota—award master's degrees in specialized fields such as tribal administration and education.

TCUs have a unique and multifaceted mission. As minority-serving colleges, they are committed to promoting educational access for American Indians, historically among the least represented minority groups in higher education. Tribally controlled community colleges also award credentials that are transferable to nontribal colleges and universities. Other features set TCUs apart from both mainstream colleges and universities and other minority-serving institutions. They are universally committed to revitalizing tribal languages, cultures, and traditions; invigorating reservation economies through locally tailored vocational and technical programs; and fostering self-determination by preparing a new generation of tribal leaders and administrators. With few exceptions, TCUs must be chartered by American Indian tribes and maintain at least 50 percent Indian enrollment to be eligible for federal assistance as authorized under the Tribally Controlled College or University Assistance Act.[4] Most TCUs easily exceed this threshold: Approximately 80 percent of students enrolled at tribal colleges identify as American Indian (AIHEC 2006), owing in large part to the location of TCUs on or near Indian reservations.

This overview of tribal and black colleges reveals sharp differences in their timing and purposes. A more thorough understanding of these differences requires an analysis of the social, political, and legal contexts in which TCUs and HBCUs emerged. The remainder of this chapter seeks to demonstrate that the emergence of postsecondary institutions for African Americans and American Indians can be traced to nature of each group's incorporation into the mainstream polity.

THE LOGICS OF INCLUSION AND EXCLUSION

Formal relationships between minority groups and the states they inhabit generally follow one of two logics of political incorporation: inclusion and exclusion. These logics assume different and even incongruous meanings over time and for different minority groups. For most African Americans, exclusion meant segregation from a society they wished to enter, whereas inclusion entailed their social, legal, and political integration as equal citizens into the mainstream polity. Conversely, for most American Indians, inclusion was experienced as forced assimilation, "the practice of forcing an historically separate people into a melting pot which scalds rather than warms" (Gross 1973: 244). Likewise, exclusion does not deprive American Indians, as racial minorities, of the right to participate freely and equally in mainstream institutions but rather provides the basis from which Indian tribes, as political communities, maintain their own institutions. Exclusion, that is, empowers Indians to exercise their collective rights as independent, institutionally complete, self-determining, quasi-sovereign nations.

These different logics of inclusion and exclusion structured each group's relationship with the American state in contradictory ways. Will Kymlicka stated the matter succinctly when he concluded that "the crucial difference between blacks and the aboriginal peoples of North America is, of course, that the latter value their separation from the mainstream life and culture of North America" (Kymlicka 1989: 145). Although HBCUs and TCUs both emerged under conditions of exclusion—the former before the Civil Rights Act of 1964, the latter after it—the terms and logic of that exclusion differed. It was not by choice that HBCUs existed as separate institutions. As W. E. B. Du Bois noted in 1933, "a Negro university . . . does not advocate segregation by race, it simply accepts the bald fact that we are segregated, apart, hammered into a separate unity by spiritual intolerance and legal sanction" (Du Bois [1933] 2001: 130). Conversely, most TCUs (excepting three federally chartered institutions) were chartered by Indian tribes in their capacity as sovereign nations, for the purpose of protecting, preserving, and promulgating their endangered languages and cultures.

These inverse dynamics of inclusion and exclusion have been shaped by two dimensions of minority-group incorporation. One dimension comprises the legal regimes that structure minority–state relations from the top down; the other dimension pertains to the efforts of minority groups to influence their relations with the state from the bottom up, through social movement activism.

Legal Dimension: Policies of Minority-Group Incorporation

Both African Americans and American Indians were initially excluded, by law, from American civil and political life. Nevertheless, the nature of each group's exclusion differed, as illustrated by the historical treatment of blacks and Indians in the U.S. Constitution. Until the Fourteenth Amendment formally extended citizenship to "all persons born or naturalized in the United States, and subject to the jurisdiction thereof" in 1868, a black slave counted as three-fifths of a person for the purposes of apportioning tax revenues and allocating representatives in Congress. American Indians, in contrast, were not counted at all. As members of sovereign nations not "subject to the jurisdiction of" the United States, they were not taxed, nor were they represented in Congress. Blacks were denied U.S. citizenship as slaves; Indians, as "citizens" of their respective tribes.

Two nineteenth-century cases decided by the Supreme Court exemplify these different logics of exclusion. In *Cherokee Nation v. Georgia* (1831), the Court was asked to determine if tribes, *as foreign governments*, could invoke the Supreme Court's original jurisdiction. Chief Justice John Marshall ultimately determined that they could not, but he also admitted that Indian tribes constituted quasi-sovereign orders of government—"domestic dependent nations"—within the federal system. By virtue of this status, Indian tribes retain all inherent rights to sovereignty except where expressly curtailed or negated by an act of Congress. In stark contrast, the question before the Supreme Court in *Dred Scott v. Sandford* (1857) was whether blacks had legal standing *as individuals*. The Court ruled that because blacks were not citizens, they did not enjoy the privileges and prerogatives of citizenship, which includes the right to file suit in courts of law. To bolster its argument, the *Dred Scott* Court drew an explicit comparison between blacks and Indians:

> The situation of this population [blacks] is altogether unlike that of the Indian race. The latter, it is true, formed no part of the colonial communities, and never amalgamated with them in social connections or in government. But although they were uncivilized, they were yet a free and independent people, associated together in nations or tribes, and governed by their own laws. . . . These Indian Governments were regarded and treated as foreign Governments, as much so as if an ocean had separated the red man from the white. . . . But they may, without doubt, like the subjects of any other foreign Government, be naturalized by the authority of Congress, and

become citizens of a State, and of the United States; and if an individual should leave his nation or tribe, and take up his abode among the white population, he would be entitled to all the rights and privileges which would belong to an emigrant from any other foreign people. (p. 403)

Incivility and barbarism notwithstanding, the status of tribes as separate, independent, and original peoples qualified their members for citizenship in ways that were denied to blacks.

Of course, the federal government did not always have sovereignty-affirming motives at heart when excluding Indian tribes. The Indian Removal Act of 1830, for example, forcibly relocated Indian tribes from the southeastern United States to the "wastelands" west of the Mississippi River in order to make their lands available for white settlement—and also to make room for the hundreds of thousands of slaves that had been imported from Africa (Wolfe 2001). And only twenty-seven years after the *Dred Scott* decision referenced the semi-foreign status of Indian tribes to justify the extension of citizenship to American Indians (and to deny citizenship to African Americans), the Supreme Court used the same reasoning in *Elk v. Wilkins* (1884) to arrive at the opposite conclusion. The petitioner, John Elk, an Indian who had voluntarily left his reservation and renounced his tribal allegiance to live among whites in Nebraska, appealed to the Supreme Court after being denied the right to vote in a local election. The Court found against Elk:

Indians born within the territorial limits of the United States, members of, and owing immediate allegiance to, one of the Indian tribes (an alien, though dependent, power), although in a geographical sense born in the United States, are no more "born in the United States and subject to the jurisdiction thereof," within the meaning of the Fourteenth Amendment, than the children of subjects of any foreign government within the domain of that government, or the children born within the United States, of ambassadors or other public ministers of foreign governments. (p. 102)

Tribal sovereignty was a double-edged sword, one the federal government could wield for or against American Indians as circumstances required.

Minority incorporation policies in the United States underwent superficial change after the Civil War, although substantive continuity with the antebellum period was ultimately preserved. The Thirteenth, Fourteenth, and Fifteenth amendments had freed the slaves, granted them citizenship, and guaranteed their right to vote, yet African Americans continued to endure segregation under state-imposed and federally sanctioned Jim Crow laws. The Supreme Court applied its imprimatur on these "separate-but-equal" legal regimes in its infamous *Plessy v. Ferguson* (1896) ruling.

The federal government's complicity in the segregation of African Americans contrasts with its efforts to integrate Indians into the mainstream polity. The cornerstone of this effort, the General Allotment (Dawes) Act of 1887, provided for the individualization of tribal lands by allotting 40-, 80-, or 160-acre parcels of Indian reservations to tribal members and making the remaining "surplus" lands available for purchase by whites. Allotted Indians then became eligible for citizenship, as did American Indians who served in World War I. Unqualified citizenship was unilaterally extended to Americans Indians under the Indian Citizenship Act of 1924, despite resistance among many tribes (Cornell 1988). The nominal incorporation of Indians into mainstream polity via allotment and enfranchisement served two related purposes: On the one hand, it gave white settlers access to Indian lands; on the other hand, it weakened Indian claims to sovereignty by dismantling tribal societies.

So it was that prior to the civil rights movement, racial policies made it exceedingly "easy" to be black but comparatively difficult to be Indian. In many states, one drop of "black" blood irrevocably qualified a person as black and hence excluded him or her from participating in the mainstream society and polity. At the same time, restrictive blood quantum thresholds of one-quarter or even one-half greatly reduced the number of American Indians who were eligible to receive federal services (thus absolving the government of responsibility) or who shared in the collective ownership of tribal land (thus clearing it for white settlement).

The policy of allotment ended with passage of the Indian Reorganization Act (IRA) in 1934, but not before Indian tribes collectively lost some 165,000 square miles of land (Frantz 1999: 40). As part of an "Indian New Deal," the IRA provided for increased tribal self-government, albeit within a distinctly Western framework: It gave tribes the opportunity to establish democratically elected councils and adopt constitutions modeled after the American system. Many tribes, including the Navajo, opted to retain their traditional systems of governance rather than be co-opted by tribal councils established under the IRA (Cornell 1988: 93).

It took only two decades for the pendulum of federal Indian policy to swing away from support of tribal self-governance and back toward the mandatory integration of American Indians into mainstream society. The civil rights movement of the 1950s provided the backdrop for this policy shift. Premised on what Patrick Wolfe (2001) calls the logic of elimination, the federal government appealed to the rhetoric of equal rights as a pretense for undermining tribal sovereignty. In 1953, Congress adopted House Concurrent Resolution 108 to authorize the "termination" of the federal government's special relationship with Indian tribes by "mak[ing] Indians . . . subject to the same laws and entitled to the same privileges and responsibilities as are applicable to other citizens of the United States" (Prucha 2000: 234). Also in 1953, Congress unilaterally transferred civil and criminal jurisdiction over selected tribes to state governments. Indians were yet again in danger of losing their distinctive "citizens-plus" status—a status that acknowledges their distinctive rights as members of quasi-sovereign tribal nations, over and above the rights that flow from U.S. citizenship—by becoming merely citizens.[5]

The policy of termination turned out to be short lived but effective. By the mid-1960s, when the practice of terminating Indian tribes ended, more than 100 tribes had lost federal recognition. As a result, Indian tribes and Alaska Native communities in Alaska, California, Minnesota, Nebraska, Oregon, and Wisconsin were placed under the jurisdiction of their respective state governments. These measures formed part of a larger trend then underway in American society, one toward racial integration and civil rights. Only a year after Congress announced its termination policy, in 1954, the Supreme Court pronounced school segregation unconstitutional in *Brown v. Board of Education*. While most black Americans welcomed desegregation, many Indian tribes resisted integration, as it deprived them of their rights to self-government. Frances Svensson (1979), for example, recounts how the Pueblo communities of the American Southwest opposed the extension of civil rights protections to Indians living on reservations, for fear that it would undermine tribal sovereignty. Self-determination, after all, implies less rather than more representation in mainstream society and political institutions (Kymlicka 1995).

The Civil Rights Act of 1964 represented a decisive turning point in government policies toward minorities. Table 5.1 summarizes the dramatic policy inversion that ensued. Prior to 1964, American Indians were coercively assimi-

TABLE 5.1.
Inversion of African American and American Indian incorporation logics, pre– and post–civil rights movement.

Logic of incorporation	Social and legal environment	
	Pre–Civil Rights	*Post–Civil Rights*
Inclusion	American Indians (coerced assimilation)	African Americans (integration)
Exclusion	African Americans (segregation)	American Indians (self-determination)

lated into, and African Americans involuntarily segregated from, mainstream society.[6] The reasons, as noted, were largely strategic: Assimilating Indians freed their lands for white settlement and chipped away at tribal sovereignty, while excluding blacks enlarged the pool of servile labor during the antebellum era and neutralized the competitive threat of cheap black labor after the Civil War (see Wolfe 2001). These policies were at odds with the prevailing desires of African Americans for equal treatment and of American Indians for recognition of their sovereignty, treaty rights, and land rights. During the 1960s, official policies came into much closer alignment with each group's modal interests. The federal government finally dismantled the legal barriers impeding African Americans' full participation in mainstream society. A concomitant reversal in federal Indian policies gave renewed force to treaty rights and restored Indian tribes that had been terminated to their former self-governing status.

In exercising this renewed right to self-government, however, Indian tribes confronted new restrictions imposed on them by Congress under the Indian Civil Rights Act of 1968. The act, which for the first time extended several constitutional guarantees and protections to tribal members vis-à-vis their respective tribal governments, represented yet another effort to integrate American Indians into the same civil rights framework as other racial minorities. But only a decade later, in 1978, a pair of Supreme Court decisions reaffirmed the inherent sovereignty of Indian tribes. The first decision, in *Santa Clara Pueblo v. Martinez*, protected tribes' sovereign immunity from suit, thereby preventing enforcement of the Indian Civil Rights Act in federal (as opposed to tribal) courts. The second ruling, in *United States v. Wheeler*, upheld the sovereign right of tribal courts to punish crimes independently of the federal government.

Social Dimension: Social Movement Activism

The legal changes just described did not occur in a vacuum, but rather were precipitated by grassroots activism. Here, too, we can discern fundamental differences in the primary claims advanced by African American and American Indian activists. African Americans sought the extension of *civil* rights to individuals previously denied their enjoyment, whereas American Indians demanded the protection of *treaty* rights to which they were entitled as political communities. Two monuments currently in the planning stages or under construction reflect these opposing claims nicely. In a powerful symbol of the struggle by African Americans for equal rights, a planned memorial to Martin Luther King Jr. in Washington, D.C., will feature a statute of the civil rights leader positioned to face the Jefferson Memorial, as though King were calling on Jefferson to make good on the principles of equality expounded in the Declaration of Independence. The Crazy Horse Memorial in the Black Hills of South Dakota, when completed, will convey a much different message. A gigantic carving of the Lakota warrior on horseback will symbolize the struggle to defend his people's autonomy against encroachments by the very army once commanded by each of the men adorning nearby Mount Rushmore.

Many of the tactics invented or employed by African Americans during the civil rights movement were later adopted by Indian activists, but for markedly different purposes. For example, the sit-ins at segregated lunch counters that drew attention to the demands of blacks for integration would inspire Indian "fish-ins" in the Pacific Northwest that spotlighted violations of tribes' treaty-protected fishing rights (Nagel 1996: 161–162). The nineteen-month takeover of Alcatraz Island between November 1968 and June 1971 and the occupation of BIA headquarters in Washington, D.C., in 1972 were somewhat more direct and confrontational manifestations of the sit-in tactic. Similarly, the March on Washington in 1963 was later adopted by Indian activists in the "Trail of Broken Treaties" caravan to the nation's capital in 1972.

Red Power formed the very core of Indian activism during the late 1960s and early 1970s. Indians wanted their treaty rights honored, their nation-to-nation relationships with the federal government restored, and their distinctive legal status as quasi-sovereign nations recognized. Civil rights alone, premised as they are on the right of individuals to be treated equally as individuals, did not satisfy these group-based claims for autonomy. In contrast, the separatist thrust of Black Power constituted a radical flank to a movement that sought desegregation and nondiscrimination—in a word, inclusion. Proposals by black nationalists to establish racially separate institutions, including black universities, were rejected in favor of integrating African Americans into existing institutions (Rojas 2007). The Black Power movement ultimately failed because its call for blacks to separate from mainstream American society *as a group* did not resonate with the idea that blacks should be integrated into American society *as individuals* (McAdam 1999: 210).

TCUs were a direct outgrowth of Red Power, and of demands by American Indian leaders for increased control over the education of Indian youth. HBCUs, of course, antedated the civil rights movement; in fact, they, together with black churches and social movement organizations, served as mobilizing structures for the movement (McAdam 1999). Ironically, the demands of black activists for desegregation may have undermined the legitimacy of HBCUs, a paradox to which I now turn.

INCORPORATION REGIMES AND MINORITY-SERVING COLLEGES

These contradictory patterns of black and Indian political incorporation had a powerful effect on minority education policies in general and the rise of minority-serving colleges in particular. When African Americans were excluded from mainstream institutions, separate schools and colleges emerged to fill the void. And when African Americans were finally given the right to attend mainstream schools, the number of separate schools—including colleges—that had accommodated them during the segregationist era began to decline. Schooling assumed a similar incorporative function for American Indians, but with a twist: Integration into mainstream schools formed part of a concerted assault on tribal cultures and sovereignty throughout the nineteenth century and into the twentieth century, whereas tribally controlled schools and colleges established since the 1960s reincorporate American Indian students into their respective tribal societies and the wider American Indian community. As with policies of minority-group incorporation in general, the Civil Rights Act of 1964 proved to be a watershed in the history of minority education.

Education Policies during the Pre–Civil Rights Era

The emergence and expansion of black colleges reflected the imperatives of a segregated society. The earliest HBCUs emerged in northern states during the antebellum era, when laws in force throughout the South prohibited blacks from attending college. The number of HBCUs spiked following the Civil War, after the postbellum constitutional amendments granted citizenship—and, hence, the right to attend college—to African Americans. Rather than admit blacks to "white" institutions, however, most southern and border states opted to establish separate colleges under legal regimes that forbade black and white students from attending the same schools. Kentucky's Day Law of 1904, for example, decreed it "unlawful for any person, corporation, or association of persons to maintain or operate any college, school, or institution where persons of the white and negro races are both received as pupils for instruction." The federal government was complicit in the injustices perpetrated on African Americans. The Supreme Court upheld the prerogative of states to maintain racially segregated colleges in *Berea College v. Kentucky* (1908), and Congress institutionalized segregated higher education in 1890, when the Second Morrill Act compelled states with dual systems to establish land-grant colleges for blacks as well as whites. Nineteen HBCUs were established as a result.

Notwithstanding the 1890 mandate to fund public higher education for African Americans and the infamous "separate-but-equal" doctrine promulgated in *Plessy v. Ferguson* six years later, lack of adequate funding ensured that all but a select few black colleges remained inferior to their all-white counterparts. According to a government review of "Negro education" in 1917, "though a large number of the schools for colored people are called 'colleges' and even 'universities,' there are very few institutions that have equipment for college work or pupils prepared to study college subjects. . . . Only three institutions—Howard University, Fisk University, and Meharry Medical College—have student body, teaching force, equipment, and income sufficient to warrant the characterization of 'college'" (U.S. Department of the Interior 1917: 16–17). It was not until 1928 that most HBCUs abandoned primary and secondary curricula in favor of college-level instruction, in part because the Supreme Court had begun to apply the *Plessy* decision more forcefully. In *Missouri ex. rel. Gaines v. Canada* (1938), for example, the Court ruled that states did not satisfy their duty to educate black citizens under the Fourteenth

Amendment's Equal Protection Clause by awarding scholarships to attend out-of-state schools. States without separate facilities for blacks were therefore obligated to admit qualified black applicants to predominantly white institutions. Despite the progressive veneer of the *Gaines* verdict, the legacy of Jim Crow remained intact. Law professor Gil Kujovich (1987: 118) notes that "although the *Gaines* Court raised the ante for segregation, it did not end the game." Indeed, "when threatened with the enrollment of black students in their white institutions, nearly all of the [southern] states elected to pay the rising price of segregation" (Kujovich 1987: 117).

While Congress, the Supreme Court, and state legislatures were busy keeping African Americans out of white schools, Indian children were being sent to boarding schools and coercively assimilated into white society. Throughout much of the nineteenth century, churches and missionary societies established schools with the intent of "civilizing" the Indian savages by teaching them Christianity and the rudiments of agriculture or vocational trades. The aptly named Civilization Fund Act of 1819 awarded congressional subsidies for this purpose. When the federal government stopped subsidizing religious education for Indians in the late 1800s due to concerns over the separation of church and state, it established its own facilities. At boarding schools such as Carlisle Indian Industrial School and the Hampton Institute, Indian children were separated from their families and communities, "indoctrinated" with Euro-American cultural values, and then injected into mainstream American society. Later policies, beginning with the Johnson-O'Malley Act of 1934, streamlined the integration of Indian students directly into public education systems.[7]

All the same, the federal government expressed very little interest in supporting higher education among American Indians. As far as it was concerned, a vocational course of study terminating in a high school diploma was sufficient for Indian students to assume their "proper" roles in American society. Only two higher education institutions established specifically to serve American Indian students—one private college and one public university—emerged during the nineteenth century (Carney 1999). The first, Bacone College, was founded by Baptist missionaries in 1880 in Muskogee, Oklahoma. The college, known simply as "Indian University" until 1910, catered specifically but never exclusively to American Indian students. Nevertheless, unlike the failed colonial experiments in Indian higher education such as Dartmouth College—which, despite its original charter to educate Indians, was never a predominantly Indian school (Oppelt 1990)—American Indians have constituted a majority of enrollments at Bacone College throughout most of its history (Carney 1999). Indian students were drawn to the school's "holistic view of education . . . in keeping with Native American philosophy" (Carney 1999: 83). Today the college emphasizes that

> all students, regardless of race, color, national origin, sex, age or religion are welcomed and encouraged to attend Bacone College. Throughout its history, the College has attracted Indian and non-Indian students. Bacone attempts to prepare students to function in the mainstream of society, without losing their culture and heritage. (Bacone College 2008a)

Bacone College currently enrolls a roughly equal proportion of American Indian and white students, although the institution continues to use the curriculum as a vehicle for expressing "the voice and culture of American Indians" and also to promote "knowledge of Christian values and perspectives" (Bacone College 2008b).

Only seven years after Bacone College was founded, the North Carolina General Assembly established Pembroke State University in 1887 as the Croatan Normal School in Pembroke, North Carolina. The university, known today as the University of North Carolina at Pembroke, is the only higher education institution for American Indians established by a state government. Although originally created to serve members of the Lumbee/Croatan tribe, which enjoys state but not federal recognition, Pembroke began enrolling American Indians regardless of tribal affiliation in 1945. Admission was extended to all students regardless of race in 1955—a change made in compliance with the previous year's ruling in *Brown v. Board of Education*—and Pembroke subsequently became a predominantly white institution.[8] Yet even when Pembroke was a majority Indian school, its "emphasis on providing a typical college curriculum" meant that "Indian culture has never played a primary role in the institution" (Carney 1999: 91).

In many respects, Pembroke State University and especially Bacone College may be seen as precursors to tribal colleges. Both schools offered collegiate-level instruction to American Indian students when other higher education institutions would not, although only Bacone College made a point of incorporating American Indian perspectives and sensibilities into the curriculum.

But Indian control of culturally relevant colleges would have to wait until the late 1960s and early 1970s, with the establishment of the first tribally chartered community colleges.

The Post–Civil Rights Policy Inversion

Race-based education policies in the United States changed dramatically in the mid-twentieth century. The logic of racial integration meant that African Americans were entitled, indeed obligated, to attend white schools, while the logic of tribal self-determination empowered Indians to take control of their own educational institutions.

Education served as the first legal battleground of the civil rights movement. A series of Supreme Court decisions at mid-century rendered school segregation unconstitutional, beginning with three cases that struck down the separation of black and white students in public law schools—*Sipuel v. Board of Regents of the University of Oklahoma* (1948), *McLaurin v. Oklahoma State Regents* (1950), and *Sweatt v. Painter* (1950). A few years later, *Brown* overturned the separate-but-equal doctrine as it applied to primary and secondary education. In 1968, the Supreme Court formulated its "just schools" standard in *Green v. School Board of New Kent County*, requiring local school boards "to convert promptly to a system without a 'white' school or a 'Negro' school, but just schools" (p. 442).[9] The *Green* ruling was later paraphrased in *Norris v. State Council of Education* (1971), in which a U.S. district court mandated the state of Virginia to "convert its white colleges and black colleges into just colleges" (p. 1373). And in *Adams v. Richardson* (1973), a federal circuit court ordered ten states to desegregate their public higher education systems.

HBCUs have since been criticized for outliving their raison d'être—to provide higher education to individuals legally prohibited from enrolling in segregated institutions—and even for perpetuating Jim Crow segregation. Questions regarding the legitimacy of publicly funded HBCUs came to a head in 1992, when the Supreme Court's ruling in *United States v. Fordice* concluded that Mississippi's system of predominantly white and historically black public universities violated the Fourteenth Amendment and the provisions of the Civil Rights Act of 1964 that prohibit racial discrimination in federally funded programs. In particular, *Fordice* held that the maintenance of higher admissions standards at predominantly white universities, the existence of widespread duplication of nonessential curricular programs between white and black institutions, and the limited institutional missions of black colleges were all traceable to the de jure segregated system.

Although the *Fordice* Court offered no concrete recommendations or remedies for black colleges, it posited that "one or more of them [might] be practicably closed or merged with other existing institutions" (*United States v. Fordice* 1992: 742). As discussed at the beginning of this chapter, recent developments in Georgia and Mississippi would seem to indicate that the elimination of black colleges through closures or mergers remains a viable policy option. Such mergers are not without precedent. In 1979, a federal circuit court ordered the University of Tennessee at Nashville, a predominantly white campus, to merge with Tennessee State University, a historically black institution also located in Nashville. The ruling, handed down in *Geier v. University of Tennessee*, cited the need to eliminate all remaining vestiges of the state's segregated higher education system by encouraging white students to attend HBCUs. The court reasoned that the existence of two institutions in such close proximity would impede integration efforts. In effect, the decisions rendered in *Geier* and *Fordice* extended the Supreme Court's landmark ruling in *Brown* to the realm of higher education (Brown 2001; Samuels 2004; Stefkovich and Leas 1994; Strasser 2000). Not only did public elementary and secondary schools have an affirmative duty to desegregate; now public colleges and universities, absent sound educational reasons to the contrary, did as well.

Nor are these integrationist imperatives felt only at HBCUs. In many ways, the history and development of women's colleges mirrors that of HBCUs. Women's and black colleges experienced analogous patterns of expansion and decline over time, propelled by a similar logic of segregation and integration. The first women's college, Georgia Female College (now Wesleyan College), was established in 1836 (Harwarth, Maline, and DeBra 1997: 17), only a year before the first HBCU opened. As with African Americans, women were generally barred from enrolling in "mainstream"—that is, white and male—colleges, thus necessitating the establishment of separate colleges.[10] And as with HBCUs, women's colleges were profoundly affected by the social, political, and legal changes of the mid-twentieth century. A combination of mergers, closures, and mission changes greatly reduced the number of women's colleges, from 233 in 1960 to fewer than sixty today (Miller-Bernal and Poulson 2006). Litigation constituted one factor in this decline. In 1982, the Supreme Court ruled in

Mississippi University for Women v. Hogan that the exclusion of male students from a state-supported women's college violated the Fourteenth Amendment's Equal Protection Clause. The *Hogan* decision was reminiscent of earlier rulings on racial segregation that mandated the integration of black colleges.

Whereas the post-1964 legal and jurisprudential emphasis on integration put an end to the establishment of additional black (and women's) colleges and raised questions about the constitutionality of those that remained, tribally controlled colleges first emerged during the late 1960s and expanded rapidly thereafter. But more than that, tribal colleges have adopted ostensibly race-based admission policies that would almost certainly be condemned as discriminatory if undertaken by black colleges. Although most TCUs maintain the same open-door policies as community colleges, some explicitly favor Indian applicants. Navajo Community College originally granted admissions priority first to Navajos living on the reservation, and then to non-Navajo reservation residents, American Indians in general, and non-Indian applicants (Navajo Community College 1977: 14). The three federally chartered tribal colleges restrict enrollment to tribal members or to individuals who can document at least one-quarter Indian blood quantum. Still other TCUs charge different tuition rates based on a student's tribal or Indian status. At Salish Kootenai College in Pablo, Montana, members of a federally recognized tribe paid $693 to carry a full credit load, whereas individuals documenting American Indian lineage to the second generation paid $859 and non-Indian residents paid $1,082 (see Table 5.2). It is difficult to imagine Congress requiring applicants to Howard University, a federally chartered historically black institution, to document their African American ancestry before enrolling. It is likewise difficult to contemplate that any HBCU, whether federally chartered or not, would charge African American and white students different tuition rates.

Why have TCUs been insulated from the legal maelstrom plaguing HBCUs? And why are race-based enrollment and tuition policies acceptable for TCUs but unthinkable for HBCUs? First off, tribal colleges were established after the era of de jure segregation, so they cannot be condemned as historical remnants of the dual system. TCUs are therefore protected from the letter of the law as handed down in *Fordice*. But what about the spirit of the law as embodied in *Brown*, that segregation is inherently unequal and hence unconstitutional?

Arguing that one class of minority-serving institutions suffers a legitimacy crisis where another does not simply because they were established on

TABLE 5.2.
Tuition costs, Salish Kootenai College, 2002–03.

Credit hours	*American Indian*	*Indian descent*	*Non-Indian resident*	*Non-Indian nonresident*
1	$58	$71	$90	$243
2	116	143	181	485
3	173	215	270	728
4	231	287	360	970
5	289	358	450	1,213
6	347	429	541	1,455
7	404	501	631	1,698
8	462	573	720	1,940
9	520	645	811	2,183
10	578	716	901	2,426
11	635	788	991	2,668
12–18	693	859	1,082	2,911

SOURCE: Salish Kootenai College (2001: 21).

Notes: "American Indian" = enrolled member of a federally recognized tribe; "Indian descent" = an individual with documentation proving lineage to the second generation; "resident" = individual who resides on the Flathead Indian Reservation.

opposite sides of the Civil Rights Act fails to take the analysis far enough. More importantly, Indians possess moral and legal claims to "segregation" that other minority groups lack. As with integration more generally, educational integration means different things for different groups. According to Kymlicka (1995: 60),

Integrated education for the Indians, like segregated education for the blacks, is a "badge of inferiority" for it fails "to recognize the importance and validity of the Indian community." In fact, the integration of Indian children in white-dominated schools had the same negative educational and emotional effects which segregation was held to have in *Brown*. The "underlying principle" which struck down the segregation of blacks—namely, that racial classifications harmful to a minority are prohibited—should also strike down legislated integration of Indians.[11]

For American Indians, separation does not create an invidious *racial* distinction but rather derives from the sovereign right of tribes as *political* groups to administer their own affairs—a right that is grounded in the law of nations (as discussed in Chapter One) and in treaties concluded with the federal government.[12]

It is no accident of history that Congress passed the Tribally Controlled Community College and University Assistance Act the same year the Supreme Court decided the aforementioned *Martinez* and *Wheeler* cases, in 1978. Federal support of tribal colleges was closely tied to the shift in federal Indian policy from termination, which sought to end the special government-to-government relationship between tribes and the federal government, to self-determination, which reaffirmed tribal sovereignty and treaty rights. Indian control of higher education, as a product of this policy shift, both indicates and facilitates tribal sovereignty. Tribal sovereignty entails the authority to establish and control separate institutions (Rosenfelt 1973). In turn, TCUs provide Indians with the tools necessary for shaping their independent political, cultural, and economic destinies.

The Implications of Tribal Sovereignty for Control of Education

American Indians exercise rights as individuals *and* as members of corporate groups—tribes—invested with sovereignty, but African Americans have legal standing only as individuals in the American polity. The civil rights movement and ensuing legislative victories did not bestow special rights on blacks; they simply extended existing rights to a class of individuals historically deprived of their full enjoyment. Conversely, as sovereign entities, tribes exercise powers not enjoyed by other minority groups. One such power is the group-based right to establish and control important social institutions such as schools. Tribal sovereignty bestows a compelling claim to community control of education, one that insulates them from charges of racial favoritism or segregation.

In addition to these positive claims to community control, tribal control of education also depends on the exclusion of American Indians from key provisions in civil rights legislation. Members of Indian tribes, for example, are exempted from Title VI of the 1964 Civil Rights Act, which prohibits discrimination in federally assisted programs. Executive Order 13160 of June 23, 2000, asserts that "discrimination on the basis of race, sex, color, national origin, disability, religion, race, sexual orientation, and status as a parent will be prohibited in Federally conducted education and training programs," but further specifies that the "order does not apply to ceremonial or similar education or training programs or activities of schools conducted by the Department of the Interior, Bureau of Indian Affairs, that are culturally relevant to the [Indian] children represented in the school" (Clinton 2000). Furthermore, according to Chapter 43 of the Code of Federal Regulations, "an individual shall not be deemed subjected to discrimination by reason of his exclusion from the benefits of a program which, in accordance with Federal law, is limited to Indians."

These exemptions have far-reaching implications for minority control of education. The federal government, in discharging its government-to-government obligation to promote tribal self-determination, does not violate antidiscrimination laws by funding TCUs. Daniel Rosenfelt (1973: 544) argues that "because of their historical relationship with the federal government, Indians occupy a unique position under the fourteenth amendment. Consequently, there are circumstances which will justify, or even require, a departure for the general rule." This unique position extends to the realm of education: "Where educational programs on the reservations are administered by Indian tribes, by tribally chartered corporations, the application of ordinary civil rights standards [are] modified to accommodate the constitutional policy of tribal sovereignty" (Rosenfelt 1973: 543). Tribal colleges are therefore buffered from accusations of segregation.[13]

In contrast, public funding for HBCUs became increasingly suspect since 1964. By providing assistance to historically black institutions, state and federal governments have been accused of supporting continued racial segregation. Unlike Indian tribes, African Americans do not have access to the kinds of legal and political claims designed to protect their institutions from such allegations. They instead rely on liberal or cultural claims in support of HBCUs. The most common of these claims, school choice and multiculturalism, provide rather weak justifications for minority control of educational institutions (Davies 1999; Olneck 1993). The Supreme Court has invalidated programs that allowed parents and pupils to select their own schools in cases where their aggregate choices resulted in persistent segregation (*Green v. School Board of New Kent County* 1968). States for which segregation continues to be a problem are therefore prohibited from hiding behind the veil of individual choice or "benign neglect." For its part, multiculturalism typically supports the creation of all-inclusive schools, rather than the more radical aim of establishing separate or "ethnocentric" schools (Cole 2006; Davies 1999). Multicultural frames therefore have a co-opting effect. As Patrick Wolfe (2001: 874) put it, minority groups that employ this rhetoric become simply "another tile in the multicultural mosaic." Stronger cultural claims arguing for separation, like Afrocentrism (Binder 2002), have proven much less successful, as they contradict liberal norms and values.

CONCLUSION

Although HBCUs and TCUs are both committed to educating historically disadvantaged minorities, their differences are many. HBCUs emerged entirely before 1965 in a racially segregated society, to provide educational access to a class of individuals otherwise forbidden to attend college. Tribal colleges, in contrast, are a comparatively recent development in American education. The first tribally chartered college was established only in 1968—four years after the Civil Rights Act prohibited the establishment of additional black colleges. As products of the policy shift toward Indian self-determination, TCUs emerged both as an expression of tribal sovereignty and as a vehicle for reinvigorating cultures that until recently were subjected to government-sponsored assimilation programs.

The history of minority-serving postsecondary education in the United States draws attention to the dynamic quality of cultural and institutional logics. In particular, it demonstrates that multiple and sometimes contradictory logics can coexist in the same institutional environment (Friedland and Alford 1991). Prior to the revolution in race relations during the mid-twentieth century, African Americans were legally segregated from mainstream schools at the same time that American Indians were coercively integrated into them. The Civil Rights Act of 1964 transposed these policy logics, so that tribally controlled colleges and universities emerged precisely when colleges and universities for African American students declined in numbers and also in legitimacy. Institutional logics, moreover, have a "polysemic" quality (Sewell 1992) inasmuch as their meanings differ over time and for different groups. Depending on the minority group targeted, inclusion can entail either the promise of equality or the specter of assimilation, and exclusion can alternately reinforce racial segregation or support political self-determination.

Civil rights legislation and litigation produced dramatic and rather discontinuous changes in the field of minority education, although these changes had contradictory effects on HBCUs and TCUs. Historically black and tribally controlled institutions operate according to distinct sets of institutional logics that make them differentially successful at managing environmental pressures, mitigating threats to legitimacy, or justifying "segregation." Tribal claims to community control of education are firmly grounded in their special quasi-sovereign status and government-to-government relationship with the federal government. African Americans, on the other hand, do not have access to compelling legal claims for community control. Indeed, the existence of separate colleges for black students is frequently denounced as a persistent form of segregation.

The institutional missions of HBCUs and TCUs were shaped by, and continue to reflect, the mode of incorporation that prevailed at the time each form emerged (Stinchcombe 1965). Even from the beginning, HBCUs deemphasized their role as "black" institutions. Lincoln University of Pennsylvania, established in 1854, acknowledges that it "was the first institution founded anywhere in the world to provide a higher education in the arts and sciences for 'youth of African descent,'" but underscores that "since its inception, Lincoln has attracted an interracial and international enrollment" (2002: 3). Likewise, Fisk University, incorporated in 1867, sought to measure itself by "the highest standards, not of Negro [*sic*] education, but of American education at its best" (2002: 7). These statements reflect deeply conventional and integrationist missions.

Tribal colleges were established under much different social, political, and cultural dynamics. TCUs sprang out of the Red Power movement, when Indians were asserting their independence from white society. Some colleges, such as Oglala Lakota College (2002: 6), situate their emergence in this explicitly political context: "With the advent of efforts to extend tribal sovereignty by American Indians . . . came a recognition by Lakotas that control of education is also the control of its destiny. On March 4, 1971, the Oglala Sioux Tribal Council exercised its sovereignty by chartering the Lakota Higher Education Center," the precursor to Oglala Lakota College. Other tribal colleges emphasize their cultural—and curricular—distinctiveness. Turtle Mountain Community College (2000: 7) in Belcourt, North Dakota, is committed to "creat[ing] an environment in which the cultural and social heritage of the Turtle Mountain Band of Chippewa can be brought to bear throughout the curriculum." These statements offer a glimpse into how the different political, legal, and social environments in which HBCUs and TCUs emerged have shaped the kinds of curricula they offer. This aspect of minority-serving colleges and universities—the extent to which their curricula incorporate culturally and ethnically distinctive content—is the focus of the next and final empirical chapter.

CHAPTER SIX

ETHNOCENTRIC CURRICULA AND THE POLITICS OF DIFFERENCE

All things in the world are two. In our minds we are two—good and evil. With our eyes we see two things—things that are fair and things that are ugly. . . . We have the right hand that strikes and makes for evil, and the left hand full of kindness, near the heart. One foot may lead us to an evil way, the other foot may lead us to good. So are all things two, all two.

Letakots-Lesa (Eagle Chief), Pawnee, late nineteenth century

A CURIOUS DUALITY CHARACTERIZES minority-serving colleges and universities.[1] On the one hand, they are deeply rooted in the history, traditions, and culture of the minority groups they serve. On the other hand, they adopt the same institutional models and curricular frameworks as "mainstream" degree-granting institutions. In this respect, they epitomize hybrid organizations "composed of two or more types that would not normally be expected to go together" (Albert and Whetten 1985: 270). TCUs and HBCUs strike a balance between these centrifugal tendencies in very different proportions, however, due in large measure to the unique conditions of their historical emergence and development.

The statement of philosophy in Navajo Community College's *General Catalog 1977–1978* suggests that tribal colleges approach the tension between tradition and modernity with a sense of pragmatic optimism:

> Today, more than ever before, the young Navajo adult is faced with the challenge and the opportunity of dealing with two worlds, the traditional and the modern. Both will remain with him, and he must be capable within both. (Navajo Community College 1977: 10)

A more recent statement declares that the college's "curriculum and services will integrate the traditional values of the Dine [Navajo] language and culture with contemporary educational mandates" (Navajo Community College 1994: 8). Students are taught to navigate between the Navajo and the white "worlds," but each remains distinct and independent. Euro-American hegemony and the onslaught of modernity, to be sure, are realities to which contemporary Indians much adjust, but indigenous traditions and cultures remain enduring components of the tribal college identity.

The outlook for black Americans, articulated most eloquently by W. E. B. Du Bois ([1903] 1989: 5) in *The Souls of Black Folk*, is much more pessimistic. Their duality is experienced as a perpetual conflict, a battle between diametrically opposing selves:

> One ever feels his twoness,—an American, a Negro; two souls, two thoughts, two unreconciled strivings; two warring ideals in one dark body, whose dogged strength alone keeps it from being torn asunder. . . . He would not Africanize America, for America has too much to teach the world and Africa. He would not bleach his Negro soul in a flood of white Americanism, for he knows that Negro blood has a message for the world.

Integrationist policies adopted some fifty years after Du Bois wrote these words did little to alleviate the sense of anxiety he conveyed. Albert Samuels (2004: 177) points out that "many blacks see integration as" an all-or-nothing enterprise, "a one-way street that requires them to surrender their cultural distinctiveness while receiving little in return." Blackness and whiteness, in this view, are mutually exclusive and hence cannot coexist, whether in "one dark body" or one organizational model.

One way these dualities play out at minority-serving colleges and universities is in the curriculum. This chapter presents evidence that TCUs incorporate distinctively "American Indian" traditions and worldviews into the formal curriculum much more extensively than HBCUs incorporate "African American" content or perspectives. I attribute this difference to the exceptional quasi-sovereign status of Indian tribes, which invests them with the authority to establish and control their own colleges and, by extension, to infuse curricula with their own cultural sensibilities. If indigenous peoples' control of independent postsecondary institutions flows from their sovereign status, sovereignty also bestows the authority to define, within certain bounds, the contours of knowledge itself. The special legal status of Indian tribes relative to other minority groups empowers them to resist—at least partially—exogenous pressures that compel colleges and universities to adopt similar kinds of curricula.

ACCOUNTING FOR CURRICULAR DISTINCTIVENESS

My approach is grounded in an open-systems organizational perspective that draws attention to "the external context as a basis for explaining internal features of organizations" (Scott and Meyer 1994: 137). I focus in particular on the institutional, political, and legal forces that shape the composition of formal curricula at TCUs and HBCUs. As with other colleges and universities, minority-serving institutions depend on external constituents for material and moral support. They are beholden to governments, tuition-paying students, alumni, foundations, and other donors for financial resources, and to accrediting agencies for certification. In addition, minority-serving colleges are also sensitive to policy changes affecting the groups they serve. Tribal sovereignty, I contend, has buffered TCUs from powerful forces operating within the field of higher education to produce curricular isomorphism or homogeneity.

The Dynamics of Curricular Convergence and Divergence

Numerous studies have documented the convergence of school curricula at all levels—primary, secondary, and tertiary—around increasingly standardized national and global models (Frank et al. 1994, 2000; Kamens, Meyer, and Benavot 1996; Meyer, Kamens, and Benavot 1992). Although nation-specific historical legacies sometimes produce distinctive curricular permutations (Ramirez and Meyer 2002), cases of "enduring exceptionalism" (Kamens 1992) are rare and generally deemed illegitimate. In fact, some scholars have suggested that curricular standardization actually precipitates the annihilation of minority cultures. "Our period," concluded Benavot and colleagues (1991: 98), "is one in which local and primordial cultures are undergoing wholesale destruction, in part as a result of mass education."

Such a view now seems misguided or shortsighted. Far from being destroyed, the cultures and worldviews of historically marginalized groups are now prominently represented in schooled knowledge. The celebration of diversity—multiculturalism—is an increasingly standard feature of modern university curricula. Consider, for example, the dramatic rise of women's and ethnic studies programs in the United States and abroad (Champagne and Stauss 2002; Olzak and Kangas 2008; Rojas 2007; Wotipka et al. 2007), the expanded representation of minority groups and non-Western regions in university history curricula (Frank et al. 1994, 2000), and the current vogue of multicultural curricula (Olneck 1993).

What accounts for this sea change away from assimilation and toward multiculturalism? Institutional theorists posit that changes in formal curricula closely track broader transformations in world-cultural models of social reality (McEneaney and Meyer 2000). For example, as the natural world became "disenchanted" and rationalized, scientific disciplines gained prominence relative to the religious canon (Drori et al. 2003; Gabler and Frank 2005; Frank and Gabler 2006). So it is, too, with the disenchantment of the nation: After World War II, the histories of subnational groups and world history began to challenge the primacy of grand nationalistic narratives in university curricula (Frank et al. 2000). The incorporation of previously neglected worldviews into formal curricula reflects improvements over the past half-century in the moral, social, and legal status of minority groups, and parallels their integration into mainstream society—including "common" schools and mainstream universities—more generally.

With so much evidence documenting curricular convergence, cases that depart fundamentally from standardized frameworks are often overlooked. Researchers analyzing deviant cases typically credit powerful geopolitical forces, usually civilizational or ideological in nature and transnational in scope, with producing isolated curricular anomalies (Kamens 1992; Ramirez and Meyer 2002). Islamic curricular models, for example, retain much of their distinctiveness, but this should not be too surprising. Islam, after all, counts over one billion adherents, and Muslim clerics control or influence the state apparatus in a number of countries. Oil revenues also afford some Islamic countries the resources needed to support unique curricula. Likewise, the former Soviet Union deviated from global instructional emphases, producing a uniquely "communist" vision of the curriculum. Superpower exceptionalism of this sort is not unexpected.

Tribally controlled colleges and universities present a case of curricular distinctiveness on a much smaller and hence more perplexing scale. As an impoverished minority group amounting to less than 2 percent of the U.S. population, American Indians are, by most accounts, powerless to effect changes in deeply entrenched curricular models. Moreover, colleges and universities serving African Americans—a much larger, geographically concentrated, and hence more powerful constituency by conventional standards—are much less likely than tribal colleges to incorporate culturally and ethnically distinctive curricular content. The ability of American Indians to establish independent colleges that emphasize their unique perspectives is therefore quite remarkable. To understand why, we must recognize that American Indians wield much more political authority than simple demographics would imply.

Bending the Bars of the Iron Cage

Tribal sovereignty plays a central role in the efforts of Indian tribes to develop and implement culturally distinctive curricula at their own colleges and universities. African Americans, who lack sovereignty, have been much less successful at doing so. This crucial difference reflects the kinds of political claims available to American Indians and African Americans. Some claims, derived from the logics of self-determination, support the establishment of culturally distinctive institutions; other claims, rooted on the imperatives of integration, do not.

By virtue of their precontact sovereignty under international law (as discussed in Chapter One) and their status as quasi-sovereign nations under domestic law (as discussed in Chapters Three and Five), tribal communities advance compelling legal claims to self-determination. In turn, this quasi-sovereign status supports the establishment of independent social and political institutions, including separate colleges. The very title of the Indian Self-Determination and Education Assistance Act, enacted by Congress in 1975 to promote greater tribal participation in federal programs affecting Indians, expressly recognizes the direct relationship between education and self-determination.

Demands by African Americans for collective self-determination, by contrast, are exceedingly weak or nonexistent. Black nationalism existed on the radical fringe of a social movement otherwise intent on securing integration and equal rights. Absent sovereignty, African Americans advance liberal claims emanating from the Constitution—equality under the law, fair treatment, and the like—that provide only a feeble justification for minority control of separate colleges and the development of culturally distinctive curricula that such control entails (Olneck 1993; Davies 1999).

The implications of these legal and political differences for curricular programming at tribal and historically black colleges are profound. The same quasi-sovereign status that authorizes Indian tribes to establish and control separate colleges in the post–civil rights era also empowers them to develop ethnically and culturally distinctive curricula. Their legal claims support what Walter Feinberg (1998: 19) calls "separatism," the principle that "groups should form their own separate educational institutions and use them to maintain their own distinctive identity." Liberal claims, conversely, find expression in "multicultural" reforms premised on the idea that a diversity of cultures should be equally represented in and valorized by school curricula. "From the multiculturalist standpoint," writes Feinberg (1998: 19), "separatism achieves one important goal of education—the development of cultural affiliation and pride—but it does so at the neglect of another goal—the understanding and recognition of different cultures." Liberal claims support the incorporation of minority cultures and sensibilities, on equal footing with the dominant culture, into the *mainstream* academy, rather than the more radical aim of establishing *separate* schools catering specifically and exclusively to one cultural group.

In this sense, liberal claims and multicultural ideals have a co-opting effect on culturally distinctive curricular content. Identities have become a matter of individual taste and preference, resulting in a form of façade diversity (Boli and Elliott 2008) that produces facile curricular representations of minority perspectives, values, and traditions. Yet the representation of American Indian or tribal perspectives in the curriculum at TCUs amounts to much more than perfunctory multiculturalism. Rather, cultural distinctiveness suffuses tribal colleges, and it is core to their institutional missions and identities.

ETHNOCENTRISM IN THE CURRICULUM

Multiculturalism stands in opposition to "ethnocentrism," a curricular orientation in which "the experiences and perspectives, the culture, and the identity of a particular group are centered as the point of reference and development" (Olneck 1993: 246). Ethnocentrism differs from multiculturalism in its focus on *one* culture or group to the exclusion of others (without necessarily implying the superiority of that culture or group). Proponents of ethnocentrism call for the complete overhaul of existing curricula and pedagogies to make them relevant to cultural minorities. Ethnocentric curricular models take their inspiration from the Afrocentric approach developed by Molefi Kete Asante (1991: 171), which he defines as "a frame of reference wherein phenomena are viewed from the perspective of the African person." The development and implementation of ethnocentric curricula generally presupposes community control of schools, so that, for example, Afrocentric curricula are taught at black-focused schools but not elsewhere (Olneck 1993). Diversity is therefore accomplished at the systemic rather than the institutional level, with curricula exhibiting between-school but not within-school variation.

Whereas Afrocentrism seeks to place Africa at the center of instruction, "Black Nationalist" curricular orientations focus more narrowly on the experiences of African Americans (Watkins 1993). As with Afrocentrism, the Black Nationalist outlook eschews multiculturalism in favor of an approach to teaching and learning that focuses on African Americans to the exclusion of other racial, ethnic, or cultural groups. Indeed, it forms part of a broader movement that "call[s] for the building of a parallel society," including parallel schools (Watkins 1993: 330). Both the Afrocentric and Black Nationalist perspectives advocate the recentering of curricula around African Americans and their historical, geographical, spiritual, and cultural roots on the African continent. More importantly, both perspectives are rooted in a "separatist" as opposed to an "inclusionary" vision of race relations (Marable and Mullings 1994). For the sake of brevity, I include both curricular models under the broad rubric of "Afrocentrism."

Afrocentrism is a controversial curricular innovation that has failed to find much success in American schools (Binder 2002). Support for Afrocentrism is limited because its basic tenants fail to resonate with wider cultural and political frames that promote integration, equality, and diversity—and also because African Americans lack the kinds of group-based claims to sovereignty that would support ethnocentric curricular innovations. Although debates raged over the particular kind of mission and curricula HBCUs should adopt, Afrocentric or black-focused curricula never garnered serious attention. In one famous debate, Booker T. Washington envisioned a predominantly vocational, technical, and agricultural course of study for black colleges, whereas W. E. B. Du Bois advocated a traditional liberal arts curriculum. The fundamental point, however, is that both models were in some sense "conventional"—neither Washington nor Du Bois assigned HBCUs the role of preserving "black" culture per se.

These debates reflected the historical legacy of HBCUs as parallel institutions. The very logic of the separate-but-equal system generally necessitated some form of curricular replication.[2] Privately controlled black colleges, for example, tended to copy the classical curriculum offered by their white counterparts (Allen and Jewell 2002; Anderson 1988; Drewry and Doermann 2001). To wit: In 1908, Du Bois advised his alma mater to adopt a rigorous curriculum. "Fisk University wants to know what . . . subjects are fittest for a college course—there are in the United States, France, and Germany, hundreds of universities and other institutions of the very highest standing, whose curricula have been matters of thought, study, and development among the best educational philosophers of the world; learn of these and copy their courses and hold their standards" (Du Bois [1908] 2001: 47). In this stunning example of what we would now call mimetic isomorphism (DiMaggio and Powell 1983), Du Bois admonished black colleges—many of which were "colleges" in aspiration only—to model their curricula after the Harvards, Sorbonnes, and Heidelbergs of the world.

Such indiscriminate copying did not go unnoticed. A government report issued in 1917 criticized the tenacity with which some black colleges clung to an antiquated curriculum:

> Th[e] emphasis on ancient languages is greatest in the schools owned and managed by the colored denominations. This devotion to the old rigid curriculum, with Latin four years, Greek two or three years, and mathematics two or three years, is not difficult to explain. The majority of the schools were established at a time when the old curriculum was the current practice. This practice has continued somewhat longer in the South than in other sections of the country and the Negroes naturally adopted the educational forms of their white neighbors." (Department of the Interior 1917: 42)

Late-nineteenth-century Howard University, a case in point, required *matriculating* students to be examined in the following:

> LATIN—Four books of Caesar, five orations of Cicero, six books of Virgil's Æneid, and twelve lessons in Jones' Latin Prose Composition;

> GREEK—Crosby's Lessons, four books of Xenophon's Anabasis, and one book of Homer's Iliad;

ENGLISH—Arithmetic (High School), including the Metric System, Algebra through Quadratic Equations, Plane Geometry, Elements of Physics and Chemistry, Orthography, Grammar, Composition, and Descriptive and Physical Geography. (Howard University 1890: 27)

Tellingly, Howard University did not implement a mandatory "Afro-American" requirement until 1987.

This insistence on the classical curriculum was at once progressive and debilitating. Although such a curriculum was premised on the assumption that black students were fundamentally "educable" and could, in time, overcome the legacies of slavery to complete the same rigorous course of study as white students (Anderson 1988), it was also largely devoid of any attention to the unique history, perspectives, and experiences of African Americans. Instead, "the prominent role of middle-class Whites in the founding of HBCUs often led to the biases of this culturally dominant majority being reflected in the culture and curriculum of these institutions" (Jewell 2002: 16).

The differential efficacy of claims rooted in sovereignty and multiculturalism are readily apparent in contemporary American higher education. It is no mere coincidence that the rise of African American and women's studies departments coincided with the decline of HBCUs and women's colleges. Consistent with the logics of integration and multiculturalism, curricular programs that cater to women and minorities became a proper subject of teaching and research in the mainstream academy during the 1960s (Olzak and Kangas 2008; Rojas 2006; Wotipka et al. 2007), precisely when separate colleges serving women and African Americans—those vestiges of the segregated era—began to close or integrate. Conversely, tribal colleges and American Indian studies programs emerged and expanded in tandem, highlighting the availability of both legal claims supporting the establishment of independent tribally controlled institutions, and multicultural claims advocating the inclusion of American Indian cultures and perspectives—which I refer to generically as "Indiocentric" curricula—into mainstream colleges and universities.

As discussed in the previous chapter, racial integration mandates threaten to undermine the very existence of separate colleges and universities for minority groups. The Civil Rights Act of 1964 prohibited the establishment of additional black colleges, and policies implemented since then have raised questions about the legitimacy of those that remain open. In 1969, for example, "the U.S.

Department of Health, Education, and Welfare (HEW) notified ten states that they were guilty of maintaining dual systems of higher education—one for blacks and one for whites—in violation of Title VI of the Civil Rights Act of 1964" (Samuels 2004: 79).[3] Four years later, in *Adams v. Richardson* (1973), a district court ordered the offending states to implement formulate higher education desegregation plans. More recently, in *United States v. Fordice* (1992), the Supreme Court denounced Mississippi's public HBCUs as remnants of institutionalized segregation. The *Fordice* Court singled out the curriculum as part of the problem. Duplication of curricular programming between historically black and predominantly white colleges, the Court argued, was part and parcel of the "separate but equal" regime. State governments therefore had an "affirmative duty" under the Fourteenth Amendment and the Civil Rights Act to eliminate all remaining distinctions between black and white colleges.

Conversely, tribal sovereignty plays a central role in the efforts of Indian tribes to establish separate colleges and develop culturally distinctive curricula. To be sure, as individual members of racial or ethnic groups, American Indians also reference liberal claims, including the right to enjoy one's cultural heritage, that are available to all Americans. Federal Indian law nevertheless treats "Indians not as a discrete racial group, but, rather, as members of quasi-sovereign tribal entities" (*Morton v. Mancari* 1974: 554). This unique *political* status of Indian tribes exempts tribal colleges (and other tribally controlled schools) from legal prohibitions against *racial* discrimination in federally assisted programs.

To consider the effect of these social, political, legal, and institutional forces on the core activities and identities of minority-serving colleges, I analyze the composition of formal curricula at TCUs and HBCUs. My basic contention is that Indiocentric curricular content at TCUs should be much more prevalent that Afrocentric curricular content at HBCUs, reflecting the different legal claims and legacies of incorporation between these groups.

ANALYZING CURRICULAR ETHNOCENTRISM

I examine the *prevalence of ethnocentric courses* offered at TCUs and HBCUs, defined as the number of undergraduate-level courses that made explicit and exclusive reference to American Indian or African American issues, perspectives, or worldviews. I systematically coded course offerings for a sample of twenty-eight TCUs and thirty-three HBCUs at five-year intervals between 1977 and 2002. I read catalogs and bulletins issued by these institutions for course titles and descriptions, recording (1) the total number of courses offered during a given academic year and, of those courses, (2) the number that referred specifically to American Indian, tribal, black, or African American—that is, to ethnocentric—content.[4] These variables, it is important to note, describe the intended rather than the enacted curriculum. I did not gauge whether classroom activities were faithful to course descriptions, nor do my data address how curricula were designed, approved, or implemented. Measuring and analyzing curricula in this manner nevertheless has several precedents in the research literature (for example, Frank et al. 1994, 2000; Gumport and Snydman 2002) and permits us to examine the ways in which colleges and universities present themselves to internal and external audiences in official publications (that is, course catalogs).

Descriptive Trends

Figure 6.1 plots the overall percentage of ethnocentric courses offered at TCUs and HBCUs between 1977 and 2002. The trends support my basic contention regarding the emphasis on ethnocentrism at tribal and black colleges. On average, 19.5 percent of courses at tribal colleges included ethnocentric content, compared with only 2.5 percent at black colleges.[5] Figure 6.2 presents a more nuanced picture by disaggregating ethnocentric curricula into broad fields of study. For both tribal and black colleges, the proportion of ethnocentric courses is greatest within the arts and humanities; however, the emphasis on ethnocentrism is between five and seven times greater at TCUs relative to HBCUs. On average, 27 percent of humanities courses at tribal colleges focus exclusively on American Indian or tribal perspectives, while only 4 percent of humanities courses at black colleges are classified as Afrocentric.[6] A similar but less pronounced pattern characterizes the social sciences.

Examples of humanities and social science courses with ethnocentric content abound. Alabama State University (1999), for example, offered an array of Afrocentric courses such as Introduction to African American Art, Black Literature, African American History to 1877, Survey of African American Music, and Blacks in the American Political System. Similar courses focusing on American Indians or tribes were also offered at tribal colleges. Students at Oglala Lakota College (2003) could enroll in Indian Art History, Lakota Music and Dance,

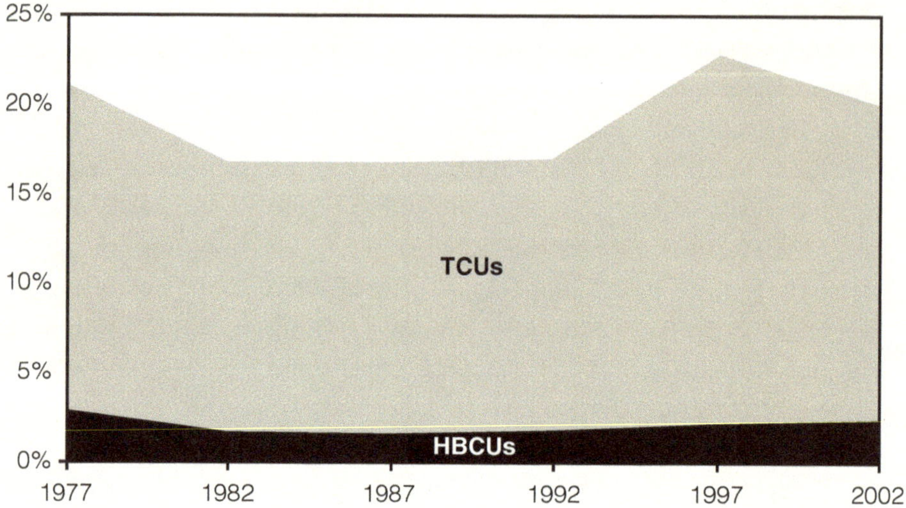

FIGURE 6.1. Ethnocentric courses as a percentage of total courses at TCUs and HBCUs, 1977–2002.

Note: HBCUs = Historically black colleges and universities; TCUs = Tribal colleges and universities.

Lakota History, Indian Law, and Lakota Philosophy. Another tribal college, Bay Mills Community College, offered a tribal literature class but only during the winter term, because stories were traditionally told when there was snow on the ground (AIHEC 1999). Also falling in this category are courses in African or tribal languages. The Department of World Languages and Cultures at Howard University included a four-course sequence in Swahili, while Saginaw Chippewa Tribal College offered instruction in the Ojibwe language.

As "negotiable" disciplines (Binder 2002), the humanities and social sciences have a greater capacity than other fields of study to incorporate ethnocentric coursework. These disciplines afford educators more flexibility to incorporate culturally relevant content, especially relative to disciplines such as mathematics and the natural sciences that are putatively more "objective" and hence more impervious to cultural influences. Nevertheless, a surprising proportion of natural science courses at TCUs includes ethnocentric content—an average of 4 percent over the period. Stone Child College (2002: 71) offered two such courses in 2002. A course in ethnobotany, housed within the biology department, "provides the opportunity to use plants in the traditional way with adherence to

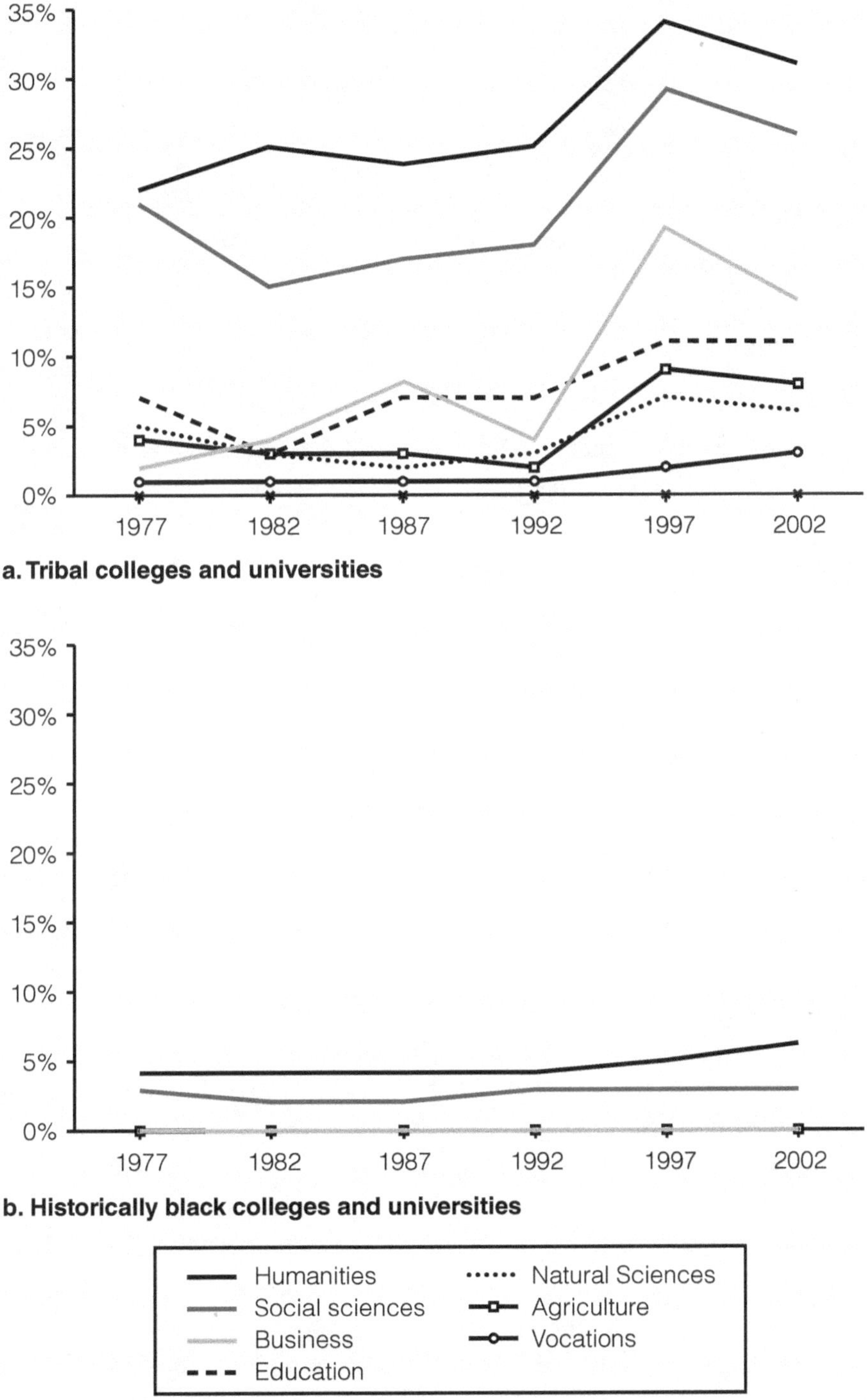

FIGURE 6.2. Percentage of ethnocentric courses per subject area, 1977–2002.

cultural protocol" and "blend[s] the cultural and scientific perspectives." Also at Stone Child College, a course titled "Fundamentals of Physics" resembled a mainstream introductory physics course in nearly every respect—it surveyed mechanics, motion, thermodynamics, magnetism, electricity, and the like—but the description further noted that "Native American understanding [of] these phenomena will be discussed" (p. 92). Similarly, a course in the "Fundamentals of Astronomy" at Diné College (2002: 37) provides a "basic introduction to the planets, solar system and galaxy" but also "relates Navajo stories of creation to the scientific view." Environmental science courses at Diné College integrated "Navajo views of the environment, science, and approaches to environmental problem-solving" (p. 45), and the geology program included "Indigenous Physical Geology," with "an emphasis on the geology of the Navajo Nation and geologic topics of significance to Navajo people" (p. 48). All told, the proportion of *science* courses with Indiocentric content at TCUs was roughly equivalent to the proportion of *humanities* courses with Afrocentric content at HBCUs.

Even the trades provide an opportunity for tribal colleges to incorporate culturally relevant content. A course in construction technology at Blackfeet Community College (1996: 77) "allow[s] students to develop skills in the construction and study of architectural and engineering techniques that were utilized in traditional Blackfeet lodge construction." And the relatively large number of locally tailored business courses at TCUs, especially with the addition of casino operations and tribal business administration programs at several tribal colleges after 1992, reflects their importance in promoting economic development on reservations. I include such courses under the rubric of "ethnocentrism" because they are instrumental to tribal nation building and self-determination projects. As indicated by Leech Lake Tribal College (1997: 38), courses in casino operations constitute a "critical area in the development of the economic and organizational infrastructure of the Reservation and in the ability of the Tribe to realize its desire to practice its sovereignty fully."

Figure 6.3 concludes the descriptive analysis by showing the distribution of courses with ethnocentric content across subject areas, such that the proportions sum to 1 within each observation year. These trends show the extent to which ethnocentric content was concentrated or "compartmentalized" in certain disciplines. Not surprisingly, humanities and social sciences accounted for the largest share of ethnocentric courses, particularly at HBCUs. Still, culture was distributed much more evenly across disciplines at TCUs than

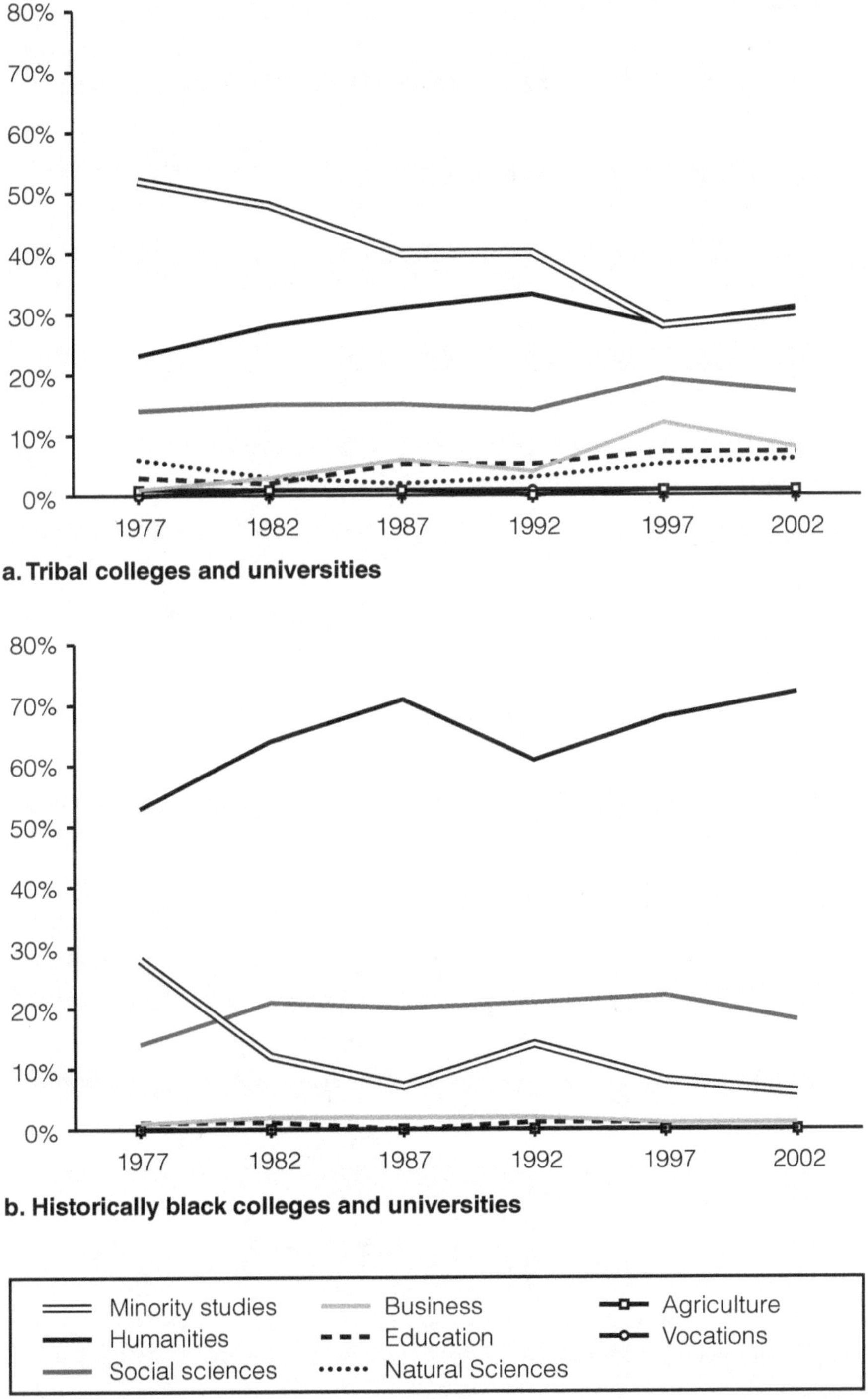

FIGURE 6.3. Distribution of ethnocentric courses across fields of study, 1977–2002.

it was at HBCUs. Afrocentric content at black colleges was overwhelmingly concentrated in arts and humanities programs—well over 50 percent in most years, and up to 72 percent in 1987 and 2002—followed by the social sciences and African American studies programs. In contrast, American Indian studies programs accounted for the largest share of ethnocentric courses at tribal colleges, although this share declined relative to other disciplines over time. As befits a holistic approach to knowledge, indigenous epistemologies are integrated throughout the curriculum rather than compartmentalized into minority studies or humanities programs (Champagne and Stauss 2002). Still, as a share of total courses, ethnic studies programs were much larger at TCUs than at HBCUs. Between 6 and 11 percent of total courses at TCUs were located in American Indian or tribal studies programs, compared with fewer than 1 percent of courses at HBCUs that were located within African American or black studies programs. The relatively low percentage of ethnic studies courses at HBCUs is consistent with prior research, which found that African American or black studies programs are no more prevalent at HBCUs than they are at mainstream colleges or universities (Olzak and Kangas 2008; Rojas 2006).

Multivariate Analysis

To examine these trends in greater detail, I conducted negative-binomial regression analyses that estimate the effect of minority-serving institutional status on the number of courses with ethnocentric content, net of other organizational characteristics.[7] These analyses include an additional sample of thirty mainstream colleges and universities that serve as a comparative baseline and are conducted for two time points, 1992 and 2002.[8] I combined my curricular data with information from the Integrated Postsecondary Educational Data System (U.S. Department of Education 1992, 2002). The resulting data set comprises 177 institution-year observations: eighty-six for 1992 and ninety-one for 2002.

In selecting mainstream institutions for analysis, I oversampled those with above-average African American and American Indian enrollments, as well as those located in the same states as TCUs and HBCUs (primarily in the West, Southwest, Midwest, and South). Geographic proximity controls for any unmeasured effects arising from shared institutional, social, and legal environments. Oversampling mainstream colleges with substantial minority enrollments is designed to isolate the effects of institutional charter (Meyer 1970) and demand-side or consumer-driven processes (Kraatz and Zajak 1996). Charter effects operate if a college's official designation as a minority-serving institution dictates curricular content, independently of enrollment composition. Explanations based on charter effects predict that HBCUs and TCUs, including those few with predominantly white enrollments, will consistently incorporate more ethnocentric content into the curriculum relative to mainstream institutions. Conversely, a market-based approach expects *all* colleges and universities, whether chartered to serve minorities or not, to offer culturally distinctive curricula in proportion to the number of minority students enrolled.

The core variables in the analysis denote whether an institution is a TCU or HBCU. I also examine the composition of student enrollments, to determine whether ethnocentric courses increase as the share of American Indian and African American enrollment increases. Other variables control for a variety of additional organizational characteristics: total number of courses offered; total undergraduate enrollment; and indicators to signify whether a college is publicly or privately controlled, a two- or four-year institution, and accredited or not. Analyses also include a series of regional indicators and a dummy variable for the year 2002, to determine whether ethnocentric content increased relative to 1992.

Table 6.1 displays the results of the multivariate analysis.[9] Positive coefficients indicate that the corresponding variable is associated with a net increase in the number of ethnocentric courses, and negative coefficients denote a net reduction in the number of ethnocentric courses. The baseline model (Model 1) includes only the control variables: total number of courses, undergraduate enrollment, organizational control, observation year, institutional sector, accreditation, institutional age (in years), and region. Model 2 adds minority enrollment variables. The fully specified equation, Model 3, enters the TCU and HBCU dummy variables to gauge the effect of minority-serving institutional charters on ethnocentric curricula, net of minority enrollment and control variables. Finally, Model 4 includes an interaction term to determine whether publicly controlled HBCUs differ from their private counterparts with respect to the prevalence of Afrocentric content in the curriculum.

The effects of three control variables—total number of courses, the year 2002, and the South—were statistically significant in every model. The total number

TABLE 6.1.

Negative binomial regression analyses of the number of ethnocentric courses, 1992 and 2002.

	Models			
Variables	*1*	*2*	*3*	*4*
Control Variables				
Total number of courses	.002*** (.004e–1)	.001*** (.003e–1)	.002*** (.003e–1)	.002*** (.003e–1)
Undergraduate enrollment (in 1,000s)	–.026 (.033)	–.019 (.031)	–.011 (.031)	–.009 (.030)
Community college (1 = yes)	–.257 (.174)	–.317 (.170)	–.170 (.148)	–.247 (.153)
Public control (1 = yes)	.006 (.171)	–.051 (.158)	.075 (.151)	.300 (.172)
Accredited (1 = yes)	.189 (.142)	.167 (.145)	.088 (.123)	.158 (.120)
Age (in years)	–.007* (.003)	.001 (.003)	.004 (.003)	.001 (.003)
Year 2002 (1 = yes)	.314*** (.064)	.254*** (.066)	.220*** (.060)	.222*** (.058)
West (1 = yes)[a]	.013 (.367)	.142 (.272)	.224 (.265)	.243 (.249)
Southwest (1 = yes)[a]	–.196 (.383)	–.191 (.263)	.402 (.304)	.330 (.290)
South (1 = yes)[a]	–1.192*** (.313)	–.832*** (.229)	–.697** (.240)	–.689** (.231)
Enrollment Composition				
% American Indian enrollment		.023*** (.003)	.005 (.004)	.003 (.004)
% African American enrollment		.007* (.003)	.005 (.004)	.003 (.004)
Minority-serving Charters				
TCUs (1 = yes)			2.251*** (.445)	2.228*** (.424)
HBCUs (1 = yes)			.359 (.354)	1.442*** (.436)
HBCUs × Public				–1.305*** (.324)
Intercept	2.834***	.557	.251	.414
Wald χ2 (versus null)	95.70***	187.62***	206.38***	242.86***
df	10	12	14	15
L.R. χ2 (versus previous)	—	36.40***	23.46***	15.84***

Note: Standard error estimates, in parentheses, are adjusted for clustering within institutions. N = 91 colleges, 177 college-year observations.

* $p \le .05$, ** $p \le .01$, *** $p \le .001$ (two-tailed tests).

[a] Relative to a combined Midwest/Mid-Atlantic reference category.

of courses offered at a college or university had a positive but infinitesimal effect on the number of ethnocentric courses offered. This finding indicates that, on average, only a tiny fraction of total courses include ethnocentric content: In precise terms, each additional course offering increased the predicted number of ethnocentric courses by only 0.2 percent.[10] Time was a much more substantial predictor. Based on results from Model 1, sampled institutions offered an estimated 37 percent more ethnocentric courses in 2002 than in 1992. Moreover, colleges and universities in the South offered slightly fewer than one-third as many ethnocentric courses as did institutions located elsewhere in the United States. Although baseline estimates also suggest that the age of an institution slightly reduces the number of ethnocentric courses, the effect disappears in subsequent models.

Model 2 adds the share of full-time American Indian and African American undergraduate student enrollments to the baseline model. Although the minority enrollment variables are statistically significant, their individual effects are neither strong nor robust. Each one-percentage-point increase in the number of American Indian and African American students who are enrolled elevated the predicted number of ethnocentric courses by only 2.3 and 0.7 percent, respectively. Moreover, these effects vanish once the TCU and HBCU dummy variables are entered into Model 3, suggesting that minority-serving charters trump consumer-driven processes. The number of Indiocentric courses at tribal colleges was nearly ten times larger than the number of ethnocentric courses (either Indio- or Afrocentric) at mainstream institutions (exp[2.251] = 9.5), but the statistically insignificant coefficient on HBCUs suggests that black colleges *as a whole* do not differ from mainstream colleges with respect to the number of Afrocentric courses.

Differences between TCUs and HBCUs may not be as straightforward as they first appear, however. The interaction term between the HBCU and public indicators in Model 4 reveals that the number of Afrocentric courses at *publicly controlled* HBCUs was an estimated 73 percent lower than the number of ethnocentric courses at mainstream institutions. However, the main HBCU effect—which, after public HBCUs are controlled, designates *private* black colleges—becomes a positive and statistically significant predictor of Afrocentric curricular content.[11] Taken together, the coefficients suggest that the number of Afrocentric courses at private HBCUs was an estimated 15 percent greater than the number of ethnocentric courses at mainstream colleges.

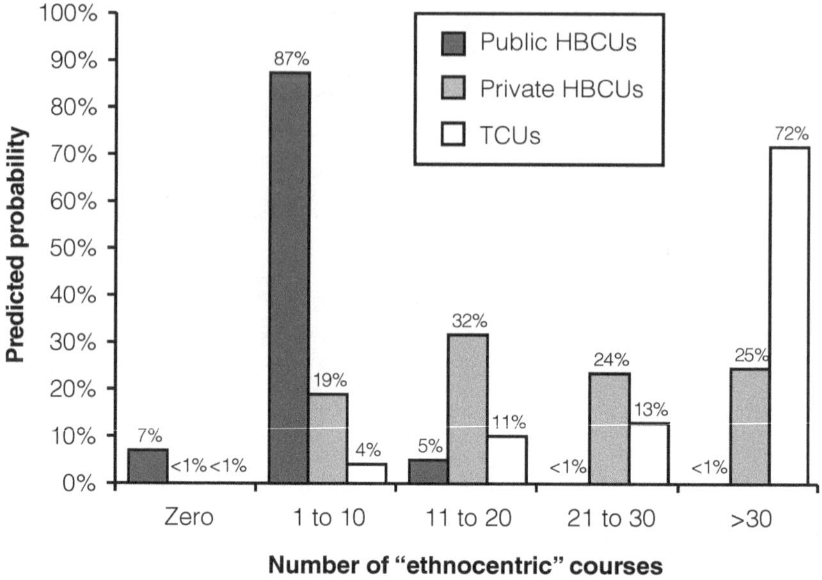

FIGURE 6.4. Estimated number of ethnocentric courses at TCUs and HBCUs in 2002.

Note: Predicted probabilities computed using coefficient estimates from Model 4 in Table 6.1 with control variables set to their group-specific mean values.

Estimates from the same model show that the number of Indiocentric courses at tribal colleges was an astounding 828 percent greater than the number of ethnocentric at mainstream institutions. Thus, the number of ethnocentric courses at private HBCUs is slightly higher than at public HBCUs but still *much lower* than at TCUs.

To illustrate this difference another way, Figure 6.4 uses coefficient estimates from regression models similar to those reported in Model 4 to derive predicted probabilities for the number of ethnocentric courses at public HBCUs, private HBCUs, and TCUs.[12] The graph plots the likelihood that an "average" TCU and an "average" public or private HBCU offered zero, one to ten, eleven to twenty, twenty-one to thirty, or more than thirty ethnocentric courses in 2002. The differences are striking. The likelihood that an average TCU or an average private HBCU did not have *any* ethnocentric courses was less than 1 percent, whereas the corresponding likelihood for an average public HBCU was 7 percent. Public HBCUs were most likely to have between one and ten Afrocentric courses, whereas private HBCUs were most likely to have between eleven and twenty such courses. The results also indicate that there was a nearly 50 percent chance that an average private HBCU offered more than twenty Afrocentric courses. Clearly, then, Afrocentric curricular content was more prevalent at private than at public HBCUs. Nevertheless, the emphasis on ethnocentrism at TCUs sets them apart from all HBCUs, whether public or private. As shown in Figure 6.4, the likelihood that an average TCU offered more than thirty Indiocentric courses stood at 72 percent in 2002, far higher than the corresponding probability for private HBCUs (25 percent) and public HBCUs (less than 1 percent).

CURRICULAR DISTINCTIVENESS AND INSTITUTIONAL MISSION

Differences in the quantitative emphasis on ethnocentric curricular content between TCUs and HBCUs reflect qualitative differences in their missions. Consider the mission statements of three HBCUs: Miles College, a private liberal arts college in Fairfield, Alabama; Harris-Stowe College, a public college in St. Louis, Missouri; and the University of Arkansas at Pine Bluff, a public university:

> Miles College is a . . . historically black, four-year liberal arts institution founded in 1905 to provide leadership to the Black Community. This mission has been expanded to include an emphasis on the personal development of all individuals, regardless of race, who, upon graduation from Miles, will possess an understanding of their own mission in a global society. (Miles College 1996: 19)

> Harris-Stowe College, though having the status of a historically black college or university (HBCU), has a student body that is diverse in age, culture, ethnicity, and experiential background. (Harris-Stowe State College 2001: 4)

> While the University of Arkansas at Pine Bluff will continue to maintain a special sensitiveness to the needs, aspirations, problems and opportunities of its historical constituents, it shall expand its mission with a high degree of excellence and with a sense of constantly improving quality. The new social context that is emerging as a result of integration requires that this mission be expanded, extended and enriched so as to become consonant with the needs and demands of a more culturally heterogeneous student clientele. (University of Arkansas at Pine Bluff 2002: 9)

Although each institution concedes that its original purpose was to serve African American students, contemporary mission statements deemphasize this role and instead underscore inclusivity and heterogeneity—in other words, the missions are multicultural rather than ethnocentric. Each statement reflects the moral and legal obligation to educate *all* individuals, regardless of race, and celebrates diversity in all its forms. The "blackness" of these black colleges is largely, if not completely, relegated to history.

A close inspection of the mission statements reveals a subtle distinction between Miles College, a private institution, and the two publicly controlled institutions. This distinction may explain why private HBCUs offer somewhat more Afrocentric courses, on average, than public HBCUs do. Miles College declares its continued intention "to provide leadership in the Black Community." Such a mandate implies that at least some curricular programs are devoted to the particular needs, desires, or aspirations of black students. But the mission of Miles College also includes programs that prepare a racially diverse student body for participation in a "global society." The imagery is "both/and," rather than "either/or," but with a marked shift toward racial diversification and a global rather than a local perspective.

By contrast, Harris-Stowe State College, a publicly controlled institution, is much more adamant in effacing its historical mission. As a college that is chartered and funded by the state, Harris-Stowe dramatizes its compliance with the mandates of integration. To that effect, the college's mission proclaims its success in attracting students from a variety of backgrounds *in spite of* its designation as an HBCU. For the same reason, the mission statement for the University of Arkansas at Pine Bluff fails even to mention black students, referring instead, euphemistically, to the institution's "historical constituents." In demonstrating their conformity to contemporary racial norms and legal standards, public HBCUs perhaps overcompensate by renouncing their historical missions and excising curricula of Afrocentric content. Organizational theorists have referred to this phenomenon as "hyperadaptation" (Hatch and Schultz 2002). As creatures of the same governments that were once responsible for enforcing segregation, public HBCUs recall their historical commitment to serve black students with indifference, if at all, while private HBCUs do so with pride.

These missions compare dramatically with the missions at TCUs. To amplify the differences, I present mission statements from Oglala Lakota College in Kyle, South Dakota; Fort Peck Community College in Poplar, Montana; and D-Q University in Davis, California:

> [Oglala Lakota College] promotes the study and practice of sovereignty; works with tribal entities toward building our nation; celebrates Lakota culture, including sacred songs and ceremonies; researches, studies and disseminates Lakota language, culture and philosophy; [and] provides leadership to maintain and revitalize Lakota culture in a diverse and changing environment. (Oglala Lakota College 2003: 4)

> To preserve Indian culture, history, and beliefs, and to perpetuate them among the Indian people of all ages is an important function of FPCC. . . . Although FPCC does not deny anyone the opportunity for higher education, the institution's primary purpose is service to the Indian population of the Fort Peck Reservation. (Fort Peck Community College 2001: 1)

> The mission of D-Q University is to provide quality education, community involvement, and learning opportunities for all California Native American Indians and Native American Indians in California. . . . The curriculum will include the spiritual and cultural truths of the past, the realities of the present and preparation for the future. . . . Inherent in the activities of the University is a fundamental concern for the self determination of Native peoples. A trilateral approach is established to support the individual's presence in a rapidly changing society: discovery of self-identity via an awareness of cultural heritage, bridging the gap between cultures, and preparing the individual for service to their community. (D-Q University 2002: 13)

The contrast with HBCUs, whether public or private, is striking. Oglala Lakota College prepares students for leadership not in a *global* society, as does Miles College, but in *Lakota* society, conceived as a sovereign nation. And it emphatically rejects multiculturalism, aiming instead to defend Lakota traditions from a "diverse and changing environment." As such, the college's mission, and hence its curriculum, "celebrates Lakota culture" and "researches . . . Lakota language, culture and philosophy."

Oglala Lakota College is certainly not unique in this regard. Fort Peck Community College officially maintains an open-door admissions policy but makes no secret of its dedication to "preserve Indian culture, history, and beliefs" and caters explicitly to American Indians living on the reservation. This mission compares starkly with a dedication to cultural pluralism and enrollment diversification, as extolled by Harris-Stowe State College. Although TCUs are also devoted, in the words of D-Q University, to "bridging the gap between cultures," the focus on American Indian cultures would seem to overshadow this nod to cosmopolitanism.

The differences between TCUs and HBCUs are not merely cultural but political as well. Instead of promoting integration, the stated goal of most black colleges, Oglala Lakota College advocates tribal sovereignty and nation building, and D-Q University fosters the "self determination of Native peoples." Sociologists have long acknowledged the importance of education to the nation-building efforts of sovereign states (Bendix 1964; Boli 1989; Marshall 1948; Ramirez and Boli 1987a; Weber 1976), and it would appear to be little different for quasi-sovereign tribes. Nation-states used common schools to invent imagined communities (Anderson 1991). Tribes, alternatively, establish "uncommon" schools—and curricula—to preserve their primordial communities.

CONCLUSION

The distinctiveness of tribal colleges and universities challenges the common presumption that institutional pressures operate more or less uniformly within a given organizational sector or field. Instead, the logics encapsulated in different institutional charters and organizational identities produce distinct, even contradictory, outcomes. Tribal college charters, rooted in sovereignty, support deviation from mainstream curricular models, whereas historically black college charters entail the replication of mainstream curricula. In turn, these opposing institutional logics subject tribal and historically black colleges to different standards of legitimacy. By emphasizing cultural distinctiveness, TCUs risk straying too far from accepted curricular standards. Sovereign or not, tribes still depend on the federal government for funding and on accrediting agencies for certification. It is worth noting in this context that some 80 percent of courses at tribal colleges did *not* incorporate explicitly ethnocentric content during the period covered by my analysis. Even those courses that incorporate distinctive subject matter are structured in rather conventional ways. Organizing ethnocentric content into credits that students accumulate toward a credential or degree forces it into a rationalistic framework. Knowledge that was once passed down orally by elders is now organized in a syllabus, advertised in a catalog, assigned three or five credits, taught by a faculty member with a master's degree or doctorate, and taken by students whose mastery of the content is evaluated and graded.

The impulse to certify and credentialize traditional knowledge is epitomized by an honorary degree program for elders at Leech Lake Tribal College in Cass Lake, Minnesota. The Elders Program awards "an Honorary Degree for Elders (HDE) who pursue a separate track of study similar to the regular two-year liberal arts program" (Leech Lake Tribal College 2008: 35). Although elders enrolled in the program are "exempted from the usual rigors of western assessment methods," participants are nevertheless required to meet with an academic advisor to "prepar[e] an Annual Education Plan" in addition to satisfactorily completing sixty-four credit hours of study.

In this fashion, educators at tribal colleges struggle to reconcile their desire for cultural relevance with the imperatives of institutional legitimacy. The process of attaining and preserving accreditation has proven especially problematic, as many TCUs are forced to "justify courses, teaching methods, administrative structures and intrinsic cultural values to visiting evaluators who are often unfamiliar with American Indian communities" (Shanley 1993: 8). It nevertheless remains true that within these parameters, TCUs have devoted a substantial share of their curriculum to the cultures, polities, and economies of the tribal communities they serve.

HBCUs confront the opposite problem. They are accused of unnecessarily duplicating programs that are offered by predominantly white institutions. The Supreme Court held in *United States v. Fordice* (1992: 719) that "the widespread duplication of programs at the historically black and historically white . . . universities is problematic . . . [because it] represents a continuation of the 'separate but equal' treatment required by the prior dual system." The Court also criticized the continued maintenance of historically black colleges alongside white institutions as "wasteful and irrational" (p. 741). To address this legal challenge, HBCUs could conceivably incorporate ethnocentric perspectives more extensively into the curriculum. Creating an Afrocentric curricular niche would distinguish HBCUs from mainstream institutions and thereby insulate them from legal accusations of programmatic duplication. Unfortunately, such a strategy may also leave HBCUs vulnerable to another sort of attack: By increasing the relative curricular focus on African American cultural perspectives, historically black colleges may inadvertently discourage students from other racial or ethnic backgrounds from attending. Were this to happen, the problem would shift from curricular replication to something potentially much more nefarious—enrollment segregation. This is precisely the sort of conflicted "twoness" of which Du Bois wrote more than a century ago.

Throughout this book I have argued that claims to sovereignty give indigenous peoples the authority to preserve their traditions, languages, and cultures in postsecondary institutions they establish (or have established for them). These sovereignty claims and the institutions they support operate within—and indeed derive from—a broader world-cultural framework that provides the justifications, content, and lexicon of indigenous peoples' struggles for self-determination. It is the same for all nonstate groups that aspire to control their own destinies: Quebecois nationalism, Basque nationalism, Kurdish nationalism, Lakota nationalism, and Maori nationalism are but particular iterations of a universal idea—*nationalism* itself is a creature of world culture. Groups seeking greater autonomy qua nations almost always adopt the language of sovereignty. Indigenous peoples' recourse to these world-cultural scripts, tailored to their unique circumstances and characteristics, has empowered them to establish separate colleges and develop ethnocentric curricula. Although some commentators (for example, Boldt and Long 1984; Corntassel and Primeau 1995) criticize indigenous peoples' use of an "alien" legal framework to protect their traditional cultures, this is precisely what American Indians have done. They have, in the language of Chapter One, deftly appropriated Western legal foundations (sovereignty) and organizational forms (postsecondary institutions) in the service of their own ends (the advancement of tribal self-determination and the preservation of tribal cultures). In so doing, American Indians and their indigenous counterparts around the world have transformed education from a weapon for assimilation into a powerful tool for cultural and political empowerment.

CONCLUSION

Summary, Challenges, and the Future of Indigenous Postsecondary Institutions

Ka whawhai tonu matou [The struggle continues].

Maori expression, quoted in Fleras and Elliott (1992: 220)

THE EMERGENCE AND INSTITUTIONALIZATION of indigenous postsecondary institutions signals the dawn of a new era in the education of indigenous peoples. After 500 years of colonial hegemony and state-sponsored assimilation, governments around the world are beginning to respect indigenous languages, cultures, and worldviews. Despite these gains, the struggle to make higher education relevant to the needs and desires of indigenous peoples continues. Many obstacles have been cleared, but many more remain. In this concluding chapter, I summarize the major findings at each level of analysis—global, cross-national, and organizational—and unify them into a coherent framework. I then consider some of the challenges facing indigenous postsecondary institutions and speculate about their future.

THE RISE AND SPREAD OF INDIGENOUS POSTSECONDARY INSTITUTIONS

In the Introduction, I presented a model for understanding the development, institutionalization, and diffusion of indigenous postsecondary institutions as an organizational innovation (look back again at Figure I.2). The model began with the constitution of "actors"—whether individuals, states, or indigenous peoples—and their identities. This is the work of global-institutional culture. World culture, in short, defines the ontological structure of the modern world system. As an obvious but necessary precondition for the establishment of indigenous postsecondary institutions, the substance and attribution of "indigeneity" itself—what it means to be indigenous, who can legitimately claim to be indigenous, and what consequences flow from being indigenous—must first be determined. Explicating indigeneity, however, is no simple task (Miller 2003). It has involved a series of political, cultural, and legal processes that are ultimately traceable to the late fifteenth century.

Chapter One argued that the world system passed through three stages, each with different sets of actors operating under historically contingent legal rules and social norms. During the first era, when Europeans made initial contact with indigenous peoples in the Americas, the Catholic Church and embryonic states tenuously acknowledged the rights and sovereignty of indigenous nations. Thus began a period of diplomacy and conquest. With the ascendance of nation-states as the dominant actors in the world polity during the eighteenth and nineteenth centuries, the autonomous legal and political standing of indigenous peoples waned. Instead, they were incorporated and assimilated directly into national polities. After World War II, an ontologically expansive world society gave more and more entities—including indigenous peoples—political standing, moral worth, and legal rights. For indigenous peoples, these rights include self-determination, which derives ultimately from the recognition of their sovereign status under the contact-era law of nations.

Among other things, claims to self-determination give indigenous peoples the authority to establish, or to have established for them, their own post-secondary institutions (Chapter Two). In this respect, the absolute timing of indigenous postsecondary institutions as an organizational innovation is the result of processes operating in the world polity: As discussed in Part I, indigenous postsecondary institutions did not surface until the political and cultural rights of indigenous peoples as self-determining groups were recognized anew under international law. However, the emergence of indigenous postsecondary institutions "on the ground" was patterned by cross-national and historical differences in the structure of indigenous–state relations (Chapter Three). Although the general *principle* of indigenous sovereignty is inscribed in world culture, its day-to-day exercise in *practice* is mediated by, and finds tangible expression in, state policies. The extent to which states acknowledge the sovereignty of indigenous peoples, together with cross-national variation in the pace and structure of higher education expansion, shaped the relative timing, number, institutional autonomy, and organizational form of indigenous postsecondary institutions (Chapter Four). I further demonstrated, in Chapters Five and Six, that the status of indigenous peoples differs markedly from that of nonindigenous minorities. The distinct and sometimes contradictory historical experiences and legal standing of American Indians and African Americans in the United States informed the emergence, purposes, legitimacy, and even the curricula of tribal and historically black colleges and universities.

The first indigenous postsecondary institution was established by the Navajo Nation in the United States in 1968. From there, indigenous postsecondary institutions emerged sequentially in Canada, New Zealand, Australia, and elsewhere. As they continued to spread across the globe, indigenous postsecondary institutions became, in effect, institutionalized. The creation of the World Indigenous Nations Higher Education Consortium (WINHEC) in 2003 by representatives from the United States, Canada, New Zealand, Australia, and Scandinavia exemplifies this process. WINHEC, which "provides an international forum and support for Indigenous Peoples to pursue common goals through higher education," aims to

- "Accelerate the articulation of Indigenous epistemology,"
- "Protect and enhance Indigenous spiritual beliefs, culture and languages through higher education,"
- "Advance the social, economical, and political status of Indigenous Peoples,"
- "Create an accreditation body for indigenous education initiatives,"
- "Create a global network for sharing knowledge," and
- "Recognize the educational rights of Indigenous Peoples." (WINHEC 2005)

Once institutionalized in this manner, innovations become available for widespread and relatively unencumbered diffusion. Institutionalized organizational models are highly elaborated and abstract, which makes diffusion "more rapid and more universal" and "renders diffusion less structured by social relations and differences across adopters" (Strang and Meyer 1993: 493). Through ventures like WINHEC, the indigenous postsecondary institutional model became disembodied from the particular contexts in which it originally emerged, giving it a modular and readily transposable quality. Consequently, indigenous postsecondary institutions have diffused from the "first-mover" countries of the United States, Canada, New Zealand, and Australia to countries around the world.

CHALLENGES: THE IMPERATIVES OF ORGANIZATIONAL SURVIVAL

Thus far I have presented indigenous postsecondary institutions as phenomenal successes. In one sense, their very existence is a success story: Indigenous peoples overcame seemingly insuperable odds—colonial oppression, political subjugation, cultural denigration, abject poverty, and demographic imbalance—to establish their own postsecondary institutions. Even more surprising is that states, which until very recently used education as an instrument for assimilating indigenous minorities, now support indigenous-controlled higher education ventures. Nevertheless, indigenous postsecondary institutions also confront two ubiquitous and closely related challenges, both of which threaten their continued viability. One is the need to strike a "proper" balance between indigenous and mainstream epistemologies to garner institutional legitimacy, earn accreditation, and prepare students for their roles in technologically advanced societies. The other is lack of adequate funding. Obtaining pecuniary resources, an ultimate goal of any organization that seeks its own survival, is predicated on the acquisition of social legitimacy, a proximate resource. Legitimacy, in turn, is contingent on an organization's dutiful adherence to externally prescribed "myths" in the form of structural models, cultural norms, and legal rules (Meyer and Rowan 1977).

But what happens in cases where legitimacy-conferring myths fail to align with, or even impede, an organization's core activities? Through "loose coupling" (Weick 1976; Meyer and Rowan 1977), organizations buffer core activities from external structures. Ritual conformity of this sort aligns an organization with its institutional environment while allowing it to function without hindrance. Given, however, that the very mandate of indigenous postsecondary institutions—to preserve and promulgate indigenous cultures—deviates from convention, it is difficult for practitioners to engage in loose coupling as a buffering mechanism or for researchers to invoke it as a theoretical deus ex machina. In fact, the survival of indigenous postsecondary institutions, as with other "nontraditional" colleges (Hall 1979), is sometimes jeopardized by their distinctiveness.

Until recently, indigenous education deemphasized academic subjects (and, for that matter, indigenous cultural content) in favor of vocational or manual training, a practice motivated by the belief that indigenous peoples were innately less intelligent than Europeans. Racial ideologies in vogue during the nineteenth and early twentieth centuries were premised on the supposed inability of indigenous students to complete an academically rigorous curriculum. Take the case of New Zealand. W. W. Bird, the quondam Inspector of Native Schools, concluded in 1907 that "the natural genius of the Maori [is] in the direction of manual skills." Similarly, teachers of that period "were of the opinion that after leaving the village schools [Maori] pupils should, as far as possible, be drafted into vocational schools or schools where their training, apart from English language should be mainly technical" (Simon and Smith 2001: 112–113).

Fast forward now one hundred years. Today's critics argue that *wananga*, the indigenous postsecondary institutions of New Zealand, focus too much on Maori culture and not enough on "conventional" academic subjects. They question how "woodcarving and boat-building can possibly equip young Maoris to make a life for themselves in a world increasingly geared toward technology" (Cohen 2005b). Nor is New Zealand the only country where the legitimacy of culturally relevant higher education alternatives for indigenous peoples is questioned. Critics typically view curricula as a zero-sum enterprise, such that an emphasis on indigenous culture detracts from studies in other, putatively more relevant or socially useful fields of study. In Australia,

> some writers have been critical of the primacy of cultural issues in Indigenous education policy, arguing that this has shifted the focus away from the need for good mainstream education. They caution against the danger that acknowledgement and incorporation of cultural differences in education systems may mean an acceptance of different, and lower, education outcomes. An assumption that Indigenous people are

less able to undertake subjects such as science and mathematics, for example, is seen as one of the dangers of an over-emphasis on cultural factors. (Australia 2000: 63)

In this way, the prevalence of culturally relevant curricula is believed to reinforce the same racial stereotypes today that a predominantly vocational curriculum implied one hundred years ago—that indigenous students simply aren't capable of succeeding academically. For this reason, "'two way' schooling"—that is, schooling that is sensitive to both Aboriginal and Euro-Australian cultures—has "attracted criticism for concentrating too much on cultural maintenance, and for placing less emphasis on mainstream educational achievement" (Australia 2000: 72). A recent audit of the Batchelor Institute of Indigenous Tertiary Education by the Australian Universities Quality Agency (2006: 15) concluded that there is "a lack of clarity and understanding of both-ways learning," suggesting that mainstream quality assurance and accreditation agencies are still reluctant to adapt their standards to accommodate the distinctive missions and practices of indigenous postsecondary institutions.

Sometimes these tensions between mainstream and indigenous educational models are built into the very structure of indigenous postsecondary institutions. Canada's only Aboriginal-controlled university, First Nations University, is federated with a mainstream institution, the University of Regina. A recent report on the system of governance at FNU described the problems that can arise from this sort of structural relationship:

The dual reality of [FNU] being on the one hand a First Nations controlled institution and on the other hand as a university college federated with the University of Regina presents another set of challenges. Classes must meet the requirements of the University of Regina for credit. Students must meet the requirements of the University of Regina to obtain their degree. . . . Professors must meet the unique needs of the First Nations students and communities while at the same time meeting the academic demands of the University of Regina. The academic staff members are part of the University of Regina Faculty Association that brings the standards of mainstream post-secondary education into the relationships within the First Nations institution. Tensions arise when the first Nations community expectations are at variance with the relationships built into the post-secondary experience. (M. A. Begay II & Associates 2010: 44)

Although these kinds of tensions between cultural relevance and mainstream standards are very real, the problem should not be overstated. Indigenous and

Western cultures are not inherently incommensurable. A prospectus issued by Te Wananga o Aotearoa (1999: 3), for example, advertises that both "Te Reo Mäori [the Maori language] and Computing are parts of every program," but assures applicants that they "don't need to know anything about either to start." In the United States, the Northern Ute Tribal Business Committee has maintained that "our language is capable of lexical expansion into modern fields such as the field of politics, economics, mathematics and science" (Reyhner and Eder 2004: 311). As anthropologist Ronald Niezen (2003: 6) has noted, "Culture is a verb, not a noun, a process, not a thing in itself." Indigenous cultures, as with all cultures, evolve and grow; they are not static and primordial, frozen in the distant past.

The creation of institutional hybrids offers one strategy for managing environmental uncertainties. As I argued in the case of the United States (Chapter Six), the quasi-sovereign status of American Indian tribes empowers them to infuse mainstream institutional models with culturally distinctive content to create an organizational bricolage, the tribal college. Innovativeness can be either adaptive or disruptive, however, and hybrid organizations tend also to "face unique obstacles to legitimacy building, resource procurement, and effectiveness. They must . . . [find] ways to articulate a multidimensional identity and clarify what are the form's boundaries and sources of accountability" (Minkoff 2002: 383).[1] In many countries, the struggle for legitimacy plays out in the accreditation process.

The need for accreditation is bound up inextricably with the need for funding. Indigenous postsecondary institutions are everywhere dependent on external sources of funding, and accreditation signals to potential resource suppliers that a college is worthy of financial investment. In some cases, in fact, accreditation is a precondition for funding.[2] Tying money to accreditation is problematic for some indigenous postsecondary institutions, though, because "mainstream" standards often do not apply to them (Putman 2001).

Systematic underfunding remains a persistent problem for indigenous postsecondary institutions. In the United States, funds appropriated to tribal colleges by the Bureau of Indian Affairs (BIA) under the Tribally Controlled College and University Assistance Act have never matched funding levels authorized by Congress. Indigenous postsecondary institutions in Canada also struggle to survive on very little funding. The First Nations University of Canada is the only indigenous postsecondary institution in that country to receive statutory funding, but even then its total revenue "is only 64% of the level of resources received by [the] province-funded universities" of Toronto, Manitoba, Saskatchewan, and Alberta (Stonechild 2006: 127). In its study of Canada's Aboriginal postsecondary institutions, the Aboriginal Institutes' Consortium (2005: 49) lamented that "there is no source of adequate funding to support Aboriginal [postsecondary] institutions, while mainstream institutions enjoy policy and legislative support for ongoing annual secure operating grant funding, as well as a host of special purpose and infrastructure grants." Current arrangements require indigenous postsecondary to partner with mainstream colleges and universities to access funding. This has its own deleterious effects. Not only do funding shortages endanger the continued financial viability of indigenous postsecondary institutions, but requiring them to enter into partnerships with mainstream colleges that serve as funding conduits and accreditation umbrellas also undermines the independent cultural integrity of indigenous ventures.

These problems are not merely an occasion for handwringing—they have real consequences. D-Q University, established in 1970 as the only tribal college in California, recently closed after losing its accreditation due to financial mismanagement and political infighting (Norrell 2005; Read 2005). At least two other tribal colleges, Little Big Horn College and Cankdeska Cikana Community College, have been threatened with a similar fate. Without accreditation, tribal colleges lose federal financial support, which accounts for between 60 and 90 percent of their total operating budgets ("Federal Funding Increases" 1991). In 2006, Si Tanka University, a tribal college in South Dakota, closed after only five years in existence due to funding cuts under the Bush II administration.[3]

Moreover, when it comes to funding indigenous-controlled education, sovereignty is a double-edged sword. The nation-to-nation relationship between Indian tribes and the federal government in the United States gives tribes the authority to establish and control separate colleges, but it also limits the sources of funding available to tribal colleges. According to Cunningham and Parker (1998: 53),

> Unlike mainstream community colleges, tribal colleges receive little or no funding from state governments; states have no obligation to fund these schools because most are located on federal trust territory. Furthermore, tribal colleges lack the ability to raise local revenues to support higher education institutions. The status of res-

ervations as federal trust territory prohibits levying property taxes—an important revenue source for most mainstream community colleges—while the impoverished conditions do not provide a sufficient base from which to draw support.

They conclude: "Mostly due to the absence of this direct state or local support . . . tribal colleges receive about two-thirds the level of government funding per full-time equivalent student than that received by public community colleges."

Indigenous sovereignty can also lead to internal divisions and power struggles that undermine the legitimacy of indigenous postsecondary institutions. Conflicts between "two warring factions" on the Board of Trustees at D-Q University contributed to that institution's demise (Read 2005); Little Big Horn College faced a similar crisis when the Northwest Association of Schools and Colleges admonished the college to "keep itself free of interference from the tribal council" or else have its accreditation revoked (Basinger 2001). This problem is widespread. Politicized boards or tribal councils removed presidents at nine tribal colleges during a two-year period in the early 2000s. Such controversies put "tribal college[s] on precarious ground in the eyes of accrediting agencies that closely examine the relationships that tribal colleges have with outside political entities such as tribal councils" (Guillory and Ward 2008: 101). Thus, although indigenous postsecondary institutions frequently enjoy substantial autonomy vis-à-vis national, provincial, or local governments (see Chapter Four), autonomy relative to indigenous governments often proves to be more elusive. This lack of autonomy from "within" poses grave challenges to indigenous postsecondary institutions.

Similar problems have befallen indigenous postsecondary institutions in Canada. In 2007 the Association of Universities and Colleges of Canada, that country's de facto accrediting agency, placed FNU on probation following reports of budget deficits running in the millions of dollars and complaints that several faculty and administrative staff had been wrongly terminated. A year later, FNU was censured by the Canadian Association of University Teachers. Both agencies attributed FNU's problems to a deeply politicized board of governors. In 2008, fifteen out of twenty-six board members were chiefs of their respective First Nations communities, and conflicts among these communities would often spill over into the day-to-day governance of the university.

FNU's inability to maintain its independence from indigenous governments has compromised its institutional autonomy more generally and indeed jeopardizes its continued existence as an indigenous postsecondary institution. As discussed in Chapter Four, FNU lost provincial and federal funding in March 2010 due to financial irregularities, corruption, mismanagement, and wasteful spending. This loss in funding totaled more than $12 million, or nearly half of FNU's budget. Provincial funding in the amount of $5.2 million was subsequently renewed in the wake of substantial restructuring and downsizing, but at the time of this writing (in November 2010) ongoing federal funding has yet to be restored.

When problems similar to those uncovered at FNU were identified at Te Wananga o Aotearoa in New Zealand, also as reported in Chapter Four, the institution was placed under the control of a government-appointed manager (Cohen 2005a; Johnston 2008; Tahana 2007). As a consequence, enrollments were cut nearly in half, several hundred jobs were culled, and the chief executive resigned. Clearly, for all their successes, indigenous postsecondary institutions confront an uncertain future as they try to balance cultural relevance with adherence to mainstream academic standards and administrative practices.

A final concern for the future stability of indigenous postsecondary institutions pertains to their continued relegation to the periphery of mainstream postsecondary education systems. Recent efforts to improve the status of indigenous postsecondary institutions have been rebuffed. BIITE in Australia, for example, aspires to achieve official "university" status within the Australian higher education system but has been criticized for "turning away from some of its community commitment as it spent more time on activities intended to make it look university-like" (Australian Universities Quality Agency 2006: 9). Similarly, in New Zealand, attempts to translate "Te Wananga o Aotearoa" into English as "The University of New Zealand" have sparked debates over the institution's academic caliber (Cohen 2005a). In this way, indigenous postsecondary institutions are kept at an arm's length from their mainstream counterparts, even while they are criticized for straying too far from mainstream institutional and curricular frameworks.

THE FUTURE OF INDIGENOUS POSTSECONDARY INSTITUTIONS

In this book I have focused at length on the historical processes that contributed to the establishment of indigenous postsecondary institutions: the source and development of indigenous peoples' sovereignty claims, the circumstances of their political incorporation into mainstream societies and polities, and the massification of tertiary enrollments, institutions, and curricula. What, now, can be said about the future of indigenous postsecondary institutions? One might expect that they will diffuse eventually to Asia, Africa, and even central Europe, where indigeneity is more ambiguous or highly contested (Aukerman 2000; Kingsbury 1998; Niezen 2003). Once a minority group establishes itself as indigenous, thereby becoming heir to the political status and legal rights accruing thereto, it also becomes "eligible" for an indigenous postsecondary institution. Put differently, once an ethnic group successfully inserts itself into the conceptually nebulous but expansive category of "indigenous peoples" as defined by global legal and normative discourses, it gains the leverage necessary to demand state support of independent and culturally relevant educational institutions.

But who, in the final analysis, is authorized to define and confer indigeneity—global institutions, national governments, or minority groups themselves? In Asia, where indigenous identities are highly contested, the Asian Development Bank (ADB) has offered its own definition of "indigenous peoples," one that is inclusive to the point of futility:

> Indigenous peoples should be regarded as those with a social or cultural identity distinct from the dominant or mainstream society, which makes them vulnerable to being disadvantaged in the process of development. (Asian Development Bank 1999: 6)

This definition makes no effort to differentiate indigenous peoples, properly defined, from other linguistic, cultural, or ethnic minorities. A distinguishing characteristic would seem to include, at minimum, historical priority or continuity with lands traditionally occupied prior to colonization. Indeed, in a footnote, ABD equates indigenous peoples—a "term used in United Nations documents, and . . . used by ABD solely for convenience"—with "cultural minorities" and "ethnic minorities" (Asian Development Bank 1999: 1).

Minority groups in Asia increasingly define themselves as indigenous, but with the understanding that indigeneity implies something more than simple minority group status. They self-consciously claim the same identity, status, and rights as indigenous groups in the United States, Canada, Australia, New Zealand, Scandinavia, and Latin America:

> Following the pattern of group mobilization established in states dominated by European settlement—in the Americas, Australasia and the Nordic countries—groups

based in different Asian states have more recently begun to participate in international institutions and gatherings of "indigenous peoples," and transnational networks have been formed in Asia under the rubric "indigenous peoples." (Kingsbury 1998: 414)

The concept of "indigeneity" developed first in regions where European colonial settlement was extensive and permanent. Most, if not all, Asian governments would continue to limit claims to indigeneity in this way. Absent a history of sustained European colonization and settlement in many parts of Asia, states such as China, Thailand, and, until recently, Japan adamantly deny that the term *indigenous peoples* is applicable to ethnic groups within their jurisdictions. However, the Japanese government's recognition of the Ainu as an indigenous people in 2008 suggests that an indigenous postsecondary institution in that country may not be long in coming.

A different argument is often made for Africa, where Europeans quite obviously colonized most of the continent but, in most cases, did not establish permanent settlements or become a majority presence. Africans could legitimately be described as "indigenous" while under the sway of colonial administrators. When Africa was decolonized, however, power reverted back to the majority "indigenous" populations. Hence, while most African peoples continue to be, in one sense, indigenous—they have precedence in the lands they occupy—the political ramifications of indigeneity may have been effaced with decolonization.

Despite the contentiousness and equivocation surrounding the concept of indigeneity, Ronald Niezen (2003: 74) suggests that "there is a seemingly irreversible momentum behind claims of indigenous identity by peoples form Asia and Africa." With respect to Japan, anthropologist Bruce Granville Miller (2003: 63) presciently declared that "the Ainus, too, are gradually becoming indigenous." Once a group is defined as indigenous, I expect the establishment of indigenous postsecondary institutions to follow.

Because indigenous peoples are clearly not fading away as colonizers had once hoped, political philosophers such as Will Kymlicka (1995) have developed a liberal defense of their rights. A fundamental tenant of liberalism, according to Kymlicka, is the right of individuals to live "in accordance with . . . beliefs about what gives value to life" (Kymlicka 1995: 81). Ideas about what constitutes the "good life" are fundamentally cultural in nature, and the rights of individuals to cultural membership are therefore paramount. Nevertheless, individuals also have the inalienable right to revise their conception of the good life and hence to partake freely in the marketplace of cultures. Two conclusions follow. First, liberal states are obligated to protect minority cultures. Freedom of choice becomes meaningless when the range of alternatives is unduly limited. Second, to protect and preserve their cultures, minority groups may, under some conditions, restrict the rights of their members, but they may never abrogate the right of individuals to opt out of the group.

Kymlicka's formulation establishes the frontiers of indigenous sovereignty. Indigenous nations, although sovereign, are curtailed by the same human rights principles as sovereign nation-states. In exercising their sovereignty, indigenous groups must not violate the human rights of their individual members, no more than nation-states are allowed to breach the human rights of their citizens. The implication for indigenous postsecondary institutions is direct, if not immediately obvious. Some indigenous postsecondary institutions engage in status closure by restricting admission to "members" or by otherwise discouraging nonmembers from enrolling. Many tribal colleges and universities, for instance, overtly favor American Indian applicants. Indigenous postsecondary institutions may also oblige students to take culturally relevant courses or to transact exclusively in an indigenous language. Blackfeet Community College in Browning, Montana, requires all students, regardless of ethnic background or program of study, to complete at least ten credit hours in Blackfeet studies. In a similar vein, Te Whare Wananga o Awanuiarangi (2004: 2) strongly encourages students to "write and present their work in the Maori language."

Although indigenous postsecondary institutions are empowered in this way to dissuade nonindigenous students from enrolling or impose indigenous points of view on students, nowhere can they impede the right of their students to exit. Indigenous students, that is, may always exercise their right of free choice in deciding where to attend college or when to "stop out."[4] Thus, even as indigenous control of education expands, the scope of that control is tempered by human rights principles.

Ultimately, the future of indigenous postsecondary institutions remains uncertain. The foundations on which they are built—the claims of indigenous peoples to self-determination—remain hotly contested, as states disdain to relinquish their monopoly over sovereignty. I have endeavored to show that the education of indigenous peoples, although an interesting topic of study in its own right, is also a bellwether of large-scale historical, structural, political, and cultural changes. Indigenous postsecondary institutions exist precisely because fledgling European states affirmed the historical sovereignty of the indigenous peoples over 500 years ago, and indigenous claims to self-determination have enjoyed a renaissance because the raw legal and moral authority of nation-states has declined in recent decades relative to supra- and subnational groups. And yet, indigenous postsecondary institutions depend on the very same states that once repressed indigenous peoples for recognition and financial support. As such, it is impossible to predict the future of indigenous postsecondary institutions with any degree of accuracy, without also prognosticating the future of the nation-state itself. This is treacherous work, and I have no intention of signaling the "end of history" or the demise of the state as it is presently constituted. It *is* safe to conclude, however, that the fate of indigenous peoples, of indigenous education, and of indigenous postsecondary institutions is bound up intimately with that of the nation-state.

Something else is also clear: Indigenous postsecondary institutions will become more and more prevalent so long as indigenous peoples around the world continue to demand, and ultimately exercise, self-government. It used to be that indigenous elites in conventional saltwater colonies learned the skills and ideologies needed to exercise sovereignty while attending metropolitan universities. In this way, indigenous peoples appropriated the knowledge of their oppressors to support decolonization and political independence. Today's internally colonized indigenous peoples take a somewhat different approach. They draw on both mainstream and traditional knowledge to realize their claims to internal self-determination, and they do so, increasingly, in their own institutions and on their own terms. That, in the end, is what uncommon schools for indigenous peoples are all about.

APPENDIX

Indigenous Postsecondary Institutions in the United States, Canada, New Zealand, and Australia

United States

Bay Mills Community College
Blackfeet Community College
Cankdeska Cikana Community College
Chief Dull Knife College
College of Menominee Nation
Diné College
Fond du Lac Tribal and Community College
Fort Belknap College
Fort Berthold Community College
Fort Peck Community College
Haskell Indian Nations University
Ilisagvik College
Institute of American Indian Arts
Lac Courte Oreilles Ojibwa Community College
Leech Lake Tribal College
Little Big Horn College
Little Priest Tribal College
Navajo Technical College
Nebraska Indian Community College
Northwest Indian College

Oglala Lakota College
Saginaw Chippewa Tribal College
Salish Kootenai College
Sinte Gleska University
Sisseton Whapeton College
Sitting Bull College
Southwestern Indian Polytechnic Institute
Stone Child College
Tohono O'odham Community College
Turtle Mountain Community College
United Tribes Technical College
White Earth Tribal and Community College
College of the Muscogee Nation
Comanche Nation College
Keweenaw Bay Ojibwa Community College
Wind River Tribal College

Canada

Blue Quills First Nation College
First Nations Technical Institute
First Nations University of Canada
Gabriel Dumont Institute of Native Studies and Applied Research
Institute of Indigenous Government
Maskwechees Cultural College
Nicola Valley Institute of Technology
Red Crow Community College
Saskatchewan Indian Institute of Technologies
Six Nations Polytechnic
Wilp Wilxo'oskwhl Nisga'a Institute
Yellowquill College

New Zealand

Te Wānanga o Raukawa
Te Wānanga o Aotearoa
Te Whare Wānanga o Awanuiarangi

Australia

Batchelor Institute of Indigenous Tertiary Education

NOTES

ENDNOTES TO INTRODUCTION

1. This definition, although widely adopted (for example, Anaya 2004; Daes 1996; Fleras and Elliott 1992; Keal 2003; Martinez Cobo 1986), is neither definitive nor uncontroversial (see Corntassel 2003). The World Bank (1991), in its Operational Directive 4.20 on Indigenous Peoples, dispenses with the criterion of continuity with precolonial societies, and Kingsbury (1998) would expand the scope of indigeneity to include Asian groups by relaxing the historical precedence and European colonization provisions. Aukerman (2000) goes so far as to regard certain ethnic groups in Central and Eastern Europe as indigenous.

2. In exceptional cases, Indian tribes also enjoy recognition by other states. At least one tribe, the Haudenosaunee (Iroquois) Confederacy, issues its own passports, which are accepted by some sixteen countries around the world (Johansen and Mann 2000: 318).

3. This definition of self-determination comes from Article 3 of the U.N. Declaration on the Rights of Indigenous Peoples and repeats verbatim a right of "peoples" enshrined in two core human rights treaties, the International Covenant on Civil and Political Rights and the International Covenant on Economic, Social and Cultural Rights.

4. William Sewell (1992) invokes the example of language to illustrate the distinction: Rules of grammar and syntax form the constitutive elements of language (*langue*), whereas the poetry, prose, and spontaneous speech created under the rubric of those rules (*parole*) is quintessentially expressive. People routinely speak without contemplating or even comprehending formal grammatical or syntactical rules, which illustrates the often tacit and taken-for-granted nature of constitutive culture. But taken-for-grantedness does not necessarily imply lack of perception or conscious awareness (Jepperson 1991) because people are sometimes aware of and fully conversant with the rules they enact. Most students memorize, and subsequently forget, the rules of grammar at some point in their education.

5. Stronger institutionalist accounts—those that view social action as powerfully shaped by institutional forces—speak of "innovative enactors" (Boli and Thomas 1999); weaker institutionalist accounts—those underscoring the importance of individual agency—refer to "institutional entrepreneurs" (Levy and Scully 2007). We need a vocabulary that captures variation in and tension among the multiple senses of the word *actor*—someone who enacts prefabricated scripts, someone who carries out the will of a principal (and, increasingly, of abstract "principles"), and someone who behaves purposively under his or her own volition.

ENDNOTES TO CHAPTER 1

1. "Glocal," a portmanteau of *global* and *local*, refers here to centrifugal forces that redistribute political authority above and below the state. The term was popularized in sociological discourse by Robertson (1992).

2. Many observers cite the Peace of Westphalia as the decisive watershed. But as Stephen Krasner (1993, 1999, 2001) repeatedly emphasizes, Westphalia was not a break point in history, after which the Church's political hegemony crumbled and a state system emerged ex nihilo. The changes, he argues, were much more gradual. The hourglass imagery in Figure 1.1 is intended to capture the gradualness of these changes, as it slowly tapers down to a world in which only states and individuals have legitimate standing.

3. Supranationalism has in many cases reinforced the articulation of subnationalisms. The twofold process is most pronounced in Europe, where the consolidation of the European Union has occurred in tandem with the emergence of various regionalisms (Hooghe and Marks 2001; Nederveen Pieterse 1995).

4. Vitoria was nevertheless enlightened for his day in his denial that Indians were slaves by nature. Instead, their savagery was "nurtured" by an uncivilized environment, which meant that Indians could, with proper guidance, achieve the same level of intelligence and reason as Europeans. In this respect, Vitoria augured the positivist bent of much nineteenth-century social theory.

5. "I should be very happy to see the clause in Adam's will," Francis I of France is reputed to have scoffed, "which excluded me from my share when the world was being divided" (Hanke 1949: 148).

6. The case involved competing Dutch and American claims to a small island located midway between Indonesia and the Philippines.

7. For this reason, Barsh (1986: 378) notes that "the phraseology 'indigenous rights' has been preferred over 'human rights of indigenous peoples' in most recent resolutions."

8. I borrow the language of a world-systems perspective (Wallerstein 1974) in part because world polity institutionalism lacks the requisite terminology but also because I wish to portray the world-systems and world polity approaches as complementary rather than competing. In world polity terms, a hegemon is simply primus inter pares, a "first" among formally and juridically equal states.

9. The Indians' status as wards of the federal government is also consistent with the notion that a child was bound by his father's consent to the social contract until attaining adulthood. As with children, Indians could not attain full citizenship until leaving the tutelage of their "Great White Father"—the president of the United States.

10. Even the right to enjoy one's culture, while on the face of it a "collective" right, is in fact fundamentally individualistic. Cultural protections exist not to preserve collective traditions per se but to afford individuals, if they so desire, the opportunity to participate in cultural life. Cultural rights accrue to classes of individuals, not to groups as such.

11. When drafting the Treaty of Waitangi, for example, British colonizers in New Zealand struggled to translate the term *sovereignty* into the Maori language.

12. This process is encapsulated most dramatically by the European Union: A Spaniard, for example, may no longer view herself as simply a citizen of Spain but also of Catalonia, Europe, and indeed the world (Hooghe and Marks 2001).

13. This proto-feudal concept of nested sovereignty appears sporadically in international and domestic legal discourses relating to indigenous peoples. Vattel, for one, asserted that a weak state can place itself under the protection of a strong state without "divesting itself of the right to government and sovereignty" (Vattel [1758] 1883: 2). John Marshall later drew on these ideas to characterize Indian tribes as "domestic dependent nations" (*Cherokee Nation v. Georgia* 1831) and to describe the special nation-to-nation relationship between Indian tribes and the federal government (*Worcester v. Georgia* 1832).

ENDNOTES TO CHAPTER 2

1. Nevertheless, the early nationalization of the academy still bore signs of religious imperatives. Catholic rulers prohibited their subjects from attending universities in Protestant regions, and vice versa (Riddle 1989: 52).

2. Incidentally, the history of nation-building in Spain and Britain repeat, in microcosm, the hourglass pattern of state consolidation and fragmentation seen in the world polity at large (see Chapter One). The crowns of Castile and Aragon were united in 1469, creating a single, consolidated Spanish state. In Britain, Wales was conquered by England in 1284 and officially absorbed into that country in 1536, and the crowns of England and Scotland were joined in 1603. The official Act of Union creating the United Kingdom followed over a century later, in 1707. These trends reversed after World War II, when the rise to various subnationalisms contributed to the devolutionary reforms mentioned here. The European Union's Council of Regions further institutionalized devolution.

3. This process was by no means limited to indigenous peoples. Weber (1976), for example, discusses the role of education in transforming "peasants into Frenchmen."

4. Barrington (1991: 317) cautions against drawing too close a parallel with the experience of African Americans in the United States: "Sensitivities within the [New Zealand] Department of Education and the country generally about race relations were pricked when a visiting American scholar criticized the separate Maori school system and described it, somewhat inaccurately, as similar to the system of segregated black schools in the American South prior to the Supreme Court decision of 1954 [*Brown v. Board of Education*]." In New Zealand, white children often attended "Maori" schools, and Maori children frequently attended "mainstream" schools. Moreover, the ultimate goal of separate Maori schools, unlike with separate schools for African Americans, was integration (Barrington 1991: 314–315).

5. Another oft-cited example of negative educational rights for minorities is *Wisconsin v. Yoder* (1972), in which the U.S. Supreme Court held that Amish parents may remove their children from public schools after the eighth grade to protect and preserve the community's religious beliefs. The ruling did not, however, confer a positive right by compelling the state to support alternative religious schools.

ENDNOTES TO CHAPTER 3

1. Recall from Chapter One that the ILO's Convention No. 169, "Concerning Indigenous and Tribal Peoples in Independent Countries," qualified its use of the term *peoples* so as not to imply indigenous peoples' right to self-determination.

2. Australia and New Zealand subsequently endorsed the declaration, in 2009 and 2010, respectively.

3. *Worcester v. Georgia* (1832). For more recent affirmations of tribal sovereignty, see *United States v. Wheeler* (1978); *Santa Clara Pueblo v. Martinez* (1978); *Oklahoma Tax Commission v. Citizen Band Potawatomi Indian Tribe* (1991).

4. The passage comes from *Coe v. Commonwealth of Australia (No. 1)*. Elsewhere, Reynolds concludes that "there was no recognition or acceptance in Australia that remnant sovereignty survived annexation permitting autonomy or self-government. The Aborigines were never allowed the status of domestic dependent nations accorded to the Indian tribes in the United States" (Reynolds 1996: xii).

5. A similar sequence also characterizes the development of indigenous–state relations in circumpolar regions; see Salvesen (1995) and Sørensen (1995).

6. Countries, it should be noted, often deviate from this periodization. For instance, its unidirectional thrust does not account for the oscillation of federal Indian policies in the United States between "tribalism" and "assimilation" (Mathieu 1976).

7. In 1830, the British Crown shifted responsibility for Indian affairs from military to civilian administration, "reflecting the view that indigenous peoples had to become a matter of concern for internal governance rather than independent allies" (Perry 1996: 139). A similar restructuring occurred in the United States in 1849, when the Bureau of Indian Affairs was relocated to the Department of the Interior from the War Department.

8. In other cases, colonial rivalries failed to empower indigenous peoples or to strengthen their sovereignty claims. This is especially true in northern Scandinavia, where the colonization of *Sápmi*, the traditional Saami homeland, was fueled by competition among three kingdoms—Denmark-Norway, Sweden-Finland, and Russia—vying to incorporate the Saami and their territories under exclusive sovereign control (Lewis 1998; Thuen 1995). Saami peoples were recognized only as objects, never as partners or allies, in these interstate conflicts.

9. The English version of the text vested ultimate sovereignty in the Crown, giving Maori rights of "governorship" only. The Maori-language version, by contrast, recognized the continued sovereignty of Maori chiefs.

10. It is of course important in this context to distinguish between indigenous peoples who signed treaties and those who did not. In Canada, the Indian Act created an invidious distinction between "status" Indians—members of Indian nations that had signed a treaty with the Crown—and "nonstatus" Indians. Until 1982, nonstatus Indians and Métis (individuals of mixed indigenous and European parentage) did not enjoy the same rights qua Aboriginal peoples as status Indians. A similar legal distinction is drawn in the United States on the basis of federal recognition (Miller 2003). Nevertheless, treaty making has made it possible, or at least easier, to confer special rights on nonstatus indigenous peoples at a later point in time. Indigenous rights, that is, did not need to be invented ex nihilo but simply extended to groups previously denied their enjoyment. In *R. v. Côté* (1996: 174), for instance, the Supreme Court of Canada concluded that the Constitution Act protects *all* Aboriginal and treaty rights, not merely "those defining features [of Aboriginal societies] which were fortunate enough to have received the legal recognition and approval of European colonizers."

11. Prior to the constitutional entrenchment of Aboriginal treaty rights in 1982, parliament was authorized "to unilaterally regulate or extinguish existing treaty rights" (Macklem 2001: 138). In *Simon v. the Queen* (1985), the Supreme Court of Canada nevertheless declared that treaties between Indian nations and the Crown are not international in character, but rather are sui generis legal instruments.

12. Maori were granted parliamentary representation fully twelve years before the Electoral Act of 1879 accorded "universal" manhood suffrage to the European population. However, it was not until 1937 that Maori voted by secret ballot (a right that had been granted to Europeans in 1870) and 1950 that Maori and Europeans voted on the same day (Alves 1999).

13. At least two unsuccessful attempts in the United States have tried to admit "Indian" states to the union. The first treaty negotiated between Congress and an Indian tribe, in 1778, encouraged "friendly tribes" to join with the Delaware Indians and "form a state whereof the Delaware nation shall be the head, and have a representation in Congress" (Prucha 1994: 33). In another example, the Five Civilized Tribes—Creek, Cherokee, Seminole, Chickasaw, and Choctaw—proposed to establish the Indian Territory as a federated Indian state named Sequoyah. Their bid failed in 1907, when Oklahoma was admitted to the Union.

14. The ratio of treaties to tribes was approximately 1:1.4 in the United States, 1:7.7 in Canada (including the fifteen "modern" treaties concluded since 1973), and 1:540 in New Zealand. These calculations are based on the existence of 562 federally recognized tribes in the United States (as reported by the U.S. Department of the Interior [2009]), 614 First Nations communities in Canada (Manderscheid 2007), and 540 tribes that signed the Treaty of Waitangi in New Zealand (Walker 1999).

15. New Zealand's decision to sign the UNDRIP in April 2010 presents an exception to this general rule. Unlike in Australia, where the left-of-center Labour Party provided the impetus for domestic support of the declaration, in New Zealand the conservative National Party government opted to sign the declaration after entering into a coalition with the five parliamentarians from the Maori Party. This political alliance gave the National-led coalition a parliamentary majority. When it was in power, New Zealand's Labour Party had refused to sign the declaration, citing inconsistencies with domestic law.

16. Protesters had originally called for the occupation of Pinchgut Island in Sydney but ultimately rejected this plan because of the perceived failure of Indian activists on Alcatraz.

ENDNOTES TO CHAPTER 4

1. See the Appendix for a list of those institutions currently in existence.

2. An additional 122 private PTEs self-identified as Maori institutions in 2003; these institutions collectively enrolled 5,518 students, of whom 3,683 were Maori (New Zealand 2005b: 91).

3. For example, the website of Te Whare Wānanga o Awanuiārangi states that "although [it] has strong links to the people of Mataatua, its doors of learning have always been open to all iwi and all New Zealanders." According to Maori tradition, Mataatua was one of the canoes by which Polynesians migrated to New Zealand, and several tribes or *iwi* trace their descent from the Mataatua voyagers.

4. It is important to bear in mind, too, that students attending indigenous postsecondary institutions are, on average, older than "traditional" college students.

5. It is impossible to overemphasize the centrality of the federal government for the fiscal health of tribal colleges. Cunningham and Parker (1998) and Boyer (1997) recount how several tribal colleges were forced to close during the federal budget impasse of 1996, while many others found it necessary to dismiss staff or take out loans to make payroll.

6. Diné College is the only TCU to receive needs-based funding in addition to per capita funding under the TCCUAA.

7. At the time of this writing (in November 2010) the federal government had agreed to provide the University of Regina with two one-time grants totaling up to $7 million for academic programming at FNU.

8. Similar patterns of stratification hold for women; see Bradley (2000); Charles and Bradley (2002); Ramirez and Wotipka (2001).

9. WINHEC does not restrict accreditation to indigenous postsecondary institutions; for example, the Department of Native American Studies at Montana State University in Bozeman became the first nonindigenous controlled institution in the world to receive accreditation from WINHEC in 2009.

ENDNOTES TO CHAPTER 5

1. Portions of this chapter are adapted from Cole (2006).

2. Other minority colleges include Hispanic-, Asian/Pacific Islander-, Alaska Native-, and Native Hawaiian-serving institutions. I selected HBCUs for comparison with TCUs because they constitute "intentional" minority-serving institutions: From their very inception, they were chartered with the explicit purpose of educating minorities. Most other minority-serving colleges and universities are "incidental" institutions: They were not chartered to serve minority students but rather earned a minority-serving designation upon surpassing preestablished enrollment thresholds (for example, enrollments must exceed 25 percent Hispanic students before a college or university qualifies as a Hispanic-serving institution).

3. The governor's proposal also recommended that the Mississippi University for Women, a historically women's college that began admitting men in the 1980s pursuant to the Supreme Court's ruling in *Mississippi University for Women v. Hogan* (1982), be merged with nearby Mississippi State University.

4. The exceptions—Haskell Indian Nations University, the Institute of American Indian Arts, and Southwestern Indian Polytechnic Institute—were chartered directly by the federal government.

5. The term "citizens plus" originates in Canada, where it was coined in a 1966 government report on the distinctive legal status of Indians (Cairns 2000).

6. I am, of course, oversimplifying historical patterns. Federal Indian policy has oscillated between periods of exclusion (removal, IRA governments, and self-determination) and inclusion (allotment, assimilation, and termination). Similarly, the exclusion of black Americans had been punctuated by attempts to incorporate them as full citizens.

7. The federal government subsidized the transfer of Indian students from federal to state schools because most Indians still lived on reservations, which, as federal trust territories, are exempt from the property taxes that help fund public school systems.

8. North Carolina has also taken the strongest measures of any state in the Deep South to desegregate the former "dual" system of black and white higher education ("The Racial Integration of Historically Black Universities" 1999/2000).

9. Notice the double-entendre implied by "just schools," which can be interpreted to mean "fair" schools or "merely" schools—that is, neither black nor white.

10. Oberlin College became the first coeducational institution in 1837, and by 1880 a majority of women enrolled in higher education attended coeducational colleges and universities (Miller-Bernal and Poulson 2006: 3).

11. The quoted passages come from Gross (1973: 242–248).

12. On the political as opposed to racial status of American Indians, see *Morton v. Mancari* (1974).

13. For much the same reason, a controversial Arizona law, enacted in 2010, that prohibits school districts and charter schools from offering courses that "are designed primarily for pupils of a particular ethnic group" exempts "courses or classes for Native American pupils" (Arizona Revised Statutes, §§ 15-112[A][3] and 15-112[E][1]).

ENDNOTES TO CHAPTER 6

1. Portions of this chapter are adapted from Cole (2006).

2. In *Gong Lum v. Rice* (1927), for example, the Supreme Court held that "separate but equal" education systems meant that white and nonwhite schools must offer the same curriculum.

3. The states in question were Arkansas, Florida, Georgia, Louisiana, Maryland, Mississippi, North Carolina, Oklahoma, Pennsylvania, and Virginia.

4. Courses that consider American Indian or African American perspectives as one of several cultures are indicative of multiculturalism, but I restrict attention to courses that focused on one minority culture over others (that is, Indiocentrism or Afrocentrism). Curricula that compared either American Indian or African American cultural perspectives *only* to the dominant (Anglo-American) culture, however, were included in the analyses. I excluded independent studies courses, most of which do not provide course descriptions and hence cannot be coded as having (or not having) ethnocentric content.

5. Unless otherwise specified, "ethnocentrism" refers to American Indian or tribal content with respect to TCUs, African American content vis-à-vis HBCUs, and either American Indian or African American content at mainstream institutions.

6. Although the proportion of ethnocentric courses remained rather stable at HBCUs over time, it vacillated considerably at TCUs. These fluctuations are attributable to (1) the shifting set of tribal colleges for which data are available over time; (2) the reduction or elimination of programs emphasizing American Indian perspectives; and (3) overall expansion in course offerings that outpaced growth in the number of ethnocentric courses. Descriptive analyses for a constant set of TCUs revealed patterns similar to those reported here.

7. What follows is a brief overview of the study design. For more details regarding methods, data, and variable descriptions, see Cole (2006).

8. I selected 1992 and 2002 for analysis to maximize the number of TCUs entering the sample, as the number of TCUs for which catalogs were available nearly doubled, from twelve to twenty-three, between 1987 and 1992.

9. Estimates were obtained using cross-sectional time-series negative-binomial regression (Long 1997; StataCorp 2003: 141–149). I used the "xtnbreg" feature of Stata 8.0 with standard error estimates adjusted for clustering within institutions over time.

10. Percentage changes are calculated by exponentiating the regression coefficient, subtracting 1, and multiplying by 100. Consequently, the effect of each additional course offering on the number of ethnocentric courses is calculated as: $(\exp[.002] - 1) \times 100\% = 0.2\%$.

11. Additional analyses revealed that HBCUs established by black religious denominations such as the African Methodist Episcopal Church or the African Methodist Episcopal Zion Church did not differ significantly from other HBCUs with respect to Afrocentric course offerings.

12. Predicted probabilities were obtained from negative-binomial regression analyses of the number of ethnocentric courses in 2002. Estimates are based on category-specific mean values for continuous variables and modal values for dichotomous variables in the analysis.

ENDNOTES TO CONCLUSION

1. The difficulties experienced by indigenous postsecondary institutions in their quest for legitimacy compares starkly with the accreditation crisis endured by black colleges in the United States. With the demise of legalized segregation in the 1950s, regional accreditation agencies in the American South abolished their two-tier systems, so that black colleges were no longer evaluated using less rigorous criteria than were applied to white colleges. This development was both a blessing and a curse for HBCUs. It constituted, on the one hand, a symbolic victory for historically black colleges by signaling their formal equivalence with white institutions. On the other hand, state governments in the South, through decades of financial neglect, had virtually guaranteed that HBCUs would not be equal to white institutions (notwithstanding the Supreme Court's "separate by equal" ruling in *Plessy v. Ferguson*). As a result, only half of the sixty-five black colleges evaluated under the common standard initially passed muster (Samuels 2004: 70–71).

2. In the United States, colleges and universities must be accredited before they can receive federal student loans. In the case of tribal colleges, federal funding is available only when they are accredited or making reasonable progress toward accreditation.

3. In at least one case, closure was a temporary setback; Keweenaw Bay Ojibwa Community College, a tribal college in Michigan, closed in 1980 and reopened in 1998.

4. The right of "exit" must be preserved in principle, but it may sometimes be constrained in practice, especially if an indigenous postsecondary institution is the only one accessible geographically, academically, or culturally to indigenous students.

REFERENCES

Abernethy, David B. 2000. *The Dynamics of Global Dominance: European Overseas Empires, 1415–1980.* New Haven, CT: Yale University Press.

Aboriginal Institutes' Consortium. 2005. *Aboriginal Institutions of Higher Education: A Struggle for the Education of Aboriginal Students, Control of Indigenous Knowledge, and Recognition of Aboriginal Institutions.* Toronto: Canadian Race Relations Foundation. Retrieved on October 29, 2005, from: www.crr.ca/divers-files/en/pub/repePubRepAboIns1.pdf.

Adams, David Wallace. 1995. *Education for Extinction: American Indians and the Boarding School Experience, 1875–1928.* Lawrence: University Press of Kansas.

Alabama State University. 1999. *General Undergraduate Catalog 1999–2001.* Montgomery: Author.

Albert, Stuart, and David A. Whetten. 1985. "Organizational Identity." *Research in Organizational Behavior* 7: 263–295.

Alfredsson, Gudmundur. 1987. "The Right to Self-Determination and Its Many Manifestations." In Ruth Thompson, ed., *The Rights of Indigenous Peoples in International Law,* 53–57. Saskatoon: University of Saskatchewan Native Law Centre.

Allen, Robert S. 1992. *His Majesty's Indian Allies: British Indian Policy in the Defence of Canada, 1774–1815.* Toronto: Dundurn Press.

Allen, Walter R., and Joseph O. Jewell. 2002. "A Backward Glance Forward: Past, Present, and Future Perspectives on Historically Black Colleges and Universities." *Review of Higher Education* 25: 241–261.

Altbach, Philip G. 1998. *Comparative Higher Education: Knowledge, the University, and Development.* Greenwich, CT: Ablex.

Alves, Dora. 1999. *The Maori and the Crown: An Indigenous People's Struggle for Self-Determination.* Westport, CT: Greenwood.

American Indian Higher Education Consortium [AIHEC]. 1999. *Tribal Colleges: An Introduction.* Washington, DC: AIHEC and the American Indian College Fund.

———. 2000. *Globalization of Tribal Colleges and Universities: Proceedings and Reference Guide*. Retrieved on July 23, 2005, from: www.aihec.org/AIHEC%20Documents/PDFS/proceedings.pdf.

———. 2006. *American Indian Measures for Success in Higher Education: Fact Book 2005*. Norwood, MA: Systematic Research, Inc.

Anaya, S. James. 2004. *Indigenous Peoples in International Law*, 2nd ed. New York: Oxford University Press.

Anderson, Benedict. 1991. *Imagined Communities*, 2nd ed. New York: Verso.

Anderson, James D. 1988. *The Education of Blacks in the South, 1860–1935*. Chapel Hill: University of North Carolina Press.

Anderson, Perry. 1974. *Lineages of the Absolutist State*. London: N.L.B.

Armitage, Andrew. 1995. *Comparing the Policy of Aboriginal Assimilation*. Vancouver: University of British Columbia Press.

Asante, Molefi Kete. 1991. "The Afrocentric Idea in Education." *Journal of Negro Education* 60: 170–180.

Asian Development Bank. 1999. *Policy on Indigenous Peoples*. Manila: Asian Development Bank.

Associated Press. 2009. "Bolivians Back New Constitution." *New York Times*, Jan. 25.

Astiz, M. Fernanda, Alexander W. Wiseman, and David P. Baker. 2002. "Slouching towards Decentralization: Consequences of Globalization for Curricular Control in National Education Systems." *Comparative Education Review* 41: 435–459.

Aukerman, Miriam J. 2000. "Definitions and Justifications: Minority and Indigenous Rights in a Central/East European Context." *Human Rights Quarterly* 22: 1011–1050.

Australia. 1937. *Aboriginal Welfare*. Report of the Initial Conference of Commonwealth and State Aboriginal Authorities. Canberra: Commonwealth Government Printer.

———. 2000. *Katu Kalpa: Report on the Inquiry into the Effectiveness of Education and Training Programs for Indigenous Australians*. Canberra: Commonwealth of Australia. Retrieved on June 7, 2002, from: www.aph.gov.au/senate/committee/EET_CTTE/indiged/.

———. 2001. *Students 2001: Selected Higher Education Statistics*. Canberra: Department of Education, Science and Training. Retrieved on October 18, 2005, from: www.dest.gov.au/sectors/higher_education/publications_resources/statistics/.

———. 2003a. "Population Characteristics, Aboriginal and Torres Strait Islander Australians." Canberra: Australian Bureau of Statistics. Retrieved on November 19, 2005, from: www.abs.gov.au.

———. 2003b. *Report on the Review of the Independent Indigenous Vocational Education and Training Providers*. Canberra: Commonwealth of Australia.

———. 2003c. *Students 2003: Selected Higher Education Statistics*. Canberra: Department of Education, Science and Training. Retrieved on October 18, 2005, from: www.dest.gov.au/sectors/higher_education/publications_resources/statistics/.

———. 2005. *National Report to Parliament on Indigenous Education and Training, 2003*. Canberra: Commonwealth of Australia.

Australian Universities Quality Agency. 2006. *Report of an Audit of Batchelor Institute of Indigenous Tertiary Education*. Melbourne: Australian Universities Quality Agency.

Bacone College. 2008a. "History and Heritage." Retrieved on February 11, 2010, from: www.bacone.edu/about.html.

———. 2008b. "Mission Statement." Retrieved on February 11, 2010, from: www.bacone.edu/about/mission.html.

Barman, Jean, Yvonne Hébert, and Don McCaskill, eds. 1986. *Indian Education in Canada*, vol. 1: *The Legacy*. Vancouver: University of British Columbia Press.

Barnhardt, Ray. 1991. "Higher Education in the Fourth World: Indigenous People Take Control." *Canadian Journal of Native Education* 18: 199–232.

Baron, James P., Frank Dobbin, and P. Devereaux Jennings. 1986. "War and Peace: The Evolution of Modern Personnel Administration in U.S. Industry." *American Journal of Sociology* 92: 250–283.

Barrington, John M. 1991. "The New Zealand Experience: Maoris." In Margaret A. Gibson and John U. Ogbu, eds., *Minority Status and Schooling: A Comparative Study of Immigrant and Involuntary Minorities*, 309–326. New York: Garland.

Barrington, J. M., and T. H. Beaglehole. 1974. *Maori Schools in a Changing Society*. Wellington: New Zealand Council for Educational Research.

Barsh, Russel Lawrence. 1986. "Indigenous Peoples: An Emerging Object of International Law." *American Journal of International Law* 80: 369–385.

———. 1994. "Indigenous Peoples in the 1990s: From Object to Subject of International Law?" *Harvard Human Rights Journal* 7: 33–86.

Bashford, Lucy, and Hans Heinzerling. 1987. "Blue Quills Native Education Centre: A Case Study." In Jean Barman, Yvonne M. Hébert, and Don N. McCaskill, eds., *Indian Education in Canada*, vol. 2: *The Challenge*, 126–141. Vancouver: University of British Columbia Press.

Basinger, Julianne. 2001. "Accreditation at Risk for Little Big Horn College." *Chronicle of Higher Education*, February 16, p. A38. Retrieved on July 14, 2005, from: http://chronicle.com/weekly/v47/i23/ 23a03801.

Batchelor Institute. 2005. "About Batchelor: History." Retrieved on November 18, 2005, from: www.batchelor.edu.au/file/webpage/about_history.html.

Battiste, Marie. 2000. "Forward." In Marlene Brant Castellano, Lynne Davis, and Louise Lahache, eds., *Aboriginal Education: Fulfilling the Promise*, vii–ix. Vancouver: University of British Columbia Press.

Beach, Hugh. 1994. "The Saami of Lapland." In Minority Rights Group, ed., *Polar Peoples: Self-Determination and Development*, 147–205. London: Minority Rights Publications.

Ben-David, Joseph, and Awraham Zloczower. 1962. "Universities and Academic Systems in Modern Societies." *European Journal of Sociology* 3: 45–84.

Benavot, Aaron, Yun-Kyung Cha, David Kamens, John W. Meyer, and Suk-Ying Wong. 1991. "Knowledge for the Masses: World Models and National Curricula, 1920–1986." *American Sociological Review* 56: 85–100.

Bendix, Reinhard. [1964] 1996. *Nation-Building and Citizenship*. New Brunswick, NJ: Transaction.

Benford, Robert D., and David A. Snow. 2000. "Framing Processes and Social Movements." *Annual Review of Sociology* 26: 611–639.

Benjamin, Don-Paul, Stephen Chambers, and Gary Reiterman. 1993. "A Focus on American Indian College Persistence." *Journal of American Indian Education* 32: 25–40.

Berger, Peter L. 1967. *The Sacred Canopy*. Garden City, NY: Doubleday.

Berger, Peter L., and Thomas Luckmann. 1966. *The Social Construction of Reality*. Garden City, NY: Anchor.

Bergesen, Albert. 1980. "From Utilitarianism to Globology: The Shift from the Individual to the World as a Whole as the Primordial Unit of Analysis." In Albert Bergesen, ed., *Studies of the Modern World-System*, 1–12. New York: Academic Press.

Binder, Amy J. 2002. *Contentious Curricula*. Princeton, NJ: Princeton University Press.

Blackfeet Community College. 1996. *1996–1998 Catalog*. Browning, MT: Author.

Blau, Peter M. 1973. *The Organization of Academic Work*. New York: Wiley.

Boldt, Menno, and J. Anthony Long. 1984. "Tribal Traditions and European-Western Political Ideologies: The Dilemma of Canada's Native Indians." *Canadian Journal of Political Science* 17: 537–554.

Boli, John. 1989. *New Citizens for a New Society.* Oxford, UK: Pergamon.

Boli, John, and Michael A. Elliott. 2008. "Façade Diversity: The Individualization of Cultural Difference." *International Sociology* 23: 540–560.

Boli, John, Francisco O. Ramirez, and John W. Meyer. 1985. "Explaining the Origins and Expansion of Mass Education." *Comparative Education Review* 29: 145–170.

Boli, John, and George M. Thomas. 1997. "World Culture in the World Polity: A Century of International Non-Governmental Organization." *American Sociological Review* 62: 171–190.

———. 1999. *Constructing World Culture: International Nongovernmental Organizations since 1875.* Stanford, CA: Stanford University Press.

Boswell, Terry. 1989. "Colonial Empires and the Capitalist World-Economy: A Time Series Analysis of Colonization, 1640–1960." *American Sociological Review* 54: 180–196.

Bourke, Colin J., Jennifer K. Burden, and Samantha Moore. 1996. *Factors Affecting Performance of Aboriginal and Torres Strait Islander Students at Australian Universities: A Case Study.* Canberra: Evaluations and Investigations Program, Higher Education Division, Department of Employment, Education, Training and Youth Affairs. Retrieved on April 27, 2010, from: www.dest.gov.au/archive/highered/eippubs/eip9618/chapter1.htm#head1.

Boychuk, Gerald W. 2000. "Differences of Degrees: Higher Education in the American States and Canadian Provinces." *Canadian Public Administration* 43: 453–472.

Boyer, Paul. 1997. *Native American Colleges: Progress and Prospects.* Princeton, NJ: The Carnegie Foundation for the Advancement of Teaching.

Bradley, Karen. 2000. "The Incorporation of Women into Higher Education: Paradoxical Outcomes?" *Sociology of Education* 73: 1–18.

Brint, Steven. 2002. "The Rise of the 'Practical Arts.'" In Steven Brint, ed., *The Future of the City of Intellect,* 231–259. Stanford, CA: Stanford University Press.

Brint, Steven, and Jerome Karabel. 1991. "Institutional Origins and Transformations: The Case of American Community Colleges." In Walter W. Powell and Paul J. DiMaggio, eds., *The New Institutionalism in Organizational Analysis,* 337–360. Chicago: University of Chicago Press.

Brown, M. Christopher II. 2001. "Collegiate Desegregation and the Public Black College: A New Policy Mandate." *Journal of Higher Education* 72: 46–62.

Brubaker, Rogers. 1992. *Citizenship and Nationhood in France and Germany.* Cambridge, MA: Harvard University Press.

Brysk, Alison. 2000. *From Tribal Village to Global Village: Indian Rights and International Relations in Latin America.* Stanford, CA: Stanford University Press.

Bull, Hedley. 1977. *The Anarchical Society: A Study of Order in World Politics.* New York: Columbia University Press.

Cairns, Alan. 2000. *Citizens Plus: Aboriginal Peoples and the Canadian State.* Vancouver: University of British Columbia Press.

———. 2003. "Afterward: International Dimensions of the Citizen Issue for Indigenous Peoples/Nations." *Citizenship Studies* 7: 497–512.

Campbell, Monica. 2006. "In Latin America, New Universities for Indigenous Students Flourish." *The Chronicle of Higher Education,* Sept. 22, pp. A40–A43.

Canada. 1996a. *Report of the Royal Commission on Aboriginal Peoples,* vol. 3: *Gathering Strength.* Ottawa: Minister of Supply and Services Canada.

———. 1996b. *Report of the Royal Commission on Aboriginal Peoples,* vol. 1: *Looking Forward Looking Back.* Ottawa: Minister of Supply and Services Canada.

———. 2000. *Information: Post-Secondary Education for Status Indians and Inuit*. Ottawa: Indian and Northern Affairs Canada. Retrieved on October 29, 2005, from: www.ainc-inac.gc.ca/pr/info/info110_e.pdf.

———. 2002. *Words First: An Evolving Terminology Relating to Aboriginal Peoples in Canada*. Ottawa: Communications Branch, Indian and Northern Affairs Canada. Retrieved on December 7, 2004, from: www.people.cornell.edu/pages/jff1/learningacadwrtg.htm.

———. 2003. *Basic Departmental Data 2003*. Ottawa: Indian and Northern Affairs Canada.

———. 2010a. *Backgrounder: Funding for the First Nations University of Canada 2010–2011*. Ottawa: Indian and Northern Affairs Canada. Retrieved on October 22, 2010, from: www.ainc-inac.gc.ca/ai/mr/nr/m-a2010/23362bg-eng.asp.

———. 2010b. *Indian Residential Schools*. Ottawa: Indian and Northern Affairs Canada. Retrieved on October 19, 2010, from: www.ainc-inac.gc.ca/ai/rqpi/index-eng.asp.

Carney, Cary Michael. 1999. *Native American Higher Education in the United States*. New Brunswick, NJ: Transaction.

Champagne, Duane, and Jay Stauss, eds. 2002. *Native American Studies in Higher Education*. Walnut Creek, CA: AltaMira Press.

Charles, Maria, and Karen Bradley. 2002. "Equal but Separate? A Cross-National Study of Sex Segregation in Higher Education." *American Sociological Review* 67: 573–599.

Chase-Dunn, Christopher, and Richard Rubinson. 1977. "Toward a Structural Perspective on the World-System." *Politics and Society* 7: 453–476.

Chesterman, John, and Brian Galligan. 1997. *Citizens without Rights: Aborigines and Australian Citizenship*. Cambridge, UK: Cambridge University Press.

Clark, Burton R. 1978. "Academic Differentiation in National Systems of Higher Education." *Comparative Education Review* 22: 242–258.

Clinton, William J. 2000. "Nondiscrimination on the Basis of Race, Sex, Color, National Origin, Disability, Religion, Age, Sexual Orientation, and Status as a Parent in Federally Conducted Education and Training Programs." Executive Order 13160 of June 23, 2000. Retrieved on April 22, 2010, from: www.justice.gov/crt/cor/Pubs/eo13160.pdf.

Cohen, David. 2005a. "U. of New Zealand Comes under Attack." *Chronicle of Higher Education*, March 11, p. A46. Retrieved on July 14, 2005, from: http://chonicle.com/weekly/v51/i27/27a04605.htm.

———. 2005b. "A Victim of Success? A Maori University in New Zealand Tries to Cope with Rapid Growth." *Chronicle of Higher Education*, July 25, p. A34. Retrieved on July 14, 2005, from: http://chonicle.com/weekly/v49/i46/46a03401.htm.

Cole, Wade M. 2006. "Accrediting Culture: An Analysis of Tribal and Black College Curricula." *Sociology of Education* 79: 355–388.

Coleman, James S. 1986. "Social Theory, Social Research, and a Theory of Action." *American Journal of Sociology* 91: 1309–1335.

Cornell, Stephen. 1988. *The Return of the Native*. New York: Oxford University Press.

Corntassel, Jeff J. 2003. "Who Is Indigenous? 'Peoplehood' and Ethnonationalist Approaches to Rearticulating Indigenous Identity." *Nationalism and Ethnic Politics* 9: 75–100.

Corntassel, Jeff J., and Tomas Hopkins Primeau. 1995. "Indigenous 'Sovereignty' and International Law: Revised Strategies for Pursuing 'Self-Determination.'" *Human Rights Quarterly* 71: 345–365.

Corson, David. 1999. "Community-Based Education for Indigenous Cultures." In Stephen May, ed., *Indigenous Community-Based Education*, 8–19. Clevedon, UK: Multilingual Matters Ltd.

Courchene, Thomas J., and Lisa M. Powell. 1992. *A First Nations Province*. Kingston, Ontario, Canada: The Institute of Intergovernmental Relations, Queen's University.

Craufurd-Lewis, Michael. 1995. "Treaties with Aboriginal Minorities." *Canadian Journal of Native Studies* 15: 1–59.

Cunningham, Alisa Federico, and Christina Parker. 1998. "Tribal Colleges as Community Institutions and Resources." In Jamie P. Merisotis and Colleen T. O'Brien, eds., *Minority-Serving Institutions: Distinct Purposes, Common Goals*, 45–56, No. 102 in *New Directions for Higher Education*. San Francisco: Jossey-Bass.

Daes, Erica-Irene A. 1996. *Standard-Setting Activities: Evolution of Standards Concerning the Rights of Indigenous People*. New York: United Nations. U.N. Doc. E/CN.4/Sub.2/AC.4/1996/2.

Darnell, Frank, and Anton Hoëm. 1996. *Taken to Extremes: Education in the Far North*. Oslo: Scandinavian University Press.

Davies, Scott. 1999. "From Moral Duty to Cultural Rights: A Case Study of Political Framing in Education." *Sociology of Education* 72: 1–21.

Davies, Scott, and Neil Guppy. 1997. "Globalization and Educational Reforms in Anglo-American Democracies." *Comparative Education Review* 41: 435–459.

Deloria, Vine Jr. 1969. *Custer Died for Your Sins*. New York: Macmillan.

———. 1985. *Behind the Trail of Broken Treaties*. Austin: University of Texas Press.

Dennison, John D., and Paul Gallagher. 1986. *Canada's Community Colleges*. Vancouver: University of British Columbia Press.

Department of Indian and Northern Affairs [DIAND]. 1969. *Statement of the Government of Canada on Indian Policy*. Ottawa: Queen's Printer.

DiMaggio, Paul J. 1988. "Interest and Agency in Institutional Theory." In Lynn G. Zucker, ed., *Institutional Patterns and Organizations*, 3–21. Cambridge, MA: Ballinger.

DiMaggio, Paul J., and Walter W. Powell. 1983. "The Iron Cage Revisited: Institutional Isomorphism and Collective Rationality in Organizational Fields." *American Sociological Review* 48: 147–160.

Diné College. 2002. *2002–2003 General Catalog*. Tsaile, AZ: Author.

Donelan, Michael. 1984. "Spain and the Indies." In Hedley Bull and Adam Watson, eds., *The Expansion of International Society*, 75–85. Oxford, UK: Clarendon.

Donnelly, Jack. 1986. "International Human Rights: A Regime Analysis." *International Organization* 40: 599–642.

———. 2003. *Universal Human Rights in Theory and Practice*, 2nd ed. Ithaca, NY: Cornell University Press.

Dorion, John, and Kwan R. Yang. 2000. "Métis Post-Secondary Education: A Case Study of the Gabriel Dumont Institute." In Marlene Brant Castellano, Lynne Davis, and Louise Lahache, eds., *Aboriginal Education: Fulfilling the Promise*, 176–189. Vancouver: University of British Columbia Press.

Dow, Coral. 2000. "Aboriginal Tent Embassy: Icon or Eyesore?" Chronology No. 3 1999–2000, Parliamentary Library, Parliament of Australia. Retrieved on August 24, 2005, from: www.aph.gov.au/library/pubs/chron/1999-2000/2000chr03.htm.

D-Q University. 2002. *2002–2004 Catalog*. Davis, CA: Author.

Drewry, Henry N., and Humphrey Doermann. 2001. *Stand and Prosper: Private Black Colleges and Their Students*. Princeton, NJ: Princeton University Press.

Drori, Gili, John W. Meyer, Francisco O. Ramirez, and Evan Schofer. 2003. *Science in the Modern World Polity: Institutionalization and Globalization*. Stanford, CA: Stanford University Press.

Du Bois, W. E. B. [1903] 1989. *The Souls of Black Folk*. New York: Penguin.

———. [1908] 2001. "Galileo Galilei." In Herbert Aptheker, ed., *The Education of Black People*, 33–48. New York: Monthly Review Press.

———. [1933] 2001. "The Field and Function of the Negro College." In Herbert Aptheker, ed., *The Education of Black People*, 111–133. New York: Monthly Review Press.

Durie, Mason. 1998. *Te Mana te Kāwanatanga: The Politics of Māori Self-Determination*. Auckland: Oxford University Press.

Elazar, Daniel J. 1987. *Exploring Federalism*. Tuscaloosa: The University of Alabama Press.

———. 1991. *Federal Systems of the World*. Harlow, UK: Longman Current Affairs.

Elliott, Michael A., and John Boli. 2008. "Human Rights Instruments and Human Rights Institutionalization, 1863–2003." Paper presented at the 38th World Congress of the International Institute of Sociology, Budapest, June 28.

"Federal Funding Increases for Tribal Colleges." 1991. *Tribal College Journal* 2: 10.

Feinberg, Walter. 1998. *Common Schools/Uncommon Identities: National Unity and Cultural Difference*. New Haven, CT: Yale University Press.

Fettes, Mark, and Ruth Norton. 2000. "Voices of Winter: Aboriginal Languages and Public Policy in Canada." In Marlene Brant Castellano, Lynne Davis, and Louise Lahache, eds., *Aboriginal Education: Fulfilling the Promise*, 29–54. Vancouver: University of British Columbia Press.

First Nations Education Steering Committee. 2008. *Aboriginal Post-Secondary Education in British Columbia: A Place for Aboriginal Institutes*. West Vancouver, BC: Author.

First Nations University of Canada. 2005. "Our History." Retrieved on August 15, 2005, from: www.firstnationsuniversity.ca/default.aspx?page=53.

———. 2009. "Our Vision." Retrieved on January 31, 2010, from: www.firstnationsuniversity.ca/default.aspx?page=52.

———. 2010. "News Release: Reorganization at First Nations University of Canada," August 19. Retrieved on October 21, 2010 from: www.firstnationsuniversity.ca/files/File/FNUniv_Media_Release_081910.pdf.

Fisk University. 2002. *Fisk University Bulletin: 2002–2004*. Nashville, TN: Author.

Flanagan, Tom. 2000. *First Nations? Second Thoughts*. Montreal and Kingston: McGill-Queen's University Press.

Fleras, Augie. 1985. "From Social Control towards Political Self-Determination? Maori Seats and the Politics of Separate Maori Representation in New Zealand." *Canadian Journal of Political Science* 18: 551–576.

———. 1999. "Politicising Indigeneity: Ethno-politics in White Settler Dominions." In Paul Havemann, ed., *Indigenous Peoples' Rights in Australia, Canada, and New Zealand*, 187–234. Melbourne: Oxford University Press.

Fleras, Augie, and Jean Leonard Elliott. 1992. *The "Nations Within": Aboriginal–State Relations in Canada, the United States, and New Zealand*. Toronto: Oxford University Press.

Fletcher, Christine. 1999. "Living Together but Not Neighbours: Cultural Imperialism in Australia." In Paul Havemann, ed., *Indigenous Peoples' Rights in Australia, Canada, and New Zealand*, 335–350. Melbourne: Oxford University Press.

Flood, Josephine. 2006. *The Original Australians: Story of the Aboriginal People*. Crows Nest, Australia: Allen & Unwin.

Fort Peck Community College. 2001. *Catalog 2001–2003*. Poplar, MT: Author.

Frank, David John, and Jay Gabler. 2006. *Reconstructing the University: Worldwide Shifts in Academia in the 20th Century*. Stanford, CA: Stanford University Press.

Frank, David John, and John W. Meyer. 2002. "The Profusion of Individual Roles and Identities in the Postwar Period." *Sociological Theory* 20: 86–105.

———. 2007. "University Expansion and the Knowledge Society." *Theory and Society* 36: 287–311.

Frank, David John, Evan Schofer, and John Charles Torres. 1994. "Rethinking History: Change in the University Curriculum, 1910–90." *Sociology of Education* 67: 231–242.

Frank, David John, Suk-Ying Wong, John W. Meyer, and Francisco O. Ramirez. 2000. "What Counts as History: A Cross-National and Longitudinal Study of University Curricula." *Comparative Education Review* 44: 29–53.

Frantz, Klaus. 1999. *Indian Reservations in the United States.* Chicago: University of Chicago Press.

Friedland, Roger, and Robert R. Alford. 1991. "Bringing Society Back In: Symbols, Practices, and Institutional Contradictions." In Walter W. Powell and Paul J. DiMaggio, eds., *The New Institutionalism in Organizational Analysis*, 232–263. Chicago: University of Chicago Press.

Friedrichs, Jörg. 2001. "The Meaning of New Medievalism." *European Journal of International Relations* 7: 475–502.

Gabler, Jay, and David John Frank. 2005. "The Natural Sciences in the University: Change and Variation over the 20th Century." *Sociology of Education* 78: 183–206.

Gardiner-Garden, John. 1999. "From Dispossession to Reconciliation." Research Paper 27, Parliamentary Library, Parliament of Australia. Retrieved on April 5, 2010, from: www.aph.gov.au/library/Pubs/RP/1998-99/99rp27.htm.

Gasman, Marybeth. 2008. "Minority-Serving Institutions: A Historical Backdrop." In Marybeth Gasman, Benjamin Baez, and Caroline Sotello Viernes Turner, eds., *Understanding Minority-Serving Institutions*, 18–27. Albany: State University of New York Press.

Gasman, Marybeth, Benjamin Baez, and Caroline Sotello Viernes Turner, eds. 2008. *Understanding Minority-Serving Institutions.* Albany: State University of New York Press.

Gilling, Bryan D. 1993. "The Maori Land Court in New Zealand: An Historical Overview." *Canadian Journal of Native Studies* 13: 17–29.

Goedegebuure, Leo C. J., and V. Lynn Meek. 1991. "Restructuring Higher Education: A Comparative Analysis between Australia and The Netherlands." *Comparative Education* 27: 7–22.

Goffman, Erving. 1959. *The Presentation of Self in Everyday Society.* New York: Doubleday.

———. 1963. *Stigma: Notes on the Management of Spoiled Identity.* New York: Simon & Schuster.

Goldstein, Joshua S. 1988. *Long Cycles: Prosperity and War in the Modern Age.* New Haven, CT: Yale University Press.

Graney, Katherine E. 1999. "Education Reform in Tatarstan and Bashkortostan: Sovereignty Projects in Post-Soviet Russia." *Europe-Asia Studies* 51: 611–632.

Green, L. C., and Olive P. Dickason. 1989. *The Law of Nations and the New World.* Edmonton: University of Alberta Press.

Gross, Michael Paul. 1973. "Indian Control for Quality Indian Education." *North Dakota Law Review* 49: 237–265.

Guillory, Justin P., and Kelly Ward. 2008. "Tribal Colleges and Universities: Identity, Invisibility, and Current Issues." In Marybeth Gasman, Benjamin Baez, and Caroline Sotello Viernes Turner, eds., *Understanding Minority-Serving Institutions*, 91–110. Albany: State University of New York Press.

Gumport, Patricia J., Maria Iannozzi, Susan Shaman, and Robert Zemsky. 1997. *Trends in United States Higher Education from Massification to Post Massification.* Stanford, CA: National Center for Postsecondary Improvement, School of Education, Stanford University.

Gumport, Patricia J., and Stuart K. Snydman. 2002. "The Formal Organization of Knowledge: An Analysis of Academic Structure." *Journal of Higher Education* 73: 375–408.

Hall, James W. 1979. "Regional Accreditation and Nontraditional Colleges: A President's Point of View." *Journal of Higher Education* 50: 171–177.

Hall, William Edward. 1909. *A Treatise on International Law.* Oxford, UK: Clarendon.

Hampton, Eber. 2000. "First Nations-Controlled University Education in Canada." In Marlene Brant Castellano, Lynne Davis, and Louise Lahache, eds., *Aboriginal Education: Fulfilling the Promise*, 208–223. Vancouver: University of British Columbia Press.

Hanke, Lewis. 1949. *The Spanish Struggle for Justice in the Conquest of America*. Philadelphia: University of Pennsylvania Press.

———. 1959. *Aristotle and the American Indians: A Study of Race Prejudice in the Modern World*. London: Hollis & Carter.

Harman, Grant. 1991. "Institutional Amalgamations and Abolition of the Binary System in Australia under John Dawkins." *Higher Education Quarterly* 45: 176–198.

Harris-Stowe State College. 2001. *Bulletin 2001–2003*. St. Louis, MO: Author.

Harwarth, Irene, Mindi Maline, and Elizabeth DeBra. 1997. *Women's Colleges in the United States: History, Issues, and Challenges*. Washington, DC: National Institute on Postsecondary Education, Libraries, and Lifelong Learning.

Hasluck, Paul. 1961. *The Policy of Assimilation: Decisions of Commonwealth and State Ministers at the Native Welfare Conference*. Canberra: A. J. Arthur, Commonwealth Government Printer.

Hatch, May Jo, and Majken Schultz. 2004. *Organizational Identity*. New York: Oxford University Press.

Havemann, Paul, ed. 1999. *Indigenous Peoples' Rights in Australia, Canada, and New Zealand*. Melbourne: Oxford University Press.

Hele, Karl. 1994. "Native People and the Socialist State: The Native Populations of Siberia and Their Experiences as Part of the Union of Soviet Socialist Republics." *Canadian Journal of Native Studies* 14: 252–272.

Henderson, James [sákéj] Youngblod. 1995. "Treaties and Indian Education." In Marie Ann Battiste and Jean Barman, eds., *First Nations Education in Canada: The Circle Unfolds*, 245–261. Vancouver: University of British Columbia Press.

Hobbes, Thomas. [1651] 1988. *The Leviathan*. New York: Prometheus.

Hooghe, Liesbet, and Gary Marks. 2001. *Multi-Level Governance and European Integration*. Lanham, MD: Rowman & Littlefield.

Howard, Bradley Reed. 2003. *Indigenous Peoples and the State: The Struggle for Native Rights*. DeKalb: Northern Illinois University Press.

Howard University. 1890. *Catalogue of the Officers and Students, from March, 1890, to March, 1891*. Washington, DC: Author.

Hyde, Charles Cheney. 1922. *International Law Chiefly as Applied by the United States*. Boston: Little, Brown, and Co.

Ilisimatusarfik. 2005. "About Ilisimatusarfik." Retrieved on August 18, 2005, from: www.ilisimatusarfik.gl/eng/ about_ili_eng-filer/about_ilisimatusarfik.htm.

Indian and Northern Affairs Canada. 2008. "Treaties with Aboriginal People in Canada." Retrieved on June 23, 2009, from: www.ainc-inac.gc.ca/al/ldc/ccl/tra-eng.asp.

Indian Country Today. 2005. "Education Milestones: Examples for the 'Long Run.'" March 18.

Jang, Yong Suk. 2003. "The Global Diffusion of Ministries of Science and Technology." In Gili S. Drori, John W. Meyer, Francisco O. Ramirez, and Evan Schofer, eds., *Science in the Modern World Polity*, 120–135. Stanford, CA: Stanford University Press.

Jaschik, Scott. 2009. "Threat to Black Colleges." *Inside Higher Ed*, November 17. Retrieved on November 17, 2009, from: www.insidehighered.com/news/2009/11/17/hbcu.

Jenkins, Andrea. 2007. "Indigenous Postsecondary Institutions in Canada and the U.S." *Higher Education Perspectives* 3: 1–27.

Jepperson, Ronald L. 1991. "Institutions, Institutional Effects, and Institutionalism." In Walter W. Powell and Paul J. DiMaggio, eds., *The New Institutionalism in Organizational Analysis*, 143–163. Chicago: University of Chicago Press.

———. 2002. "Political Modernities: Disentangling Two Underlying Dimensions of Institutional Differentiation." *Sociological Theory* 20: 61–85.

Jepperson, Ronald L., and Ann Swidler. 1994. "What Properties of Culture Should We Measure?" *Poetics* 22: 359–371.

Jewell, Joseph O. 2002. "To Set an Example: The Tradition of Diversity at Historically Black Colleges and Universities." *Urban Education* 37: 7–21.

Johansen, Bruce Elliott, and Barbara Alice Mann. 2000. *Encyclopedia of the Haudenosaunee (Iroquois Confederacy)*. Westport, CT: Greenwood.

Johnson, Ralph W. 1991. "Fragile Gains: Two Centuries of Canadian and United States Policy toward Indians." *Washington Law Review* 66: 643–718.

Johnston, Grant. 2008. "Wananga Ready for Next 25 Years." *Te Awamutu Courier*, Oct. 7.

Kamens, David H. 1992. "Variant Forms: Cases of Countries with Distinct Curricula." In John W. Meyer, David H. Kamens, and Aaron Benavot, eds., *School Knowledge for the Masses*, 74–82. Washington, DC: Falmer.

Kamens, David H., John W. Meyer, and Aaron Benavot. 1996. "Worldwide Patterns in Academic Secondary Education Curricula." *Comparative Education Review* 40: 116–138.

Keal, Paul. 2003. *European Conquest and the Rights of Indigenous Peoples*. Cambridge, UK: Cambridge University Press.

Kidd, Ros. 2006. *Taken on Trust: Inquiry into Stolen Wages*. Canberra: Senate Legal and Constitutional References Committee. Retrieved on February 13, 2009, from: www.aph.gov.au/SENATE/COMMITTEE/ legcon_ctte/completed_inquiries/2004-07/stolen_wages/submissions/sub49.pdf.

Kingsbury, Benedict. 1992. "Claims by Non-State Groups in International Law." *Cornell International Law Journal* 25: 481–513.

———. 1998. "'Indigenous Peoples' in International Law: A Constructivist Approach to the Asian Controversy." *American Journal of International Law* 92: 414–457.

Kitschelt, Herbert P. 1986. "Political Opportunity Structures and Political Protest: Anti-Nuclear Movements in Four Democracies." *British Journal of Political Science* 16: 57–85.

Koopmans, Ruud, and Paul Statham. 1999. "Challenging the Liberal Nation-State? Postnationalism, Multiculturalism, and the Collective Claims Making of Migrants and Ethnic Minorities in Britain and Germany." *American Journal of Sociology* 105: 652–696.

Kobrin, Stephen J. 1998. "Back to the Future: Neomedievalism and the Postmodern Digital World Economy." *Journal of International Affairs* 51: 361–386.

Kraatz, Matthew S., and Edward J. Zajak. 1996. "Exploring the Limits of the New Institutionalism: The Causes and Consequences of Illegitimate Organizational Change." *American Sociological Review* 61: 812–836.

Krasner, Stephen D. 1982. "Structural Causes and Regime Consequences: Regimes as Intervening Variables." *International Organization* 36: 185–205.

———. 1993. "Westphalia and All That." In Judith Goldstein and Robert O. Keohane, eds., *Ideas and Foreign Policy*, 235–264. Ithaca, NY: Cornell University Press.

———. 1999. *Sovereignty: Organized Hypocrisy*. Princeton, NJ: Princeton University Press.

———. 2001. "Rethinking the Sovereign State Model." *Review of International Studies* 27: 17–42.

Kriesi, Hanspeter, Ruud Koopmands, Jan Willem Duyvendak, and Marco G. Giugni. 1995. *New Social Movements in Western Europe: A Comparative Analysis*. Minneapolis: University of Minnesota Press.

Kujovich, Gil. 1987. "Equal Opportunity in Higher Education and the Black Public College: The Era of Separate but Equal." *Minnesota Law Review* 72: 29–172.

Kymlicka, Will. 1989. *Liberalism, Community and Culture*. Oxford, UK: Clarendon Press.

———. 1995. *Multicultural Citizenship*. New York: Oxford University Press.

———. 2001. *Politics in the Vernacular*. Oxford, UK: Oxford University Press.

Kymlicka, Will, and Wayne Norman. 2000. "Citizenship in Culturally Diverse Societies: Issues, Contexts, Concepts." In Will Kymlicka and Wayne Norman, eds., *Citizenship in Diverse Societies*, 1–41. Oxford, UK: Oxford University Press.

Las Casas, Bartolomé. [1542] 1992. *A Short Account of the Destruction of the Indies*, translated by N. Griffin. London: Penguin.

Laurie, Nina, Robert Andolina, and Sarah Radcliffe. 2005. "Ethnodevelopment: Social Movements, Creating Experts and Professionalising Indigenous Knowledge in Ecuador." *Antipode* 37: 470–496.

Lechner, Frank J., and John Boli. 2005. *World Culture: Origins and Consequences*. Malden, MA: Blackwell.

Leech Lake Tribal College. 1997. *Catalog of Courses & Degree Requirements 1997–98*. Cass Lake, MN: Author.

———. 2008. *Catalog 2008–2011*. Cass Lake, MN: Author.

Levy, David, and Maureen Scully. 2007. "The Institutional Entrepreneur as Modern Prince: The Strategic Face of Power in Contested Fields." *Organization Studies* 28: 971–991.

Levi, Margaret. 1999. "Producing an Analytical Narrative." In John Bowen and Roger Petersen, eds., *Critical Comparisons in Politics and Culture*, 152–172. New York: Cambridge University Press.

León-Portilla, Miguel, and Earl Shorris. 2001. *In the Language of Kings: An Anthology of Mesoamerican Literature—Pre-Columbian to the Present*. New York: W. W. Norton.

Lewis, Dave. 1998. *Indigenous Rights Claims in Welfare Capitalist Society: Recognition and Implementation. The Case of the Sami People in Norway, Sweden and Finland*. Rovaniemi, Finland: Arctic Centre, University of Lapland.

Lincoln University. 2002. *2002–2003 Bulletin*. Lincoln University, PA: Author.

Lindley, M. F. 1926. *The Acquisition and Government of Backward Territory in International Law*. London: Longmans, Green and Co. Ltd.

Lipset, Seymour Martin. 1990. *Continental Divide: The Values and Institutions of the United States and Canada*. New York: Routledge.

Lloyd, Marion. 2003. "Educating Mexico's Indians: Eagar Students at a New University Must Teach Themselves in Stark Conditions." *Chronicle of Higher Education*, January 24. Retrieved on October 18, 2004, from: http://chronicle.com/weekly/v49/i20/20a03801.htm.

Locke, John. [1690] 1960. "An Essay Concerning the True Original, Extent and End of Civil Government." In E. Barker, ed., *Social Contract*, 1–144. New York: Oxford University Press.

Long, J. Anthony, and Menno Boldt. 1988. "Introduction." In J. Anthony Long, Menno Boldt, and Leroy Little Bear, eds., *Governments in Conflict? Provinces and Indian Nations in Canada*, 3–20. Toronto: University of Toronto Press.

Long, J. Scott. 1997. *Regression Models for Categorical and Limited Dependent Variables*. Thousand Oaks, CA: Sage.

Lupher, David A. 2003. *Romans in a New World: Classical Models in Sixteenth-Century Spanish America*. Ann Arbor: University of Michigan Press.

Lyall, Sarah. 2009. "Fondly, Greenland Loosens Danish Rule." *New York Times*, June 21, p. A4.

Macklem, Patrick. 1993. "Distributing Sovereignty: Indian Nations and Equality of Peoples." *Stanford Law Review* 45: 1312–1367.

———. 2001. *Indigenous Difference and the Constitution of Canada*. Toronto: University of Toronto Press.

M. A. Begay II & Associates. 2010. *First Nations University of Canada Governance Plan: An Opportunity to Lead the World in First Nations Higher Education*. Tuscon, AZ: Author.

Manderscheid, Don J. 2007. "First Nations and Self-Government: A Matter of Trust." *Canadian Journal of Law and Society* 22: 109–121.

Marable, Manning, and Leith Mullings. 1994. "The Divided Mind of Black America: Race, Ideology and Politics in the Post Civil Rights Era." *Race & Class* 36: 61–72.

Marginson, Simon. 2006. "Australia." In James J. F. Forest and Philip G. Altbach, eds., *International Handbook of Higher Education*, vol. 2, 587–611. Dordrecht, The Netherlands: Springer.

Marshall, T. H. 1948. *Class, Citizenship, and Social Development*. Garden City, NY: Doubleday.

Martinez Cobo, José 1986. *Study of the Problem of Discrimination against Indigenous Populations*. New York: United Nations. U.N. Doc. E/CN.4/Sub.2/1986/7.

Mathews, Jessica T. 1997. "Power Shift." *Foreign Affairs* 76: 50–66.

Mathieu, David J. 1976. *Indian Education*, Part I. Spearfish, SD: Black Hills State College, Center of Indian Studies.

McAdam, Doug. 1996. "Conceptual Origins, Current Problems, Future Directions." In Doug McAdam, John D. McCarthy, and Mayer N. Zald, eds., *Comparative Perspectives on Social Movements: Political Opportunities, Mobilizing Structures, and Cultural Framings*, 23–40. New York: Cambridge University Press.

———. 1999. *Political Process and the Development of Black Insurgency, 1930–1970*, 2nd ed. Chicago: University of Chicago Press.

McCarty, Teresa L. 2002. *A Place to Be Navajo: Rough Rock and the Struggle for Self-Determination in Indigenous Schooling*. Mahwah, NJ: Lawrence Erlbaum Associates.

McEneaney, Elizabeth H., and John W. Meyer. 2000. "The Content of the Curriculum: An Institutionalist Perspective." In Maureen T. Hallinan, ed., *Handbook of the Sociology of Education*, 189–211. New York: Academic/Plenum.

McHugh, P. G. 2004. *Aboriginal Societies and the Common Law: A History of Sovereignty, Status, and Self-Determination*. Oxford, UK: Oxford University Press.

McSloy, Steven Paul. 1996. "'Because the Bible Tells Me So': Manifest Destiny and American Indians." *St. Thomas Law Review* 9: 37–47.

Merisotis, Jamie P., and Colleen T. O'Brien, eds. 1998. *Minority Serving Institutions: Distinct Purposes, Common Goals*, No. 102 in *New Directions for Higher Education*. San Francisco: Jossey-Bass.

Meyer, John W. 1970. "The Charter: Conditions of Diffuse Socialization in Schools." In W. Richard Scott, ed., *Social Processes and Social Structures*, 564–578. New York: Holt.

———. 1980. "The World Polity and the Authority of the Nation-State." In Albert Bergesen, ed., *Studies of the Modern World-System*, 109–137. New York: Academic Press.

———. 1999. "The Changing Cultural Content of the Nation-State: A World Society Perspective." In George Steinmetz, ed., *State/Culture: State-Formation after the Cultural Turn*, 123–143. Ithaca, NY: Cornell University Press.

———. 2000. "Globalization: Sources and Effects on National States and Societies." *International Sociology* 15: 233–248.

Meyer, John W., John Boli, and George M. Thomas. 1987. "Ontology and Rationalization in the Western Cultural Account." In George M. Thomas, John W. Meyer, Francisco O. Ramirez, and John Boli, eds., *Institutional Structure: Constituting State, Society, and the Individual*, 12–37. Newbury Park, CA: Sage.

Meyer, John W., John Boli, George M. Thomas, and Francisco O. Ramirez. 1997a. "World Society and the Nation-State." *American Journal of Sociology* 103: 144–181.

Meyer, John W., David John Frank, Ann Hironaka, Evan Schofer, and Nancy Brandon Tuma. 1997b. "The Structuring of a World Environmental Regime, 1870–1990." *International Organization* 51: 623–651.

Meyer, John W., and Ronald L. Jepperson. 2000. "The 'Actors' of Modern Society: The Cultural Construction of Social Agency." *Sociological Theory* 18: 100–120.

Meyer, John W., David H. Kamens, and Aaron Benavot. 1992a. *School Knowledge for the Masses.* Washington, DC: Falmer.

Meyer, John W., Francisco O. Ramirez, and Yasemin Nuhoğlu Soysal. 1992b. "World Expansion of Mass Education, 1870–1980." *Sociology of Education* 65: 128–149.

Meyer, John W., and Brian Rowan. 1977. "Institutionalized Organizations: Formal Structure as Myth and Ceremony." *American Journal of Sociology* 83: 340–363.

———. 1978. "The Structure of Educational Organizations." In M. W. Meyer, ed., *Environments and Organizations*, 78–109. San Francisco: Jossey-Bass.

Meyer, John W., and W. Richard Scott. 1983. "Centralization and the Legitimacy Problems of Local Government." In John W. Meyer and W. Richard Scott, eds., *Organizational Environments: Ritual and Rationality*, 199–215. Beverly Hills, CA: Sage.

Miles College. 1996. *Catalog 1996–2000.* Fairfield, AL: Author.

Miller, Bruce Granville. 2003. *Invisible Indigenes: The Politics of Nonrecognition.* Lincoln: University of Nebraska Press.

Miller-Bernal, Leslie, and Susan L. Poulson, eds. 2006. *Challenged by Coeducation: Women's Colleges since the 1960s.* Nashville, TN: Vanderbilt University Press.

Minkoff, Debra C. 2002. "The Emergence of Hybrid Organizational Forms: Combining Identity-Based Service Provision and Political Action." *Nonprofit and Voluntary Sector Quarterly* 31: 377–401.

Morgan, Rhiannon. 2004. "Advancing Indigenous Rights at the United Nations: Strategic Framing and its Impact on the Normative Development of International Law." *Social & Legal Studies* 13: 481–500.

Morse, Bradford. 1988. "Aboriginal-Government Relations in Australia and the Implications for Canada." In J. Anthony Long, Menno Boldt, and Leroy Little Bear, eds.. *Governments in Conflict? Provinces and Indian Nations in Canada*, 209–221. Toronto: University of Toronto Press.

Nagel, Joane. 1996. *American Indian Ethnic Renewal: Red Power and the Resurgence of Identity and Culture.* New York: Oxford University Press.

National Inquiry into the Separation of Aboriginal and Torres Strait Islander Children from Their Families (Australia). 1997. *Bringing Them Home: Report of the National Inquiry into the Separation of Aboriginal and Torres Strait Islander Children from their Families.* Sydney: Human Rights and Equal Opportunity Commission.

Navajo Community College. 1977. *Navajo Community College General Catalog 1977–1978.* Tsaile, AZ: Author.

———. 1994. *Navajo Community College 1994–95 College Catalog.* Tsaile, AZ: Author.

Nederveen Pieterse, Jan. 1995. "Globalization as Hybridization." In Mike Featherstone, Scott Lash, and Roland Robertson, eds., *Global Modernities*, 45–68. Sage: London.

Nettheim, Garth. 2007. "The Influence of Canadian and International Law on the Evolution of Australian Aboriginal Title." In Hamar Foster, Heather Raven, and Jeremy Webber, eds., *Let Right be Done: Aboriginal Title, the* Calder *Case, and the Future of Indigenous Rights*, 177–197. Vancouver: University of British Columbia Press.

New Zealand. 2000. *New Zealand's Tertiary Education Sector 1999: Profile and Trends.* Wellington: Ministry of Education. Retrieved on November 5, 2010, from: www.educationcounts.govt.nz/__data/assets/pdf_file/0020/9245/PT-1999.pdf.

———. 2003. *Participation in Tertiary Education 2003*. Wellington: Ministry of Education. Retrieved on November 2, 2005, from: www.minedu.govt.nz/web/downloadable/dl8811_v1/participation-in-tertiary-education-2003-web-vers.pdf.

———. 2005a. *Maori in Tertiary Education: A Picture of the Trends*. Wellington: Ministry of Education.

———. 2005b. *Ngā Haeata Mātauranga: Annual Report on Māori Education 2004*. Wellington: Ministry of Education.

———. 2005c. *Tertiary Statistics 2004*. Wellington: Ministry of Education. Retrieved on October 18, 2004, from: www.minedu.govt.nz/index.cfm?layout=document&documentid=10508&indexid=7552&indexparentid=6142.

———. 2008. *Provider-Based Enrolments*. Wellington: Ministry of Education. Retrieved on January 20, 2010, from: www.educationcounts.govt.nz/statistics/tertiary_education/participation.

Niezen, Ronald. 2003. *The Origins of Indigenism*. Berkley: University of California Press.

Norrell, Brenda. 2005. "D-Q University Closure Exposes Mysteries." *Indian Country Today*, March 4. Retrieved on August 13, 2005, from: www.indiancountry.com/content.cfm?id=1096410491.

Nuttall, Mark. 1994. "Greenland: Emergence of an Inuit Homeland." In Minority Rights Group, ed., *Polar Peoples: Self-Determination and Development*, 1–28. London: Minority Rights Publications.

Office of Aboriginal and Torres Strait Islander Affairs. 2003. "Fact Sheet 4—Indigenous Higher Education Advisory Council." Retrieved on November 1, 2005, from: www.atsia.gov.au/facts/fs_cdep4.pdf.

Oglala Lakota College. 2003. *2003–2004 Catalog*. Kyle: SD: Author.

Olneck, Michael R. 1993. "Terms of Inclusion: Has Multiculturalism Redefined Equality in American Education?" *American Journal of Education* 101: 234–260.

Olzak, Susan, and Nicole Kangas. 2008. "Ethnic, Women's, and African American Studies Majors in U.S. Institutions of Higher Education." *Sociology of Education* 81: 163–188.

Oppelt, Norman T. 1990. *The Tribally Controlled Indian College*. Tsaile, AZ: Navajo Community College Press.

Oppenheim, L. 1928. *International Law*. London: Longmans, Green and Co. Ltd.

Orton, Larry. 2009. *Statistics Canada's Definition and Classification of Postsecondary and Adult Education Providers in Canada*. Ottawa: Minister of Industry.

Osiander, Andreas. 2001. "Sovereignty, International Relations, and the Westphalian Myth." *International Organization* 55: 251–287.

Pagden, Anthony. 1995. *Lords of All the World*. New Haven, CT: Yale University Press.

———. 2001. *Peoples and Empires*. New York: The Modern Library.

Paine, Robert. 1985. "Ethnodrama and the 'Fourth World': The Saami Action Group in Norway, 1979–81." In Noel Dyck, ed., *Indigenous Peoples and the Nation State: 'Fourth World' Politics in Canada, Australia and Norway*, 190–235. St. John's, Canada: Institute of Social and Economic Research, Memorial University of Newfoundland.

Peddie, R. 1992. "New Zealand." In Burton R. Clark and Guy R. Neave, eds., *The Encyclopedia of Higher Education*, vol. 1: *National Systems of Higher Education*, 504–510. Oxford, UK: Pergamon.

Perkin, Harold. 2006. "History of Universities." In James J. F. Forest and Philip G. Altbach, eds., *International Handbook of Higher Education*, Part One: *Global Themes and Contemporary Challenges*, 159–205. Dordrecht, The Netherlands: Springer.

Perry, Richard J. 1996. *From Time Immemorial: Indigenous Peoples and State Systems*. Austin: University of Texas Press.

Persson, Diane. 1986. "The Changing Experience of Indian Residential Schooling: Blue Quills, 1931–1970." In Jean Barman, Yvonne M. Hébert, and Don N. McCaskill, eds., *Indian Education in Canada*, vol. 1: *The Legacy*, 150–167. Vancouver: University of British Columbia Press.

Peterson, Nicolas, and Will Sanders. 1998. "Introduction." In Nicolas Peterson and Will Sanders, eds., *Citizenship and Indigenous Australians*, 1–32. Cambridge, UK: Cambridge University Press.

Pevar, Stephen L. 2002. *The Rights of Indians and Tribes*, 3rd ed. Carbondale and Edwardsville: Southern Illinois University Press.

Pfeffer, Jeffrey, and Gerald R. Salancik. 1978. *The External Control of Organizations: A Resource Dependence Perspective*. New York: Harper & Row.

Provasnik, Stephen, Linda L. Shafer, and Thomas D. Snyder. *Historically Black Colleges and Universities, 1976–2001*. Washington, DC: National Center for Education Statistics, Institute of Education Sciences.

Prucha, Francis Paul. 1994. *American Indian Treaties: The History of a Political Anomaly*. Berkeley: University of California Press.

———, ed. 2000. *Documents of United States Indian Policy*, 3rd ed. Lincoln: University of Nebraska Press.

Putman, Betsy Mennell. 2001. "Can Tribal Colleges Maintain Identity while Seeking Legitimacy?" *Tribal College Journal* 13: 18–25.

"The Racial Integration of Historically Black Universities: High Praise for the State of North Carolina." 1999/2000. *Journal of Blacks in Higher Education* 26: 74–75.

Ragin, Charles C. 2000. *Fuzzy-Set Social Science*. Chicago: University of Chicago Press.

Ramirez, Francisco O. 2006. "From Citizen to Person? Rethinking Education as Incorporation." *International Perspectives on Education and Society* 7: 367–387.

Ramirez, Francisco O., and John Boli. 1987a. "Global Patterns of Educational Institutionalization." In George M. Thomas, John W. Meyer, Francisco O. Ramirez, and John Boli, eds., *Institutional Structure: Constituting State, Society, and the Individual*, pp. 150–172. Newbury Park, CA: Sage.

Ramirez, Francisco O., and John Boli. 1987b. "The Political Construction of Mass Schooling: European Origins and Worldwide Institutionalization." *Sociology of Education* 60: 2–17.

Ramirez, Francisco O., and John W. Meyer. 2002. "National Curricula: World Models and National Historical Legacies." In M. Caruso and H.-E. Tenorth, eds., *Internationalisation: Comparing Educational Systems and Semantics*, 91–107. Frankfurt am Main, Germany: Lang.

Ramirez, Francisco O., and Richard Rubinson. 1979. "Creating Members: The Political Incorporation and Expansion of Public Education. In John W. Meyer and Michael T. Hannan, eds., *National Development and the World System*, 72–82. Chicago: University of Chicago Press.

Ramirez, Francisco O., Yasemin Soysal, and Suzanne Shanahan. 1997. "The Changing Logic of Political Citizenship: Cross-National Acquisition of Women's Suffrage Rights, 1890 to 1990." *American Sociological Review* 62: 735–745.

Ramirez, Francisco O., and Christine Min Wotipka. 2001. "Slowly but Surely? The Global Expansion of Women's Participation in Science and Engineering Fields of Study, 1972–1992." *Sociology of Education* 74: 231–251.

Read, Brock. 2005. "California's Only Tribal College Shuts Its Doors." *Chronicle of Higher Education*, March 4, p. A26.

Reyes, Adrián. 2005. "Indigenous Peoples Day: New Universities for a Multicultural Mexico." *Inter Press Service News Agency*, Aug. 9. Retrieved on November 11, 2005, from: http://ipsnews.net/news.asp?idnews=29824.

Reyhner, Jon, and Jeanne Eder. 2004. *American Indian Education: A History*. Norman: University of Oklahoma Press.

Reynolds, Henry. 1989. *Dispossession: Black Australians and White Invaders*. St Leonards, Australia: Allen & Unwin.

———. 1996. *Aboriginal Sovereignty: Three Nations, One Australia?* St Leonards, Australia: Allen & Unwin.

Riddle, Phyllis. 1989. *University and State: Political Competition and the Rise of Universities, 1200–1985*. PhD dissertation, Department of Sociology, Stanford University.

———. 1993. "Political Authority and University Formation in Europe, 1200–1800." *Sociological Perspectives* 36: 45–62.

———. 1996. "The University and Political Authority: Historical Trends and Contemporary Possibilities." *Research in Sociology of Education and Socialization* 11: 43–62.

Robertson, Roland. 1992. *Globalization*. London: Sage.

Rojas, Fabio. 2006. "Social Movement Tactics, Organizational Change and the Spread of African-American Studies." *Social Forces* 84: 2139–2158.

———. 2007. *From Black Power to Black Studies: How a Radical Social Movement Became an Academic Discipline*. Baltimore: The Johns Hopkins University Press.

Rosenfelt, Daniel M. 1973. "Indian Schools and Community Control." *Stanford Law Review* 25: 489–550.

Roy, Bernadette, and Gudmunder Alfredsson. 1987. "Indigenous Rights: The Literature Explosion." *Transnational Perspectives* 13: 19–24.

Saami College. 2005. "Saami University College—The Saami Guiding Star." Retrieved on November 22, 2005, from: www.samiskhs.no/eng/about_SUC.htm.

Salish Kootenai College. 2001. *2001–2003 Catalog*. Pablo, MT: Author.

Salvesen, Helge. 1995. "Sami Ædnan: Four States—One Nation?" In Sven Tägil, ed., *Ethnicity and Nation Building in the Nordic World*, 106–144. Carbondale: Southern Illinois University Press.

Samuels, Albert L. 2004. *Is Separate Unequal? Black Colleges and the Challenge to Desegregation*. Lawrence: University Press of Kansas.

Sanders, Douglas. 1989. "The UN Working Group on Indigenous Populations." *Human Rights Quarterly* 11: 406–433.

Sanders, Joe. 1991. "First Nations Sovereignty and Self-Determination." In Frank Cassidy, ed., *Aboriginal Self-Determination*, 186–196. Lantzville, BC, and Montreal: Oolichan Books and The Institute for Research on Public Policy.

Sassen, Saskia. 2006. *Territory, Authority, Rights: From Medieval to Global Assemblages*. Princeton, NJ: Princeton University Press.

Schofer, Evan, and John W. Meyer. 2005. "The Worldwide Expansion of Higher Education in the Twentieth Century." *American Sociological Review* 70: 898–920.

Scott, James C. 1985. *Weapons of the Weak: Everyday Forms of Peasant Resistance*. New Haven, CT: Yale University Press.

Scott, W. Richard. 1994. "Institutional Analysis: Variance and Process Theory Approaches." In W. Richard Scott and John W. Meyer, eds., *Institutional Environments and Organizations*, 81–99. Thousand Oaks, CA: Sage.

———. 2003. *Organizations: Rational, Natural, and Open Systems*, 5th ed. Upper Saddle River, NJ: Prentice Hall.

Scott, W. Richard, and John W. Meyer. 1994. "Environmental Linkages and Organizational Complexity." In W. Richard Scott and John W. Meyer, eds., *Institutional Environments and Organizations*, 137–159. Thousand Oaks, CA: Sage.

Senese, Guy B. 1991. *Self-Determination and the Social Education of Native Americans*. New York: Praeger.

Sewell, William H. Jr. 1992. "A Theory of Structure: Duality, Agency, and Transformation." *American Journal of Sociology* 98: 1–29.
Shanley, James. 1993. "Whose College Is It Anyway?" *Tribal College Journal* 5: 8–9.
Short, Damien. 2003. "Reconciliation, Assimilation, and the Indigenous Peoples of Australia." *International Political Science Review* 24: 491–513.
Sikkink, Kathryn. 1993. "Human Rights, Principled Issue-Networks, and Sovereignty in Latin America." *International Organization* 47: 411–441.
Simeon, Richard. 1998. *Ngā Kura Māori: The Native Schools System, 1867–1969*. Auckland: Auckland University Press.
Simon, Judith, and Linda Tuhiwai Smith. 2001. *A Civilizing Mission? Perceptions and Representations of the New Zealand Native Schools System*. Auckland: Auckland University Press.
Skrentny, John D. 2002. *The Minority Rights Revolution*. Cambridge, MA: Belknap.
Snow, David A., E. Burke Rochford Jr., Steven K. Worden, and Robert D. Benford. 1986. "Frame Alignment Processes, Micromobilization, and Movement Participation." *American Sociological Review* 51: 464–481.
Soysal, Yasemin Nuhoğlu. 1994. *Limits of Citizenship*. Chicago: University of Chicago Press.
Soysal, Yasemin Nuhoğlu, and David Strang. 1989. "Construction of the First Mass Education Systems in Nineteenth-Century Europe." *Sociology of Education* 62: 277–288.
Sørensen, Axel Kjær. 1995. "Greenland: From Colony to Home Rule." In Sven Tägil, ed., *Ethnicity and Nation Building in the Nordic World*, 85–105. Carbondale: Southern Illinois University Press.
Stark, Rodney. 2005. *The Victory of Reason: How Christianity Led to Freedom, Capitalism, and Western Success*. New York: Random House.
StataCorp. 2003. *Cross-Sectional Time-Series Reference Manual: Release 8.0*. College Station, TX: Stata Corporation.
Statistics Canada. 2007. *Register of Postsecondary and Adult Education Institutions*. Retrieved on September 12, 2007, from: www27.statcan.ca/IP_Internet/English/Browse/EntryForm.asp.
Stefkovich, Jacqueline A., and Terrence Leas. 1994. "A Legal History of Desegregation in Higher Education." *Journal of Negro Education* 63: 406–420.
Stein, Wayne J. 1990. "The Funding of Tribally Controlled Colleges." *Journal of American Indian Education* 30: 1–7.
———. 1992. *Tribally Controlled Colleges: Making Good Medicine*. New York: Peter Lang.
Stinchcombe, Arthur L. 1965. "Social Structure and Organizations." In James G. March, ed., *Handbook of Organizations*, 153–193. Chicago: Rand McNally.
Stone Child College. 2002. *2002–2004 Catalog*. Box Elder, MT: Author.
Stonechild, Blair. 2006. *The New Buffalo: The Struggle for Aboriginal Post-Secondary Education in Canada*. Winnipeg: University of Manitoba Press.
Strang, David. 1990. "From Dependency to Sovereignty: An Event History Analysis of Decolonization, 1870–1987." *American Sociological Review* 55: 846–860.
———. 1991. "Global Patterns of Decolonization, 1500–1987." *International Studies Quarterly* 35: 429–454.
Strang, David, and John W. Meyer. 1993. "Institutional Conditions for Diffusion." *Theory and Society* 22: 487–511.
Strang, David, and Sarah A. Soule. 1998. "Diffusion in Organizations and Social Movements: From Hybrid Corn to Poison Pills." *Annual Review of Sociology* 24: 265–90.
Strasser, Mark. 2000. "*Plessy, Brown*, and HBCUs: On the Imposition of Stigma and the Court's Mechanical Equal Protection Jurisprudence." *Washburn Law Journal* 40: 48–69.
Stripling, Jack. 2009. "HBCUs Drawing Scrutiny." *Inside Higher Ed*, January 30. Retrieved on November 17, 2009, from: www.insidehighered.com/news/2009/01/30/hbcu.

Stuart, Paul. 1987. *Nations within a Nation: Historical Statistics of American Indians*. New York: Greenwood.

Svensson, Frances. 1979. "Liberal Democracy and Group Rights: The Legacy of Individualism and Its Impact on American Indian Tribes." *Political Studies* 27: 421–439.

Swidler, Ann. 1986. "Culture in Action: Symbols and Strategies." *American Sociological Review* 51: 273–286.

Szasz, Margaret Connell. 1988. *Indian Education in the American Colonies, 1607–1783*. Albuquerque: University of New Mexico Press.

Tahana, Yvonne. 2007. "Wananga Heads for Profit after Years of Struggle." *New Zealand Herald*, Oct. 24.

Tarr, G. Alan, Robert F. Williams, and Josef Marko, eds. 2004. *Federalism, Subnational Constitutions, and Minority Rights*. Westport, CT: Praeger.

Tarrow, Sidney. 1998. *Power in Movement*, 2nd ed. New York: Cambridge University Press.

Te Wananga o Aotearoa. 1999. *Prospectus 2000*. Te Awamutu, New Zealand: Author.

———. 2009. *Te Pūrongo ā-Tau: Annual Report 2008*. Te Awamutu, New Zealand: Author.

Te Wananga o Raukawa. 2000. *2000 Prospectus*. Otaki, New Zealand: Author.

Te Whare Wananga o Awanuiarangi. 2004. *Student Study Guidelines*. Retrieved on December 20, 2005, from www.wananga.ac.nz/Student_Handbook/StdGuidelines_2004.pdf.

Thelen, Kathleen. 1999. "Historical Institutionalism in Comparative Perspective." *Annual Review of Political Science* 2: 369–404.

Thomas, George M., John W. Meyer, Francisco O. Ramirez, and John Boli, eds. 1987. *Institutional Structure: Constituting State, Society, and the Individual*. Newbury Park, CA: Sage.

Thompson, Thomas, ed. 1978. *The Schooling of Native America*. Washington, DC: American Association of Colleges for Teacher Education.

Thornberry, Patrick. 2002. *Indigenous Peoples and Human Rights*. Manchester, UK: Manchester University Press.

Thuen, Trond. 1995. *Quest for Equity: Norway and the Saami Challenge*. St. John's: Institute of Social and Economic Research, Memorial University of Newfoundland.

Tilly, Charles. 1984. *Big Structures, Large Processes, Huge Comparisons*. New York: Russell Sage Foundation.

Tocqueville, Alexis de. [1835] 2000. *Democracy in America*. New York: Bantam.

Tolbert, Pamela S., and Lynne G. Zucker. 1983. "Institutional Sources of Change in the Formal Structure of Organizations: The Diffusion of Civil Service Reform, 1880–1935." *Administrative Science Quarterly* 28: 22–39.

Tranby Aboriginal College. 2004. "History." Retrieved on July 26, 2004, from: www.tranby.com.au/.

Trow, Martin. 1970. "Reflections on the Transition from Mass to Universal Higher Education." *Daedalus* 99: 1–42.

———. 2006. "Reflections on the Transition from Elite to Mass to Universal Access: Forms and Phases of Higher Education in Modern Societies since WWII." In James J. F. Forest and Philip G. Altbach, eds., *International Handbook of Higher Education*, Part One: *Global Themes and Contemporary Challenges*, 243–280. Dordrecht, The Netherlands: Springer.

Turtle Mountain Community College. 2000. *2000–2002 Catalog*. Belcourt, ND: Author.

Tyack, David. 2003. *Seeking Common Ground: Public Schools in a Diverse Society*. Cambridge, MA: Harvard University Press.

Union of International Associations [UIA]. 1983 and 2001. *Yearbook of International Organizations*. Geneva: Author.

United Nations. 1960. *Convention against Discrimination in Education.* Paris: UNESCO.

———. 1966. *International Covenant on Civil and Political Rights.* U.N. Doc. A/6316.

———. 1992. *Declaration on the Rights of Persons Belonging to National or Ethnic, Religious or Linguistic Minorities.* U.N. Doc. A/RES/47/135.

———. 1996. "Annex." *Programme of Activities for the International Decade of the World's Indigenous People.* U.N. Doc. A/RES/50/157.

———. 1999. "Recommendations." *Report on the Workshop on Higher Education and Indigenous Peoples.* U.N. Doc. E/CN.4/Sub.2/AC.4/1999/5.

———. 2003. *Permanent Forum on Indigenous Issues: Report on the Second Session.* U.N. Doc. E/2003/43-E/C.19/2003/22.

———. 2004. *Report of the Special Rapporteur on the Situation of Human Rights and Fundamental Freedoms of Indigenous People, Rodolfo Stavenhagen. Addendum: Conclusions and Recommendations of the Expert Seminar on Indigenous Peoples and Education.* U.N. Doc. E/CN.4/2005/88/Add.4.

———. 2007. *United Nations Declaration on the Rights of Indigenous Peoples.* U.N. Doc. A/RES/61/295.

UNESCO (United Nations Educational, Scientific and Cultural Organization). 1994. *Statistical Yearbook.* Paris: UNESCO.

———. 1996. *World Guide to Higher Education: A Comparative Survey of Systems, Degrees, and Qualifications,* 3rd ed. Paris: UNESCO.

———. 1997. *International Standard Classification of Education.* Paris: UNESCO.

———. 1998. *Statistical Yearbook.* Paris: UNESCO.

———. 1999. *Statistical Yearbook.* Paris: UNESCO.

———. 2003. "Higher Education." Retrieved on February 4, 2010, from: http://portal.unesco.org/culture/en/ev.php-URL_ID=3107&URL_DO=DO_TOPIC&URL_SECTION=201.html.

U.S. Census Bureau. 2000. *American Indian and Alaska Native Population, by Age and Sex for the United States: 2000.* Retrieved on November 21, 2005, from: www.census.gov/population/www/cen2000/ phc-t08.html.

U.S. Department of Education. 1992 and 2002. *Integrated Postsecondary Education Data System* [IPEDS]. Washington, DC: National Center for Education Statistics.

———. 1998. *American Indians and Alaska Natives in Postsecondary Education.* Washington, DC: National Center for Education Statistics.

———. 2001. *Digest of Education Statistics.* Washington, DC: National Center for Education Statistics.

U.S. Department of the Interior. 2009. *About the Department of the Interior.* Retrieved on October 21, 2010, from: www.doi.gov/facts.html.

U.S. Department of the Interior, Bureau of Education. 1917. *Negro Education: A Study of the Private and Higher Schools for Colored People in the United States,* vol. 2. Washington, DC: U.S. Government Printing Office.

University of Arkansas at Pine Bluff. 2002. *Catalog 2002–2004.* Pine Bluff, AR: Author.

Vattel, Emmerich de. [1758] 1883. *The Law of Nations or, Principles of the Law of Nature, Applied to the Conduct and Affairs of Nations and Sovereigns,* translated by Joseph Chitty. Philadelphia: T. & J. W. Johnson & Co.

Vitoria, Franciscus de. [1557] 1917. *De Indis et de Ivre Belli Relectiones,* Ernest Nys, ed. Washington, DC: Carnegie Institution.

Wabaunsee, Rissa. 1998. *Accreditation, Tribal Governments, and the Development of Governing Boards at Tribal Colleges in Montana and Washington.* Ed.D. dissertation, School of Education, University of Washington.

Waitangi Tribunal. 1998. *Wananga Capital Establishment Report (Wai 718)*. Wellington: GP Publications. Retrieved on January 21, 2010, from: www.waitangi-tribunal.govt.nz/reports/view.asp?ReportID=39E13093-2F4D-4971-ACA0-28E811572755.

———. 2005. *The Report on the Aotearoa Institute Claim Concerning Te Wananga o Aotearoa (Wai 1298)*. Wellington: GP Publications. Retrieved on January 21, 2010, from: www.waitangi-tribunal.govt.nz/reports/view.asp?reportid=9982adf5-40c6-420e-8899-a86640da6doc.

Walker, Ranginui J. 1999. "Maori Sovereignty, Colonial and Post-Colonial Discourses." In Paul Havemann, ed., *Indigenous Peoples' Rights in Australia, Canada, and New Zealand*, 108–122. Melbourne, Australia: Oxford University Press.

———. 2005. "Quality Assurance in Tertiary Education from a Maori (Indigenous) Perspective." Paper presented at the INQAAHE Biennial Conference, March 29–April 1, Wellington, New Zealand.

Wallerstein, Immanuel. 1974. *The Modern World System: Capitalist Agriculture and the Origins of the European World Economy in the Sixteenth Century*. New York: Academic Press.

———. 1983. "The Three Instances of Hegemony in the History of the Capitalist World-Economy." *International Journal of Comparative Sociology* 24: 100–108.

Walsh, Catherine E. 2002. "The (Re)articulation of Political Subjectivities and Colonial Difference in Ecuador." *Nepantla: Views from the South* 3: 61–97.

Washburn, Wilcomb E. 1995. *Red Man's Land, White Man's Law*, 2nd ed. Norman: University of Oklahoma Press.

Watkins, William H. 1993. "Black Curriculum Orientations: A Preliminary Inquiry." *Harvard Educational Review* 63: 321–338.

Weber, Eugen. 1976. *Peasants into Frenchmen: The Modernization of Rural France, 1870–1914*. Stanford, CA: Stanford University Press.

Weick, Karl. 1976. "Educational Organizations as Loosely Coupled Systems." *Administrative Science Quarterly* 21: 1–19.

Werther, Guntram F. A. 1992. *Self-Determination in Western Democracies: Aboriginal Politics in a Comparative Perspective*. Westport, CT: Greenwood.

Westlake, John. 1894. *Chapters on the Principles of International Law*. Cambridge, UK: Cambridge University Press.

Wiessner, Siegfried. 1999. "Rights and Status of Indigenous Peoples: A Global Comparative and International Legal Analysis." *Harvard Human Rights Journal* 12: 57–128.

Wilkinson, Charles F., and Eric R. Biggs. 1977. "The Evolution of the Termination Policy." *American Indian Law Review* 5: 139–184.

Williams, David V. 2007. "Customary Rights and Crown Claims: *Calder* and Aboriginal Title in Aotearoa New Zealand." In Hamar Foster, Heather Raven, and Jeremy Webber, eds., *Let Right Be Done: Aboriginal Title, the* Calder *Case, and the Future of Indigenous Rights*, 155–176. Vancouver: UBC Press.

Williams, Robert A. Jr. 1983. "The Medieval and Renaissance Origins of the Status of the American Indian in Western Legal Thought." *Southern California Law Review* 57: 1–99.

———. 1990. *The American Indian in Western Legal Thought: The Discourses of Conquest*. New York: Oxford University Press.

Windolf, Paul. 1992. "Cycles of Expansion in Higher Education, 1870–1985: An International Comparison." *Higher Education* 23: 3–19.

Wolfe, Patrick. 2001. "Land, Labor, and Difference: Elementary Structures of Race." *American Historical Review* 106: 866–905.

Wolfley, Jeanette. 1990. "Jim Crow, Indian Style: The Disenfranchisement of Native Americans." *American Indian Law Review* 16: 167–202.

World Bank. 1991. "Operational Directive 4.20: Indigenous Peoples." *World Bank Operational Manual.* Washington, DC: World Bank.

World Indigenous Nations Higher Education Consortium [WINHEC]. 2003. *WINHEC Accreditation Handbook,* 1st ed. Retrieved on September 21, 2004, from: www.win-hec.org/docs/pdfs/Accreditation%20Handbook.pdf.

———. 2005. "History." Retrieved on July 23, 2005, from: www.win-hec.org/.

Wotipka, Christine Min, Francisco O. Ramirez, and Capitolina Diaz Martinez. 2007. "A Transnational Analysis of the Rise and Institutionalization of Women's Studies." *Revista Española de Sociología* 117: 35–59.

Yashar, Deborah J. 2005. *Contesting Citizenship in Latin America: The Rise of Indigenous Movements and the Postliberal Challenge.* New York: Cambridge University Press.

LEGAL CASES

Australia

Coe v. Commonwealth of Australia (No. 1), 24 ALR 118 (1979)

Cooper v. Stuart (1889) 14 App Cas 286.

Mabo v. Queensland [No. 1] (1988), 166 C.L.R. 186.

Mabo v. Queensland [No. 2] (1992), 175 C.L.R. 1.

Milirrpum v. Nabalco (1971) 17 FLR 141.

Canada

Calder v. Attorney General of British Columbia, [1973] S.C.R. 313.

Delgamuukw v. British Columbia, [1991] 3 W.W.R. 97 (B.C.S.C.).

Delgamuukw v. British Columbia, [1997] 3 S.C.R. 1010.

Greyeyes v. The Queen, [1978] 2 F.C. 385.

Guerin v. The Queen, [1984] 2 S.C.R. 335.

Nowegijick v. The Queen, [1983] 1 S.C.R. 29.

R. v. Côté [1996] 3 S.C.R. 139.

R. v. Sioui, [1990] 1 S.C.R. 1025.

R. v. Syliboy, [1929] 1 D.L.R. 307 (N.S. Co. Ct.).

Re Eskimos, [1939] S.C.R. 104.

Simon v. The Queen, [1985] 2 S.C.R. 387.

St. Catherines Milling and Lumber Co. v. The Queen (1888), 14 App. Cas. 46 (J.C.P.C.).

New Zealand

R. v. Symonds (1847) N.Z.P.C.C. 387.

Te Weehi v. Regional Fisheries Officer [1986] 1 NZLR 680 (HC).

Wi Parata v. Bishop of Wellington (1877) 3 NZ Jur (NS) 72.

United States

Adams v. Richardson, 356 F. Supp. 92 (1973).

Berea College v. Kentucky, 211 U.S. 45 (1908).

Brown v. Board of Education, 347 U.S. 483 (1954).

Cherokee Nation v. Georgia, 30 U.S. (5 Pet.) 1 (1831).

Dred Scott v. Sandford, 60 U.S. 393 (1857).

Elk v. Wilkins, 112 U.S. 94 (1884).

Fletcher v. Peck, 10 U.S. 87 (1810).

Geier v. University of Tennessee, 597 F.2d 1056 (6th Cir. 1979).

Gong Lum v. Rice, 275 U.S. 78 (1927).
Green v. School Board of New Kent County, 391 U.S. 430 (1968).
Johnson v. McIntosh, 21 U.S. (8 Wheat.) 543 (1823).
Lone Wolf v. Hitchcock, 187 U.S. 553 (1903).
McLaurin v. Oklahoma State Regents, 339 U.S. 637 (1950).
Mississippi University for Women v. Hogan, 458 U.S. 718 (1982).
Missouri ex. rel. Gaines v. Canada, 305 U.S. 337 (1938).
Morton v. Mancari, 417 U.S. 535 (1974).
Native American Church v. Navajo Tribal Council, 272 F.2d 131 (10th Cir. 1959).
Norris v. State Council of Education, 327 F. Supp. 1368 (1971).
Oklahoma Tax Commission v. Citizen Band Potawatomi Indian Tribe, 498 U.S. 505 (1991).
Plessy v. Ferguson, 163 U.S. 537 (1896).
Santa Clara Pueblo v. Martinez, 436 U.S. 49 (1978).
Sipuel v. Board of Regents of the University of Oklahoma, 332 U.S. 631 (1948).
Sweatt v. Painter, 339 U.S. 629 (1950).
United States v. Fordice, 505 U.S. 717 (1992).
United States v. Kagama, 118 U.S. 375 (1886).
United States v. Washington, 384 F. Supp. 312 (W.D. Wash. 1974).
United States v. Wheeler, 435 U.S. 313 (1978).
Wisconsin v. Yoder, 406 U.S. 205 (1972).
Worcester v. Georgia, 31 U.S. (6 Pet.) 515 (1832).

International

Cayuga Indians (Great Britain) v. United States, 6 R.I.A.A. 173 (1926).
Island of Palmas, 11 R.I.A.A. 829 (1928).
Legal Status of Eastern Greenland [1933] PCIJ, Ser. A./B., No. 53.
Minority Schools in Albania [1935] PCIJ, Ser. A./B., No. 64.
Western Sahara, [1975] I.C.J. 12.

INDEX

Note: Figures and tables are indicated by *f* or *t*, respectively, following the page number.

FSC
www.fsc.org
MIX
Papier | Fördert
gute Waldnutzung
FSC® C083411

Kolibri 360 GmbH
Ferdinand-Jühlke-Straße 7
99095 Erfurt, Deutschland
produktsicherheit@kolibri360.de